RED
REBELS

RED
REBELS

The Glazers and the FC Revolution

JOHN-PAUL O'NEILL

YELLOW JERSEY PRESS
LONDON

1 3 5 7 9 10 8 6 4 2

Yellow Jersey Press, an imprint of Vintage
20 Vauxhall Bridge Road
London SW1V 2SA

Yellow Jersey Press is part of the Penguin Random House group of companies
whose addresses can be found at global.penguinrandomhouse.com.

Penguin
Random House
UK

First published by Yellow Jersey Press in 2017

www.vintage-books.co.uk

A CIP catalogue record for this book is available from the British Library

ISBN 9781787290099

Extract from *Manchester Disunited*, by Mihir Bose reprinted with permission of
Aurum Press.
Extract from *This is the One*, by Daniel Taylor reprinted with permission of
Aurum Press.
Extract from *An Undividable Glow*, by Robert Brady reprinted with permission
of Robert Brady. The entire cover price for this publication is donated to
The Working Class Movement Library.

Typeset in 10.5/16 pt ITC Galliard by Jouve UK, Milton Keynes
Printed and bound in Great Britain by Clays Ltd, St Ives plc

Penguin Random House is committed to a sustainable future for our business,
our readers and our planet. This book is made from Forest Stewardship
Council® certified paper.

MIX
Paper from
responsible sources
FSC
www.fsc.org   FSC® C018179

"Do not imagine, comrades, that leadership is a pleasure! On the contrary, it is a deep and heavy responsibility. No one believes more firmly than Comrade Napoleon that all animals are equal. He would be only too happy to let you make your decisions for yourselves. But sometimes you might make the wrong decisions, comrades, and then where should we be?"

— *George Orwell, Animal Farm*

contents

Introduction   ix

Preface   xv

1. Mercantilism   1

2. March Of The Blanketeers   25

3. Universal Suffrage   42

4. Utopian Socialism   57

5. The People's Charter   81

6. Salford Yeomanry   94

7. Your Lost Country Bought And Sold   110

8. Windmill Street   129

9. A Sense Awakening   152

10. I Am God, And King, And Law!   164

11. The Prostrate Multitude   181

12. Rise Like Lions After Slumber   199

13. Masque Of Anarchy   208

14. Ye Are Many, They Are Few   221

15. By Wisdom And Effort   236

Epilogue   257

League Structure   267

National Cup Competitions   267

FC United Steering Committee   268

Evolution of the FC United Board Members   268

INTRODUCTION

I don't recall any conscious decision to become a United fan; it's probably because my dad was one before me. Where he got it from I've never actually asked. One of his older sisters was a big City fan, and used to watch them regularly – even heading down to Wembley for the Cup Final in the '50s – but my dad evidently had more sense. He'd sometimes tell us about being coached as a kid by Johnny Carey, United's 1948 FA Cup-winning captain. The family certainly had Red roots geographically – my grandparents met in Cornbrook, Old Trafford, where they'd both lived, before moving out to Wythenshawe after they married.

One of my earliest football-related memories, certainly that I can date, is my dad jumping out of his chair when Norman Whiteside scored the winner against Everton in the 1985 Cup final. The following day we went to Sale to see the team parade the trophy. That was it for a few years as far as football was concerned as my parents then dragged the five of us (all under the age of eight) off to the South Pacific. As you do. My dad had given up his job, having taken a post teaching in the Solomon Islands, and off we went to live in Honiara on Guadalcanal. History buffs might recognise it as the scene of tumultuous battles between the Americans and Japanese in World War

Two; or perhaps as the setting for *The Thin Red Line*, the book centred on that campaign.

In spite of such gallivanting, somewhere along the line I became obsessed with United, with my hero being the captain Bryan Robson. After much pestering, my dad eventually took me and one of my younger brothers to a game at Old Trafford in the midst of a gruesome 11-game run without a league victory. Needless to say, Robson didn't play, once again being out injured. It didn't matter though, as the experience was mesmerising: from the seemingly tiny slits that passed for turnstiles to the continual hum of the crowd, the fog of smoke hanging over the terraces to the glare of the floodlights, and the bright, vivid clash of the teams' colours against the green(ish) pitch.

From then on pretty much all I wanted to do was watch United, and within a year I was going without my dad: being 11 years old on the Stretford End would probably seem a big deal to some parents nowadays; back then it was just how it was. By then I had six siblings, so to pay my way, even with admittance costing only £2.30, I did regular paper rounds – trudging the streets every morning from 7 a.m., delivering the day's news. For a Saturday game I'd get to Old Trafford for 12:30 p.m., with the gates opening about 1 p.m. When the Stretford End was demolished I kept the same routine, even though the ground didn't open until probably an hour later. That meant hanging around on Warwick Road, where I quickly learnt who the regular characters and personalities were. From there, I started selling the fanzine *United We Stand* when I was 14 – away match tickets meant more income was required – and about 18 months later, *Red Issue*. By then I'd left school, although still only 15. I'd long lost interest in formal education and, as I'd already done my GCSEs having been promoted a year, headed off to find more lucrative work to feed my football habit.

A mate sorted me out with a job as a bike courier for a printing firm in Manchester: £95 cash in hand for cycling round town all day, picking up and dropping off site plans from architects and building companies that they needed copying. After paying my mum rent, it worked out little better than £1 per hour but it saw me through the 1995/96 season, including a summer trip to Milan where United played Inter in a friendly as part of Paul Ince's transfer. The following autumn, still only 16, I grudgingly headed back to college to do A-Levels. By then I'd known *Red Issue* contributors like Richard Kurt and Pete Boyle for a few years, and decided to try my hand at writing and, eventually, the editor Chris Robinson was short enough on material to print something I'd produced. He even paid for the honour.

The best part of watching United was undoubtedly the trips abroad. In 1998, for the fourth summer in a row, a few of us headed off overseas to watch the team during pre-season. A fortnight in Scandinavia beckoned and one older Red warned how expensive it was, suggesting that it would probably be cheaper to fly home in between the games than stay out there for the duration. We'd prepared by taking a load of United pin badges to sell to the locals at Scandinavian rates: a working holiday was the only way we could afford to do it.

During halftime of one game in Oslo we were sat by the pitch while United's substitutes warmed up. 'Come on,' I said to the others, 'let's have a kick around,' and walked over to David May, one of United's players at the time. He didn't look too surprised at the sight of three interlopers and had a chat with us all. Just before the second half we headed over to sit on the team bench but Brian Kidd, Alex Ferguson's assistant, came out and said: 'You'd better scarper quick before the boss sees you.' Although the other two headed back to their places, I remained where I was. The players filed out and took their seats alongside me, with the likes of Teddy Sheringham and Dennis Irwin casting a puzzled glance, clearly wondering who I was. The local kids behind the dugout were soon demanding autographs and, as I was sat on the end, began to pass their programmes and scraps of paper down the line. Eventually the Swedish player Jesper Blomqvist told me 'No more!' but I felt bad turning the fans down so started signing them myself.

It was the closest I'd come to turning out for United, and one of the few tales from the foreign jaunts around that time suitable for any respectable publication. With the 1998/99 season imminent I joined the herd being aimlessly funnelled into a university course for which I had no motivation. But it came with access to a student loan, and that would prove useful given the number of games and trips ahead, as United closed in on the Treble. The European Cup final in Barcelona coincided with end of year exams, and I was firmly told that there was no chance of progressing with the course if I didn't sit them. Oh well. Back into the world of work it was. A job cropped up on site building the new runway at Manchester Airport. £185 for a 45-hour week didn't sound too bad until I realised I was left with £40 after tax, rent to my mum and the expense of the car the job required. It wasn't hard to see why some people just didn't bother working, only the alternative was actually worse: I'd signed on once and vowed to never do so again given the dole payment simply wasn't worth the exchange of being treated like a complete moron.

As 1999 turned into 2000 I was heading to Rio in Brazil to watch United in the Club World Championship. Somehow I'd scraped together just enough money to afford it. Once back home in the reality of a cold Mancunian January, I insisted I wouldn't be going back to the drudgery of some pointless job; I just needed some opportunity to pop up. As fate would have it, not long afterwards it did: *Red Issue*'s editor Chris Robinson had his sights set on doing other things and wanted someone to take over running the magazine. Would I be interested? I didn't have the first clue how to do it, but yeah, why not. It had to be better than doing slump tests on a building site in the Bollin Valley.

Red Issue always had a caustic, cynical attitude and I had no intention of changing it. Not least because, in time, United and football in general lent itself to being viewed that way. United fans were used to being suspicious about United's long-term owner Martin Edwards and his eagerness to eke as much money as possible out of the club, and latterly, the plc, but it was another thing altogether when supposed 'football people' were doing likewise. When we started hearing rumours about the size of transfer payments being made to agents and their ilk, and calculating them in how many *thousands* of annual season tickets at Old Trafford that equated to, it became apparent that something was fundamentally wrong. I knew only too well how much young lads had to graft to turn a wage to afford to watch the team, and yet from 2001 onwards it seemed fortunes were being spunked away, while fans were being charged ever higher prices to underwrite them.

In the early 1990s, when the terraces were demolished at Old Trafford, it had the almost immediate impact of freezing out a generation of kids. While a standing area initially remained in the Scoreboard Paddock for another two seasons, its capacity was only a fraction of what the Stretford End had been. United's success over the ensuing years meant tickets were hard to come by, and so the crowd tended to grow older together, without the new, younger influx that would otherwise have occurred. I noticed it particularly for several seasons in the '90s because I was often by far the youngest on many away trips, yet I was already a few years older than when I'd first started going.

The people in charge of Manchester United plc seemed solely concerned with profit, and had little or no interest in petitions from the club's Independent Manchester United Supporters Association to facilitate local youngsters being given preferred access to match tickets. To me, this was akin to a dereliction of their duty to the club and its community. Because it *was* still a club, however much the 'business' side might have been prioritised by those in charge. For better or worse, I often tend to view things very much in black and white. If someone takes on a responsibility to others, be it an MP, a football club official, or even someone running a poxy fanzine, then they ought to act in the interests of that community. There are no excuses for doing otherwise. If you want to, say, pursue self-enrichment through questionable means, then abdicate the responsibility and fill yer boots. Why betray people's faith in you?

Another thing I'd always had drilled into me, especially being part of a big family, was if you can't afford something you couldn't have it. Yet in 2004, the Glazers came along threatening our football club – *my* football club. They couldn't afford it and were only interested in squeezing it for all its money. This would inevitably mean ever higher ticket prices, further disenfranchisement of the local youngsters and community, and even more dilution of the intoxicating Old Trafford matchday experience which I, and so many others, had fallen in love with. We might not succeed in fending them off, but there was no way they'd get their hands on it without an almighty fight.

PREFACE

29 June 2005, Old Trafford: *10:30 p.m. on a balmy summer evening and the new owners of Manchester United are under police protection as an angry crowd rains down missiles on a van ferrying them to safety away from the stadium. Officers on foot attempt to clear a path through barricades that supporters have hastily erected a few hours earlier, happily cracking a few heads with their truncheons along the way. The terrace song that has provided a backdrop to so many United games as the takeover battle raged for most of the season – 'How we kill him I don't know, cut him up from head to toe, all I know is Glazer's gonna die!' – has rung out all evening. The couple of hundred fans present are making it clear that, regardless of any share transactions that took place on the London Stock Exchange the previous month, this 127-year-old football institution still isn't the Glazers' to enjoy as they please.*

On their first visit to Manchester, United's new owners had been all but chased out of the area under a Greater Manchester Police (GMP) escort. If this was what a 200-strong crowd could do in the closed season, what would it be like if they ever tried to attend a game? Former United star Arthur Albiston echoed the thoughts of many when he told the BBC: 'I can't see Glazer or his sons actually turning up because the repercussions would be enormous.' It was an understandable viewpoint, but hopelessly misplaced. To the outside world, the television images of a midsummer riot at Old Trafford suggested as vibrant an opposition as ever; the reality was very different. If the evening's events had shown anything, it was that, although a hefty portion of United's following had voiced their opposition to the take-over, only a tiny proportion was sufficiently bothered to show up and demonstrate that dissent.

This was a last hurrah. The Glazers had come for Manchester United's pot of gold to take back to their Florida mansions and ultim-ately it had been handed over with barely a murmur. Come August, tickets at Old Trafford would still be sold out, and a team in United's red would still be playing games of football, regardless of whether its owners now operated it solely as a cash cow.

The Glazers had got away with implementing their leveraged take-over, a ghastly scheme whereby they were allowed to borrow hundreds of millions of pounds to buy out the shareholdings, before flipping the debt onto United and securing it against the club's assets rather than their own. This meant that Manchester United was now saddled with an enormous bill and crippling interest rates – all for the dubious pleasure of being controlled by this dysfunctional family of weirdo American chancers. How had it ever come to this?

1

MERCANTILISM

The sequence of events leading up to Malcolm Glazer's takeover of Manchester United can be traced back to the Munich air disaster of 6 February 1958. One of the victims of that fateful flight, which crashed trying to take off following a refuelling stop in West Germany, was Willie Satinoff, a supporter of the club and friend of Matt Busby, the team manager. At that time, Satinoff had looked set to become a director of the club, replacing George Whittaker who had suffered a fatal heart attack in London ahead of United's thrilling 5–4 victory at Highbury the previous weekend. None of the club's remaining directors had travelled to United's game in Yugoslavia, opting instead to stay behind for Whittaker's funeral. Another who cancelled his trip in order to pay his respects was Louis Edwards, also a friend of Busby's as well as a successful meat trader. He'd had his own hopes of election to the board blocked by Whittaker just two weeks earlier.

The day after the crash, an emergency board meeting was convened at vice-chairman Alan Gibson's house, and a motion to promote Edwards was put forward again. It was passed unanimously by the three remaining directors: Gibson, William Petherbridge and Harold Hardman. Gibson was the son of James Gibson, a local businessman who had rescued Manchester United from bankruptcy in December 1931, subsequently investing his own money into building the club up and re-establishing it as a First Division side. The stability he'd brought about led to the formation of the Manchester United Junior Athletic Club, which laid the foundations for the club's policy of developing youngsters into talent good enough to represent a first team that would prove so successful in the 1950s and 60s.

Gibson was also instrumental in persuading the Midland Railway to include stops at Old Trafford station on match days in 1933, making the club far more accessible to people from all across Manchester. After the Luftwaffe had destroyed much of Old Trafford during bombing raids in World War Two, Gibson hosted the club's operations at a business he owned in Trafford Park. When the Football League started up again in 1946 the team played home games at Manchester City's Maine Road ground while Old Trafford was reconstructed with funds that Gibson successfully petitioned from the War Damage Commission. However his greatest legacy to the club was the appointment in February 1945 of Matt Busby, who – unusually for the time – was granted total control over team affairs, free from any directorial interference.

Almost immediately, under Busby, Manchester United acquired a reputation for thrilling, attacking football, and his team won the FA Cup in 1948 and League Championship in 1952. Further successes followed with the 'Busby Babes', the flock of youth team graduates gradually introduced to the first team from 1952 onwards. Following a second championship triumph in 1956, Busby defied the Football League to lead United into the European Cup. The League dismissed the new competition as a 'gimmick', with its powerful secretary Alan Hardaker commenting, 'I don't like dealing with Europe. Too many wogs and dagoes.' The principal objection seemed to be that there was a risk to the integrity of the domestic competition, and it was clear that United would face harsh punishment if delays on their foreign travels caused the postponement of any subsequent league fixtures.

United would face the best teams the continent had to offer and, in April 1957, they reached the semi-finals before losing to the defending champions, Real Madrid. The following year Busby's team overcame Red Star Belgrade to reach the semi-finals once again, where they would face AC Milan for a place in the final. On the way home from Belgrade, the team's plane had a refuelling stop in Munich, and bad weather led to two aborted take-off attempts. A third attempt was made, in part so as not to return home late and risk jeopardising the upcoming league game against Wolves. In the crash that followed, 23 people died, including eight Manchester United players and Willie Satinoff. Busby was left fighting for his life and was twice read the last rites; both times he pulled through, eventually making a full recovery. In time, he rebuilt the team, going on to lead the club to one of the unlikeliest of triumphs by winning the European Cup in 1968, only a decade on from Munich. He retired from management the following year and became a club director.

Louis Edwards had gradually built up a substantial shareholding in Manchester United and, by early 1964, directors Harold Hardman and Alan Gibson, wary of the danger in any one person gaining too much control, insisted on a deal whereby none of them would buy any more shares. Following Hardman's death in 1965, Edwards became the club's chairman, and in 1970 was instrumental in appointing his son, Martin, as a club director. By 1978, with the Edwards family company in trouble, they brought in the business academic Roland Smith to advise on what to do. In *Manchester United: The Betrayal Of A Legend* (1990), the journalist (and United fan) Michael Crick revealed what happened next: following Smith's recommendations, Martin Edwards began buying up small shareholdings in the club, aware that there was to be an impending rights issue giving shareholders the chance to buy 208 new shares for every one pound's worth held. Edwards Jnr managed to persuade Alan Gibson to relinquish his holding, and did the same with the niece of Walter Crickmer, the club secretary who had died at Munich. It was blatant insider trading – albeit then still legal, if unethical, in the UK. Such a transparent way of extracting cash from the club was bitterly opposed by fans, led by local businessman John Fletcher, as well as by Busby, but to no avail.

The following year, dividends rocketed from £312 to £50,419, most of which went straight into the Edwards family's pockets. The club's vast support meant its profitability was not hampered by a lack of success on the pitch – United had won just one FA Cup in the decade following the European Cup triumph in 1968, while the team had also suffered the indignity of relegation and a season in the Second Division. Louis Edwards cashed in further, selling the family meat company to Argyll Foods. But, unfortunately for him, the Manchester-based Granada Television's investigatory programme *World In Action* had started sniffing around. In January 1980, they broadcast an episode alleging Edwards had supplied contaminated meat to Manchester schools that was unfit for human consumption, and that supply contracts had been won by bribing officials. There were also allegations of corruption linked to his dealings at Old Trafford, with claims of bribes being paid to schoolboys' parents, and of illegal share dealings involving false documentation.

Greater Manchester Police and the FA opened investigations but a fortnight later Louis Edwards was dead, having suffered a fatal heart attack in the bath. Martin blamed the Granada programme for his father's death, saying later, 'If Matt [Busby] had gone along with the rights issue, *World In Action* would probably not have had a story, but the publicity from Matt opposing it got people interested and they started to dig.' Edwards Jnr took over as United's chairman and, when the FA subsequently relaxed its rules around the payment of full-time directors, he appointed himself as chief executive on a salary of £30,000. Being a keen rugby fan, it seemed to many supporters that the younger Edwards had little emotional attachment to Manchester United, beyond the money he could extract from it. In 1984, despite huge opposition from United supporters, he entered into discussions to sell the club to the former MP and businessman Robert Maxwell, though he ultimately refused to pay Edwards' asking price and bought the *Daily Mirror* instead. (It was a lucky escape: following Maxwell's death in 1991, the paper's parent company was plunged into crisis when banks called in loans. It emerged he had been using hundreds of millions of pounds from the company's pension fund to stave off bankruptcy.)

Left without a buyer, Edwards decided to shake things up and invited a Manchester solicitor, Maurice Watkins (previously retained as the club's solicitor by Edwards' father) onto the board, along with the legendary ex-player Bobby Charlton.

In 1989, Martin Edwards again tried to offload United, this time to the businessman Michael Knighton, in a deal worth £20 million. Half the sum was to go to buying out Edwards, with the other half committed to redeveloping the Stretford End. (This would increase the revenue the club could generate through more executive boxes and seated areas replacing the large terraces. Although the Hillsborough disaster had occurred in April 1989, a requirement for all-seater stadia only came about following the Taylor Report, which was not published until January 1990.) Despite a deal being agreed, Knighton felt obliged to abandon his plans when his backers pulled out. He would still briefly serve on United's board, before moving on and buying Carlisle United in 1992. There he became notorious for claiming he'd had an encounter with aliens. While Edwards remained deeply unpopular with supporters, it was nevertheless felt that there had to be a better alternative for the club than the likes of Maxwell or Knighton.

An interesting suggestion was put forward in the United fanzine *Red Issue* in December 1989. The magazine had started up earlier that year and was sold outside Old Trafford on match days. In the wake of Knighton's failed takeover, Russ Delaney, a financial advisor and friend of the editor Chris Robinson, wrote to readers:

'I am writing to you to appeal to raise money to purchase shares in MUFC. The reason is to have a say in the inevitable takeover that is going to happen at the end of this season. The minimum amount for shares to get a seat on the board is £20,000. The more shares that can be bought by genuine supporters, the more difficult it becomes for any

potential bidder. I know at this stage it would be virtually impossible to gain a controlling interest in the club; however, this is a realistic long-term objective.

'The idea I have is to pool donations into a fund and buy shares as and when they become available. Once we have gained a significant shareholding, we can elect someone from those who have donated onto the board. This way we can represent the views of the grassroots supporters. I am prepared to donate a sum of money to get things moving if people are interested in this proposition.'

It was a visionary idea. But owning stocks and shares was not something with which many fans on the Stretford End were familiar. Edwards remained desperate to cash in, and once again turned to Roland Smith, who advised him to float the club on the stock market. (Smith would be knighted, despite being embroiled in a political scandal that forced his resignation as the chair of British Aerospace. It emerged that his company's purchase of the Rover car company had been facilitated by a £44 million government sweetener. A House of Commons Trade and Industry Select Committee accused Smith of 'asset stripping'.) Smith would become the chairman of Manchester United plc.

The 1991 prospectus for the flotation revealed its intention: to raise £6.7m to redevelop the Stretford End; to widen ownership of the club by giving employees and supporters the chance to invest; and to provide increased liquidity to current shareholders. Many fans suspected which might be the most important to Edwards. With the UK in the grip of a crippling recession and unemployment rocketing, the idea that large numbers of working class supporters would have the £194 necessary to meet the minimum investment was absurd – not least given that the application deadline fell when season ticket renewals were also due, and just after tens of thousands of fans had undertaken an expensive trip to watch the team in the European Cup Winners' Cup final in the Netherlands. Many fans were also turned off the idea of buying shares simply to line Edwards' pockets.

The flotation immediately valued the club at £47 million – more than double the price Knighton had been set to pay less than two years earlier. Edwards kept three million shares while offloading another 1.7 million, netting himself around £6.4 million. Over the next seven years, the club would pay out around £23 million in dividends – almost four times the amount raised to bring the Stretford End in line with post-Hillsborough requirements. The following season, supporters were incensed when it was announced that ticket prices would shoot up to compensate the club – i.e. its shareholders – for the revenue lost while the rebuilding work was undertaken. Edwards sought to justify it by saying, 'We were losing something like 12,000 or 13,000 spaces. We sat down with a calculator and a pencil and said, "What do we need to make up that lost income? What do we need to charge?" And that is exactly how we arrived at the [prices] for this season.'

The cost of a League Match Ticket Book on the terraces doubled from £76 in 1990 to £152 in 1992. A fan moving from the terrace in the 1991/92 season to a seat in 1992/93 would see the price jump from £108 to £266. Fans were outraged, and the protest group HOSTAGE (Holders Of Season Tickets Against Gross Exploitation) was set up, led by long-standing fan Jonny Flacks. The group staged a public meeting at Old Trafford Cricket Ground to discuss what action to try and take but, ultimately, it was all to no avail, beyond planting a seed in some fans' minds that they needed to get organised.

The phasing-out of the terraces resulted in a decline in the quality of the match-day experience for many supporters, forced into ever more expensive seats after a lifetime of cheap terracing. But Old Trafford's capacity shrank by several thousand at the same time as the club broke its 26-year-long championship drought. Increased demand for reduced supply meant the club was not immediately concerned about any adverse economic effect of alienating long-standing fans, especially since Alex Ferguson had just led United to its first Championship since 1967, and the likes of Eric Cantona, Mark Hughes, Peter

Schmeichel, Ryan Giggs and Paul Ince were helping the team to dominate the fledgling Premier League era.

The imposition of behavioural strictures that accompanied this tightening supply began to exacerbate fan-club relations. The pages of *Red Issue* and other fanzines regularly bemoaned the club's heavy-handed treatment. The 'offences' for which 'troublesome' supporters were targeted by the club's stewards and security team became increasingly petty. Those wanting to stand in the newly seated areas were singled out for special attention. In March 1995, with the team stuttering in its bid for a third successive league title, United played Arsenal at Old Trafford. Despite regular appeals from Alex Ferguson for increased vocal support, an announcement was made during the match by an employee who *Red Issue* subsequently named 'Tannoy Woman', which instructed supporters to remain seated or else be thrown out. In response, the section known as K-Stand rose virtually as one, challenging security to do their worst, and the rest of the ground followed suit. The fans won that battle but the war with the stewards would continue throughout the rest of the season. Even Alex Ferguson was eventually roped in to perform a startling reverse-ferret. Rather than side with the supporters, he did his masters' bidding, and pleaded for people to stay seated. (Though *terracing* was phased out, standing was never actually illegal. The impossibility of making it so meant it was permitted by MUFC within seated areas but only in dubiously defined 'moments of high excitement'.) The incident had marked a turning point; and after the game, a dozen or so fans met up in the Gorse Hill pub in Stretford to discuss how to proceed. HOSTAGE may have failed in 1992, but its 1995 offspring would learn the lessons well.

The following Saturday the local Piccadilly Radio station held a football phone-in, inviting onto the airwaves *Red Issue*'s Chris Robinson and *United We Stand* editor Andy Mitten. I knew both of the guests, and called the programme to suggest that fans needed to get together and form some sort of group to oppose the increasingly draconian actions of the club's powers-that-be. It turned out that both Mitten and Robinson had been part of the Gorse Hill meeting a few nights earlier, at which the very same idea had been proposed. The pair announced their intention to each put up £500 to start just such an organisation, which would be wholly independent of the club and represent match-going supporters. With Jonny Flacks also involved, the fanzines organised a meeting at Old Trafford Cricket Ground to gauge support, and Kevin Miles from an established Newcastle United independent fan group was invited along to give advice on the best way to proceed. After a positive initial reaction, on 22 April, the inaugural meeting of the Independent Manchester United Supporters Association (IMUSA) was held at the Free Trade Hall in the city centre. It was an important moment in United's recent history: finally match-going fans had representation and, over the coming years, the group's activism and determination would ensure that the club had to start taking their concerns seriously, rather than dismissing or ignoring them as they had in the past.

Elected to leading roles were Flacks, Robinson and the politically astute Andy Walsh, who had been invited along to the Gorse Hill meeting by Peter Boyle, a well-known United fan and friend of the fanzines. Walsh had previously been the chairman of the Greater Manchester Anti Poll Tax Federation, at one point even being imprisoned for his principled refusal to pay, and he was well versed in political protest. The football writer Richard Kurt was friends with both Boyle and Walsh, and had helped introduce Walsh into the world of football politicking a couple of months earlier:

> 'Boylie and I had set up an ad hoc group called the Cantona Defence Campaign that January, after Eric's kung-fu kick and the hysteria which followed. We organised stunts, TV appearances, supportive newspaper articles, courtroom mobs and so forth. (We even released a single – top ten in the indie charts, as Boylie will eagerly remind anyone.) At that time, it was rather unusual to see fans playing "the media

game" in the way that we were doing, and I think we all got the taste for it – not to mention the fact that we all learned some tricks of the trade that would later prove useful in bigger causes.

'Pete had suggested Andy might fancy helping out because his previous political activism had inculcated certain gifts; I quickly concluded he was a born leader, and also someone who would be good with the media. I think we all enjoyed working together on Eric's behalf, and Andy's was certainly the first name I always thought of when we were all discussing the creation of IMUSA, and who might form its leadership.'

Over the next few years, IMUSA would gain a great reputation for its work on behalf of both United supporters and football fans more generally, with one of the most notable incidences of its activism coming when the Labour government's Football Task Force turned up at Manchester Town Hall in early 1998. The task force was a populist move, having been set up in the wake of Labour's 1997 election victory with a brief to investigate football's problems and propose solutions.

Unfortunately, its narrow remit didn't seem to extend to anything that actually mattered to fans. With Hillsborough still fresh in the memory, there was no appetite amongst politicians for discussion of the introduction of 'safe standing', of which IMUSA was strongly in favour. Adam Brown, an IMUSA member, was a researcher at Manchester Metropolitan University's Institute for Popular Culture and had been appointed as a member of the Task Force. He quietly urged IMUSA members not to let government mandarins set the agenda. As a result, United supporters turned up for the meeting en masse with Brown barely able to conceal his glee as speaker after speaker got up to talk, initially about an issue that was on the Task Force's approved list, before quickly diverting the matter: '. . . but of course, we wouldn't have this problem if safe standing was to be introduced.' As the majority of the floor roared its support, the meeting's chairman – the ridiculously snooty Lord Faulkner, who was clearly unused to dealing with such oiks – desperately tried to get things back on track. 'They hijacked the whole meeting,' moaned one Task Force member afterwards.

In September 1998, IMUSA began involving itself in the national news agenda after the *Sunday Telegraph* broke a sensational story: Rupert Murdoch's BSkyB wanted to buy Manchester United for £575 million. *Red Issue's* contributors exchanged knowing nods. One of them had been tipped off six months earlier by well-connected London snouts that Murdoch was planning this move. At subsequent IMUSA meetings, *Red Issue* representatives, including writer Richard Kurt, raised the Murdoch issue on more than one occasion, urging that leadership mindsets be readied for such an assault. 'To be fair, IMUSA had such a lot on its plate at the time that I don't think it could have been expected to start drawing up battle plans on spec,' remembers Kurt. 'After all, it was simply one tip in one publication. You don't gear up a war machine on so flimsy a basis.' In any event, IMUSA's organisational reaction to the news soon compensated for the effects of being caught short, as Kurt recalls. 'It was a very English-at-war scene: for a few hours, we were all running around like Corporal Jones, until suddenly a total calm set in, and improvisational flair took over.'

The main reason for the opposition to BSkyB's bid could probably be concisely summed up as: Rupert Murdoch. Andy Walsh later expanded on IMUSA's motivation for their campaigning:

There was a belief that this was the last stand. The game may have been heading down this road for some time, but this next disastrous step was not going to have the fans' acquiescence. A United takeover would open the floodgates with other clubs being targeted by media companies and commercial concerns. Football would become a battleground for TV and sponsorship rights and the interests of supporters would be further trampled in the rush. The fact that it was Murdoch did harden opinion, but the belief that a TV company owning Manchester United was wrong would have been there regardless. Above all, there was a recognition that once again fundamental decisions were being made without any input from supporters.'

This latter point was one of the main factors in the politicisation of many fans at Old Trafford: as more and more money flooded into football, the voice of the average supporter became ever more irrelevant to those running the game and clubs like Manchester United. It seemed that decisions were consistently being taken with the viewpoint of supporters – the game's biggest stakeholders – simply ignored (at best). This was in contrast to some of the giants of European football, such as Barcelona and Real Madrid, where fans had and have a direct say in who runs their club, with members able to vote accordingly. While the Spanish model wasn't necessarily perfect, with electioneering by prospective club presidents tending to be linked to promises of star signings, it provided a democratic model that was unheard of in English football.

A key early planning meeting took place under Adam Brown's auspices at Manchester Metropolitan University, which Kurt attended along with various IMUSA heads.

'Adam and I shared a similar analysis of the situation. But he was able to express it in that meeting in a way that didn't minimise how difficult a task we faced, yet also offered a crystal clear and cogent way forward. I remember bouncing out of that room in delight, happy to have discovered someone who could think strategically. We had plenty of tacticians in our squad, but Adam could also see the bigger picture.'

Media contacts began to rely on IMUSA representatives for their reaction and guidance; and with everyone at the organisation instinctively and implacably opposed to the takeover, IMUSA's narrative took hold. The story created a massive stir, not least because BSkyB owned the broadcasting rights to Premier League matches – by own-ing United, the company would have influence on both sides of the negotiating table. With Murdoch's *Sun* newspaper headlines screaming 'GOLD TRAFFORD', imagining all the extra millions the club would supposedly have to buy players, few people believed there was any-thing that could be done to stop it. Nearly all of the defiant were in two small groups of United fans: IMUSA, led by Andy Walsh in Manchester, and the newly-formed SUAM (Shareholders United Against Murdoch), under Michael Crick's direction in London.

Crick's position as a BBC reporter led to great controversy when, having stated his opposition to Murdoch, Sky complained about his lack of objectivity when he subsequently covered the story for *News-night*. Crick later admitted that the BBC 'weren't very pleased' with his involvement. Crick and Walsh formed a somewhat unlikely alliance: the latter a former Trotskyist and 'Full-Timer' in Militant Tendency; Crick the man who, in 1984, had written the book *Militant*, an exposé of the radical socialist group's infiltration of, and attempt to take over, the Labour Party in the 1970s and 80s. The pair devoted much of the next seven months to fighting the BSkyB bid, as the deal was referred in turn to the Office of Fair Trading and the Monopolies and Mergers Commission (MMC). Neither referral would be predicted by the conventional wisdom which suggested that the deal would be waved through; both would require tireless lobbying and activism to achieve. The scale and imagination of the campaign mobilised by both IMUSA and SUAM was phenomenal.

Perhaps the most important event during the campaign was the forced resignation in December 1998 of the Murdoch-friendly Peter Mandelson. He had been Secretary of State for Trade and Industry, which oversaw the MMC. It was feared that Mandelson would have ruled in favour of Murdoch, whatever the MMC eventually reported, but with his replacement by Stephen Byers, there was hope of the bid being blocked. A friendly United fan at the Department of Cul-ture, Media and Sport regularly risked his job to feed information to

IMUSA as to how things were progressing. It therefore didn't come as *that* much of a surprise when, on 9 April 1999, it was announced that the bid had been blocked on competition grounds. It was a stunning victory for people power, and Martin Edwards petulantly hit out, echoing Richard Nixon by claiming the bid had the support of a 'silent majority' of United fans.

For several years, one of the untold stories of the campaign was of Alex Ferguson's involvement. Publicly, he maintained silence through-out, with not even Walsh and Brown's 1999 published account of the takeover battle, *Not For Sale*, indicating otherwise. In it, they excused Ferguson's refusal to get involved, referring to his need 'to look after his own interests', even though he did, in fact, privately encourage Walsh, urging him to help keep the club out of Murdoch's clutches. In 2015, Walsh spoke about it in an interview with the *Red News* fanzine:

> *'We heard that Alex Ferguson wasn't happy about the takeover. Jonny Flacks made contact with Ferguson and passed on his details to me. I was given Alex Ferguson's direct line . . . we used to have regular chats when I would update him about where we were up to with the campaign.'*

Michael Crick would also go on to reveal in *The Boss* (2002), his magisterial biography of United's manager, that Ferguson had been secretly seeking to pull together a rival consortium to snatch the club from Murdoch's grasp. Ferguson's son Mark, then a fund manager with Schroders in the City of London, was instrumental in the sub-terfuge. Though it didn't come to fruition, it was an indication of Ferguson's ambition, connections and ready access to people in high finance, all of which would have been enhanced when Mark later moved to Goldman Sachs, where he was named the City's 'Fund Manager of the Year'.

With Murdoch seen off, SUAM renamed itself Shareholders United (SU), stating its aim was to, 'campaign both to preserve United's independence, and to maintain one of the aims of the 1991 flotation: "to allow as many fans and employees as possible to own shares in Manchester United".' Echoing Russ Delaney's letter in *Red Issue* a decade earlier, it reminded people, 'The best way to keep United out of the clutches of people like Murdoch is for every ordinary fan to buy as many shares as they can.' It was a call far too few would heed.

IMUSA reverted to campaigning on the week-to-week issues affecting match-going fans and, although he remained involved, Andy Walsh stood down as chairman. The organisation owed him well over £10,000 in expenses that had been racked up during the takeover battle, yet had no funds to pay him. This was incredible, given the amount of donations made by United supporters and people all over the world during the fight against Murdoch. I got a well-sourced tip that an IMUSA official had been pocketing large sums of the money and passed the information on to Walsh. However, weeks later, it became evident that the person in question had managed to fob off all requests for further information. It seemed that the allegation wasn't being treated very seriously, so I pushed for answers. It transpired that the official had, over a long period, been forging the other two signatures required to authorise withdrawals from IMUSA's account. The lack of proper oversight from the rest of IMUSA's committee was shocking. Walsh didn't publicly discuss the matter until 2015, when he admitted in the *Red News* fanzine:

'I was in quite a bit of debt at the end of the Murdoch campaign. Later on, we found out that IMUSA did have more money, but it had been stolen from us. We estimated that something in excess of £20,000 had been taken. Signatures had been forged on cheques and the bank had allowed other cheques to be drawn in contravention of our bank mandate.

'[The bank] tried to argue that it was our fault because we didn't look after our account properly. We successfully countered that. We had direct evidence of over £20,000 of fraud and estimated that there was

probably more as well but we couldn't prove it. In the end, after a long hard slog, NatWest refunded £20,000 back to IMUSA.

'As an officer of IMUSA, I felt a great deal of responsibility. We should have been tighter on our finances but we naively trusted those who we worked alongside, and did not believe that one of our own would rip us off.'

By this time, the writer Richard Kurt and I were running *Red Issue* magazine's news and gossip column, and also overseeing the website's popular news service. Ever more supporters were devouring content about United online, and the website's forum grew, which in turn helped cultivate more sources and networks for further tips. It was in this way, for example, that *Red Issue* exposed Alison Ryan, appointed in 2000 as Manchester United's first head of PR until it was revealed that she had falsified her CV. The *Financial Times* journalist Paddy Harverson subsequently got the job instead. Richard Kurt reveals that *Red Issue* had an extra motivation in ensuring Ryan's exposure:

'Of course, we enjoyed showing up United's headhunters, and highlighting the board's incompetence, as a matter of ideological taste. But we had also wanted Harverson to get the job from the moment the shortlist was compiled. A Red Issue *reader working high up at the* Financial Times *had contacted us to sing Paddy's praises, and assure us he'd do a sound job for the club – while also respecting the likes of us, complaining from the cheap seats. Paddy lived up to that billing. He was fairly "hard", but that strong personality could handle Fergie's idiosyncrasies. Plus he treated* Red Issue *properly; no unfair favours, but always answering our queries fully, without trying to mislead us.'*

Harverson's star would rise to such an extent that he would eventually move on to represent Prince Charles, playing a key role in the success of William and Kate's wedding in 2011 – *Red Issue*'s invitation evidently getting lost in the post.

In late 2002, a much more interesting story would be plucked from the grapevine. Trot forward 'Rock Of Gibraltar', the horse which won an unprecedented seven consecutive Group One races, and which Ferguson was said to part-own with the wife of the Irish billionaire John Magnier. *Red Issue* reported, with a knowing wink:

> *'Much has been made in the Press about Fergie's foresight in investing in such a promising prospect but could it be right he only bought into a share of the steed's prize winnings and not its stud rights, where potentially the real millions are? If true, then even if Fergie has already seen a return on Gibraltar, the deal would be reminiscent of the OT [Old Trafford] contract wrangle when he rejected plc share options, instead holding out for a bigger increase in hard cash.'*

Along with JP McManus, Magnier was part of the so-called 'Coolmore Mafia', a group of hugely wealthy Irish businessmen with vast interests in horseracing, notably the Coolmore stud farm which has bases in Ireland, France, Australia and the United States. Ferguson, a keen racing fan, had been introduced to McManus by a friend-in-common at Cheltenham in March 1997, and in the following years he became increasingly friendly with both McManus and his business partner Magnier. Following the MMC's block on BSkyB's takeover of Manchester United in 1999, at various points over the next couple of years the club's share price hovered little above £1, valuing the club at less than half the £623 million that Sky had offered. Coolmore started buying up shares through an offshore investment company called Cubic Expression, increasing its holding to become the second largest investor by mid-2001.

At that time, Alex Ferguson had just emerged from a major power struggle with the plc board. Martin Edwards had quit as chief executive in August 2000, to be replaced by Peter Kenyon, the oleaginous former head of sportswear company Umbro. Ferguson indicated his intention to retire from football in May 2002 but, after winning a European Cup and three successive league championships from 1999–2001 with a team chock full of talent like Roy Keane, David Beckham, Dwight Yorke and Jaap Stam, he sought an improved deal going into his final year. In May 2001 Ferguson entered talks with Kenyon but these quickly hit a dead end, as *The Observer* reported:

'*[There was] a huge gap between what Ferguson was seeking and what the club was offering. He wanted £1m-a-year to work as an ambassador for United, while all the club had offered was £100,000 for a highly vague role which, one Ferguson ally said, "seemed to be to hang around, do nothing, keep quiet, look after the development of young players and maybe cut a few ribbons here and there".*

'*Another meeting proved short and just as acrimonious. When Jason Ferguson [Alex Ferguson's son and advisor] learnt the club was not prepared to make a better offer, he left at once. As far as the manager and his advisers – Jason, accountant Alan Baines and lawyer Kevin Jaquiss – were concerned, negotiations were now over.*

'*That afternoon Jaquiss rang Michael Crick, and told him that no deal had been reached, and Ferguson felt "insulted" by the club's "derisory" offer and would probably not be staying on after all. Ferguson's camp was happy this information was leaked to a newspaper, and the next day's* Daily Mail *duly led its back page with the news.*'

Ahead of United's last game of the season at Tottenham Hotspur, Ferguson gave an interview to the club's in-house TV station, insisting that he was going to quit in 2002 and sever all ties with Old Trafford. It looked increasingly likely that Ferguson would actually walk out following the game at White Hart Lane – not the first time he had seemed set to quit the club in a battle over wages – and fans gave him non-stop support throughout the first half. The following week the club's share price began tumbling, piling pressure on the plc board to secure Ferguson's future. As a result he was handed a

£10,000 per week pay rise and a £1 million-a-year post-retirement stipend to work as a club ambassador. More importantly, he had won the power struggle.

By the time Ferguson had performed a U-turn on his retirement decision, announced midway through the 2001/02 season, he was even more secure in his position. Not only had he cowed the board and gained a massive pay increase to boot, his Coolmore friends were now heavily invested in the club, with much talk that they were even planning a takeover themselves. While some fans welcomed the prospect – deeming anything better than the likes of Edwards and Kenyon – Andy Walsh quietly warned of the parallels with Busby and Louis Edwards back in the 1950s. It was a prescient call. *Red Issue*'s information about Ferguson not having rights to ownership of the superstar Rock Of Gibraltar would prove correct. In August 2003, the *Sunday Telegraph* reported that a huge legal wrangle loomed between Manchester United's manager and the club's second largest shareholders. Although the horse had run in Ferguson's colours, word in the racing world was that Coolmore had only ever gifted him some sort of 'ceremonial' rights, allowing Ferguson to act as a sort of 'mascot', having recognised that his association with a champion horse could be mutually beneficial. Ferguson saw it differently, believing that he'd acquired a part-share in the steed, and that he was therefore entitled to an equivalent proportion of the resulting stud fees, estimated to be worth £100,000 a time. The dispute had disastrous potential for both Ferguson and the club. In the *Daily Telegraph*, Michael Crick worried over how it would play out:

> '*I have always been sceptical over whether Alex ever had a 50-50 share of Rock Of Gibraltar. Industry people have suggested to me that Magnier is always careful of maintaining control in these situations rather than handing it over to a third party.*
>
> '*It has always been assumed that Ferguson wants to take a greater stake in the club with the help of his friends from Ireland. If the rift over*

the Rock proves permanent, it could change the face of the world's biggest football club.'

As a goodwill gesture, Magnier initially offered Ferguson one stud nomination per year and, when this was refused, raised it to two per year. Ferguson refused to back down on his claim to 50 per cent of the horse and initiated legal action against Coolmore, claiming damages of £110 million. In turn, the Irish duo put the squeeze on him by ramping up their United shareholding. By November 2003, the case was set for Dublin's High Court. Yet at Manchester United's AGM, the board was blasé about the potential ramifications. An editorial in *Red Issue* warned:

'For now the board may well sit back and declare it a "private matter" but ultimately they will have to take action to prevent the club becoming mired in such a damaging situation. For Fergie, a clearer case of professional suicide would be difficult to envisage. Magnier's team will dig up every little incident that could possibly cast doubt on his integrity.'

By January 2004, Cubic Expression owed over 25 per cent of the club making Coolmore by far the largest shareholders. They started to toy with Ferguson, issuing a list of 99 questions to which they demanded answers from the plc board, many of which zoomed in on its allegedly poor stewardship of the club and on the payments it had made to agents in transfer deals. The involvement of Ferguson's son Jason in United deals came in for special attention, just as it had in Crick's *The Boss* two years earlier. On 25 January, the *Sunday Times* ran a number of articles which hinted that Coolmore were ready to move in for the kill. At United's FA Cup game at Northampton that day, a group of us believed it would be difficult for Ferguson to survive, not least given he was in negotiations over a contract extension at the time, which Coolmore would be sure to try to veto. On

Wednesday 4 February, the plc delivered its responses to the 99 questions. The Press Association reported:

> *'[Plc chairman Roy] Gardner and chief executive David Gill [Kenyon's replacement in mid-2003] will spend an anxious few days awaiting further developments, knowing their future with the club could hinge on the eventual outcome. If the response is not satisfactory, it is thought the Irish duo will pursue the option of either calling for an emergency general meeting, demanding a seat on the United board or reporting their concerns to the Financial Services Authority.'*

Two days later came a stunning development that completely altered the dynamic of the increasingly bitter dispute. A group calling itself the Manchester Education Committee (MEC) invaded the course during a race meeting at Hereford, disrupting the 16:20 that featured the Coolmore-owned Majestic Moonbeam. The footage led bulletins on SkySports, and the following day's press ran extensive quotes from a statement the group had issued, headlined 'Operation Moonbeam'. It said that they believed 'this course of action to be the most effective way of applying pressure on Coolmore to take heed of Manchester United fans' wishes when it comes to the ownership and running of Manchester United Football Club', warning the Irish not to 'deliberately allow this dispute to publicly infringe upon and undermine the running of MUFC' – while also threatening a further 'spectacular' to come.

Importantly, it also made clear that the protest was not some blind support of Ferguson – 'The list of 99 questions submitted by Coolmore to MUFC plc regarding corporate governance of the organisation raises many legitimate concerns' – but it insisted that the MEC would not allow the club to be used as a pawn in rich men's arguments. It also urged Coolmore to 'strike up a dialogue with leading supporters' groups and abide by supporters' wishes for the future direction of the club', wishes which included not offloading their holding to parties who could be 'detrimental to the good of MUFC.'

The protest meant that the focus of the story was now completely switched: rather than being all about Coolmore meddling in the football world, the football world was now meddling in theirs. The following midweek, United were at home to Middlesbrough and another small attempt was made to take matters onto Coolmore's turf. It was discovered that Kroll, the company whose private investigators John Magnier had hired to pore over Ferguson's business dealings and private life, had an office in Manchester. A pantomime horse was hired, a small band of United supporters recruited, and the horse was led to Kroll's office doors, where it got a little bit excited and tried to kick it in, while banners urged 'Stop the horseplay Coolmore'.

An Irish United fan, Sean Murphy, subsequently popped up in the media claiming to represent a group called United4action, and requested permission from Cheltenham racecourse to stage a protest against Coolmore during the annual festival in March. Combined with the MEC's statement threatening further action, this caused reverberations around the racing world. Magnier and McManus reacted by increasing their shareholding to 28.89 per cent, marginally below the 29.9 per cent at which stock-market rules would compel them to make an offer for the whole club. Despite this, there was little doubt that they were suddenly on the back foot, and needed to find a resolution quickly.

Ferguson was feeling the heat and was just as eager to reach an agreement. He had even requested help from the United-supporting Irish prime minister Bertie Ahern, although Ahern's office declined the request, believing it would be inappropriate. Ferguson instead turned to Dermot Desmond, the owner of Celtic and a friend-cum-business partner of the Coolmore pair, who also owned a small tranche of shares in United. After a meeting with Desmond in London, Ferguson rang Magnier at his hotel retreat in Barbados. Shortly thereafter, and just three weeks after the Hereford disruption, Ferguson called upon supporters to abandon plans to target Cheltenham. 'It is effectively the equivalent of the FA Cup final to horse racing fans,' he said.

'I would not wish this special festival to be marred in any way. I am therefore asking supporters to refrain from any form of protest which may reflect badly on the club and its supporters in general.'

Sean Murphy reacted by withdrawing his request to be allowed to protest but the MEC more or less told Ferguson to butt out, mimicking his statement thus:

> *'[The club] is effectively the equivalent of a family member to many United fans and the MEC do not wish this special institution to be marred in any way. The MEC are therefore asking Sir Alex Ferguson to refrain from giving his name to any form of statement opposing action by United supporters.'*

A week later it was revealed that Ferguson and Coolmore had reached a settlement, with the United manager offered four stud fees annually or a lump sum of £2.5 million. He chose the latter, an estimated £500,000 of which would be swallowed up by legal fees. Martin Hannan, the author of *Rock Of Gibraltar* (2004) later claimed Ferguson made the wrong decision in grabbing the lump sum: 'This horse is now getting silly money for its stud fees; he would almost certainly have recouped that £2.5m in just a few years. And the horse could have another ten years in him after that, so he may have missed out on millions.'

It was a humiliating climb down for Ferguson, albeit a humiliation that he was soon prepared to overlook. The following year, the *Daily Telegraph* reported he had purchased a yearling son of Rock Of Gibraltar, quoting him as claiming, 'Grown men move on.'

The BBC could have been forgiven for wondering why their own 80-year-old institution didn't qualify as a 'grown man' in Ferguson's eyes. For it would take a decade for Ferguson to 'move on' from his Rock-like spat with the broadcasting corporation. In May 2004, the BBC ran a documentary on the Jason Ferguson financial dealings upon which Coolmore had previously focused. Among its allegations were details of Manchester United having paid Mike Morris, a close business associate of Jason Ferguson, hundreds of thousands of pounds to act for them in the defender Jaap Stam's transfer to Lazio. It also highlighted glaring contradictions in what Peter Kenyon and Jason's Elite agency had said about the move, while the player's agent expressed surprise that Elite had been paid at all: 'It sounds strange. It seems a lot of people made a lot of money for not a lot of work.' Just days before the programme was aired, in the wake of a review sparked by Coolmore's questioning, Manchester United announced that 'tighter internal procedures' would now mean that Jason would never 'act for the club' again. Despite this, Ferguson demanded the BBC apologise for the claims it had made, calling them:

'A whole lot of nonsense, all made-up stuff, brown paper bags and all that kind of carry-on. It was a horrible attack on my son's honour and he should never have been accused of that. But it is such a huge organisation that they will never apologise. They don't even care if you sue them or whatever, because they are so huge and have insurance. They carry on regardless and it's breathtaking.'

Perhaps in an attempt to show that he was capable of maintaining *some* sort of principle, Ferguson would boycott the corporation for the next seven years.

2

MARCH OF THE BLANKETEERS

Even as Coolmore added to their Manchester United shareholding in early 2004, there was talk of them selling up once Ferguson had been forced to back out of his legal action against them. By mid-February, businessman Malcolm Glazer, owner of the Tampa Bay Buccaneers American football team, had quietly built up his own holding to over 16 per cent. From a family of Lithuanian immigrants who had settled in Rochester, New York, Malcolm inherited the family watch business after his father died and built up a fortune. Expansion followed into real estate investment, centring on giant trailer parks that were home to some of the country's poorest communities. Investment in a variety of other businesses followed, not all of which were successful and Glazer soon came to be regarded as a corporate raider, targeting undervalued companies to drive up the share price, before cashing out with a big profit. One such incident involved Harley-Davidson, who ultimately took legal action against him. Glazer was described by the judge hearing the case as 'a snake in sheep's clothing'.

Glazer's reputation as a money-obsessed chancer was underlined when his sister Jeanette was asked for her views of his interest in Manchester United. 'He's centred on one thing. He's like a machine – money, money, money. There's no other dimension. He's always striving for more which, I suppose, is why he wants your soccer team.' She knew only too well: after their mother died in 1980, Malcolm's belief in his sole entitlement to her estate led him to wage a 15-year court battle against his siblings. In Tampa Bay, Glazer had threatened to move the Buccaneers franchise to Baltimore unless the city built the team a new stadium. The politicians caved in and gave him what he wanted, while Glazer subsequently reneged on his promise to fund half the venture. Though the Buccaneers won the 2003 Super Bowl, fans were unhappy with ever-increasing ticket prices and a lack of investment in the team. In 2000, some fans sued the club regarding the pricing and seating provision in the new stadium; Glazer counter-sued them for defamation. The case was eventually settled out of court.

In 2003 when Glazer first began to invest in Manchester United, his record of corporate raiding meant that he was widely regarded as a stalking horse, only looking to capitalise on the expected increase in United's share price to pocket a quick profit. The journalist Mihir Bose later claimed that the Glazers were actually encouraged to mount a full takeover by the plc board:

'Near the end of 2003 the Glazers had given no thought to mounting a takeover of United. The idea was planted in their heads when they first met David Gill. It was at this meeting that they realised how much the United board felt under siege from the Irish. At their meeting with Joel and Avi Glazer, Gill and the board made it clear they saw the Americans as their saviours. They told them that if they offered £3 a share to the Irish they would sell, and that such a move would be welcomed by the board with open arms.'

In the summer of 2004, the chairman of IMUSA, Julian ('Jules') Spencer, reacted to the growing speculation by bringing together his organisation, Shareholders United and the three fanzines, *Red Issue*, *Red News* and *United We Stand*, into a 'Not For Sale' coalition. Its aim was to present a unified front to oppose any suitors for the club, while urging supporters to buy shares with the intention of creating a 10 per cent holding to help keep the club out of private control. The two big unknowns with the potential to undermine this ambition were the intentions of Coolmore (were they long-term investors or would they now be looking to cash out?) and of Glazer – was *he* a long term investor or just a speculator after a quick buck? On 3 October, the Glazer question was answered when details broke in the press that he was set to launch a full bid for the club. His plan was to execute a leveraged takeover, borrowing the money required to buy Manchester United, before flipping the loans onto the club and repaying them through its profits – profits which would be ramped up by increased ticket prices. The plan was fraught with danger due to the crippling interest rates chargeable on some of the loans. With United as the ultimate security against the loans, in the event of any default on payments, there was a risk of the club being taken over by hedge funds and possibly even Old Trafford being sold off, a humiliating and needless prospect for a club that, in 2004, boasted being the richest club in the world.

Predictably, fans were outraged. Whereas in previous years a public meeting would've been called to gauge the strength of feeling, this was now the internet age. Thousands of people visited *Red Issue*'s website every single day, devouring its comprehensive United news service and whiling time away on the site's forum where the collective view on the news was in no doubt. *Red Issue*'s web of contacts was soon feeding in information from the City of London, which was regurgitated in more digestible form for the readers.

Within hours of anyone appearing in the media acting in any capacity for the Glazers, their name, email address, employer, phone number and even their home address would be splashed on internet forums, leaving them at the mercy of the mob. In this way, Brunswick, an international financial PR firm, was forced to take its website offline, remove all staff's contact details and instruct switchboard operators not to divulge the identity of anyone working on Glazer's bid; their offices were hit with a deluge of unsolicited pizza orders and skip deliveries. Paul Ridley, a PR consultant and former sports editor of the *Sun* newspaper, was also targeted.

It wasn't long before *Red Issue* received an email titled 'Urgent – Warning' from a reader at a London law firm. The email said the firm had been instructed by 'a certain PR company with a view to taking action regarding the anti-Glazer disruption caused to it by United fans'. The Glazers' own City law firm had also already come under siege, word of which had got around the industry. The source claimed, 'My firm is obviously concerned about the possible retaliation if it accepts these instructions, but already a couple of our trainees have had to register on the site so they can monitor the message board to take evidence.' *Red Issue* obtained the company's IP address and promptly banned it from accessing the forum.

Information on Glazers' bankers was also obtained, a friendly informant emailing *Red Issue*:

'JP Morgan's Dublin office are handling the modelling work for Glazer's bid. The idea is for the London office to pass a good deal of the background work over to Dublin to keep it out of sight, specifically the financial model for handling the debt long term. It seems it will be done in conjunction with another bank in the US who would be kept out of the limelight. The Dublin employees involved are being made to sign all kinds of confidentiality agreements in addition to the usual rules they have to abide by.'

A United fan in Florida sent in Malcolm Glazer's home address ('his neighbours include Rod Stewart and Donald Trump') while another with Home Office contacts forwarded details of anyone called Glazer who'd entered the UK in the previous few months, with a promise to track future movements. With every day came a fresh leak, a new cunning stunt, or some new 'mob justice' outrage to infuriate the financial press.

But there was plenty occurring elsewhere besides pizzas and skips. When the news of Glazer's move had broken, Andy Walsh was despondent, believing it spelled the end for hopes of fan ownership of the club. Commentator David Cummings, of Standard Life Investments, agreed: 'I do not think there is anything that Manchester United fans can do about it. They can complain about it but it is curtains for them. They may not want him but they are going to get him.'

I was adamant that, as with Coolmore, there could be a way – it just needed working out what that was. In the meantime, Richard Kurt and I aimed to coax Walsh out of self-imposed semi-retirement in order to bring his experience and array of contacts from the BSkyB battle into play.

Through an intermediary, Kurt and Russ Delaney set up a meeting between Walsh and Keith Harris, a United-supporting investment banker who had recently been involved in a number of football club takeovers, as well as advising BSkyB on its bid for United back in 1998. Harris flew up to Manchester and the pair discussed the options in the kitchen of Walsh's house in Stretford. Walsh wanted the meeting kept secret, if only until he handed matters over to IMUSA and SU's leadership to take on from there. However, word leaked to the *Daily Mirror*, and they splashed the development on their back page, claiming Harris and United fans' groups were putting together a rival bid.

In spite of being informed of the Harris meeting, SU's suspicious spokesperson Oliver Houston decided to mark some cards in the press. 'Fans will remember Harris as the man who tried, as a broker, to flog United to Rupert Murdoch. If anyone wants to talk to us about a bid where fans are truly at the centre, they know where we are.' But over in Dublin, it would be Russ Delaney with whom a Coolmore representative chose to make contact, and it seemed the Irish might be amenable to talks about selling their stake – if supporters could raise the finance. Around £250 million was believed to be the figure

Coolmore wanted. That was clearly a major obstacle but, incredibly, the *Mirror* story had also smoked out a possible backer: the Japanese investment bank Nomura, keen to help explore structuring some sort of deal. A meeting in London between them, IMUSA and SU was quickly scheduled for later in the month.

The ground war would continue though. On Thursday 7 October, the MEC reappeared, this time at Altrincham's Moss Lane ground where United's reserve team played. Twenty balaclava-clad men invaded the pitch to disrupt a game being broadcast live on the club's MUTV channel. In *The Guardian* Danny Taylor reported:

> '*The same group, going by the name of the Manchester Education Committee (MEC), is believed to be responsible for an incident at the home of the United director Maurice Watkins on Monday night, when paint was thrown over his car. Watkins was targeted after selling one million shares to Glazer.*
>
> '*Information has been passed to* The Guardian *that other directors, notably Nick Humby and Andy Anson, are being seen as legitimate targets. The MEC believes both men are not averse to the idea of Glazer taking control. Acts of violence have not been ruled out and United are fully aware that it is not merely the work of a few individuals but a well organised group armed with addresses, contact details and inside information.*
>
> '*In a statement the MEC said last night: "For far too long the wishes of Manchester United fans, and football fans in general, have been ignored as clubs sacrifice everything at the altar of commercialism.*
>
> '*"The Manchester Education Committee would like to stress that in the event of the wishes of Manchester United supporters being ignored in any takeover situation, we intend to initiate a civil war effectively setting the football club – the supporters – against the company. In such a situation it is our intention to render the club ungovernable and actively disrupt all manner of commercial activity associated with Manchester United."*

'Pointedly it added: "The club's sponsors and commercial partners should note that the Manchester Education Committee will view them as legitimate targets."'

Manchester United condemned the protest, and employees of the club's security company subsequently approached at least one well-known hooligan to quietly request help in bringing the MEC to heel. Cooperation was not forthcoming.

At October's monthly IMUSA meeting, discussions were held as to the best way to proceed. The next game on 24 October was one of the biggest of the season, with champions Arsenal visiting Old Trafford. I suggested that fans had to take the MEC's promises into their own hands by targeting the club's sponsors, and that the best way to do so was via the Old Trafford megastore, owned and operated by the kit suppliers Nike. Before the game, a large group of protestors brought together by IMUSA flash-mobbed the store, causing chaos and forcing its closure, which left legions of tat-tourists disappointed. It wasn't quite Jesus driving the moneylenders out of the temple but the symbolism was there for many of the more traditional fans involved. The atmosphere in the ground continued the mutinous vibe and, at half-time, an effigy of Glazer was hung from the Stretford End in front of a flag bearing a skull and crossbones that declared, 'WARNING – USING MUFC MAY RESULT IN SERIOUS DAMAGE TO YOUR HEALTH.' Clearly the occasion helped matters, and as the chant 'United, United, not for sale!' continually rang out all around the ground, United ended Arsenal's supposed Invincibles' quest for a fiftieth game unbeaten, Van Nistelrooy and Rooney scoring in a 2–0 win.

A couple of days earlier, news of Nomura's talks with IMUSA and SU had been broken by the *Financial Times*:

'Nomura, the largest Japanese investment bank, is exploring ways of blocking a takeover of Manchester United by Malcolm Glazer, after

being enlisted by Keith Harris, chairman of Seymour Pierce, the UK investment bank.

'The Japanese bank has been working on a financing package with Mr Harris, a long-term United fan, for several weeks. Mr Harris wants to build up a stake in the FA Cup holders which would be held by supporters and would be substantial enough to ensure that United could never be taken over without their consent or involvement.

'The bank had initially earmarked £200m for use by Mr Harris and the supporters. The loan would have been partly repaid with funds released from a securitisation of future ticket sales or revenues from media rights.

'However, recent share buying by Mr Glazer and his family – which lifted their stake above 28 per cent – would now make that difficult. With more than 25 per cent of the equity Mr Glazer could veto any proposed securitisation, which would require 75 per cent of shareholders to back the plan.

'In spite of this apparent setback, however, Nomura is continuing to work on a financing proposal. The bank declined to comment.

'The Glazers, owners of the Tampa Bay Buccaneers NFL franchise, have in the last week lifted their stake from 19.2 per cent to 28.1 per cent, paying 285p a share from institutional investors such as UBS.'

On 25 October, the plc released a statement that seemed to kill off Glazer's hope of any imminent deal: 'The board has decided to inform all shareholders that it would regard an offer which it believes to be overly leveraged as not being in the best interests of the Company.' David Gill went further, saying, 'The Club has 126 years of history and is recognised as one of the most successful football clubs in the world. I don't think any sensible person would think we could recommend a proposal that could jeopardise something that has been built up over so many years.'

With the plc's AGM approaching on 12 November, Glazer plotted his revenge. The directors Maurice Watkins, Andy Anson and Philip Yea were all up for re-election and, with Glazer expected to vote against them, the club appealed to Magnier and McManus for support. The Irish abstained and the trio were booted off the board. However, it was a self-defeating act, as Glazer's backers JP Morgan and Brunswick now withdrew their services, having no desire to be part of a hostile takeover. The prospects of a buy-out looked even more remote a week later when Jim O'Neill, a United fan and Goldman Sachs' head of global economics, was appointed by the plc as a non-executive director. He had links to both Coolmore and Ferguson, while his appointment also ensured Glazer couldn't turn to Goldman Sachs to replace JP Morgan. The move was also beneficial for David Gill, who cashed in over £500,000 of share options by selling them to O'Neill.

Everyone at the club seemed confident that Glazer had been seen off, not least Alex Ferguson. Having kept quiet thus far, he took the opportunity to issue a statement on the club's website:

> *'I have always tried to be the bridge between the club and the fans. I have tried to support the fans in a lot of their pleas and causes. It's important for the club to recognise the fans. We are a special club in that respect.*
>
> *'When the plc started, there were grave doubts about it – I had them myself – but I think the supporters have come round to that. There's a stronger rapport between the club and the fans than there's ever been. We are both of a common denominator: we don't want the club to be in anyone else's hands.'*

David Gill was equally keen to be seen as a man of the people and attended a SU meeting at which he insisted Glazer's plan was 'unworkable' and that 'debt is a road to ruin'. He also pledged solidarity to SU's chairman Nick Towle, saying, 'If I wasn't in the position I'm in now, I would be behind the barricades with you.' However, in spite of that promise, there was no sign of him when Glazer returned to the attack in February 2005 with JP Morgan now back on board. Reacting to the news Glazer was seeking to conduct due diligence through a thorough review of United's book, SU sent out an urgent email:

'Tonight – Go straight from work to Old Trafford. Or leave early if you have to travel further. Talk to other Reds and get them to come too. Take your car/van/lorry if you have one. From 5.30 building up to 7 p.m. we want to see cars parked on the car park opposite the Megastore with your lights on full beam and your horn sounding. Make sure they know we will not accept Glazer.'

While SU bizarrely urged people to beep horns, others focused on United's sponsors. On Saturday 12 February, a large group of fans met up in Shambles Square in Manchester and flash-mobbed the Vodafone shop on Market Street and various outlets of Ladbrokes – both of whom had commercial arrangements with the club. IMUSA organised a huge protest march before a European Cup game against AC Milan, with thousands meeting by Old Trafford Cricket Ground and heading down to Old Trafford. Oliver Houston had continued SU's increasingly quixotic pronouncements by telling reporters, 'It'll probably be like something out of a Steven Spielberg movie: we're telling people to bring down torches. A sea of several thousand torches being carried down Matt Busby Way might look quite awesome.'

Both *Red Issue* and IMUSA were starting to believe they might have a problem with Houston. An impression of solipsism was only strengthened when a full-page profile on him appeared in the *Manchester Evening News*, complete with him laying out his future career hopes. While *Red Issue* and IMUSA had historically close links – Jules Spencer had been involved with the magazine since 1991 – there was a growing suspicion that some at SU didn't quite share the same aims as everyone else. This was summed up by an internal message sent by one of their officials at a moment when the Glazers were rumoured to be in the UK: 'We are trying to find out where he's staying, but we don't want the MEC to get there and do something silly before we can do something peaceful and powerful.'

Duncan Drasdo, who was both an IMUSA committee member and heavily involved with SU, might have been ideal to act as a bridge between the two organisations but he was deeply suspicious that *Red Issue* was pulling IMUSA's strings. Much later, it transpired that this extended to a general belief within SU that *Red Issue* had 'entered into secret talks with Keith Harris' over a period of several months, to the 'exclusion of SU and IMUSA'. SU believed these non-existent talks had been 'likely to reduce the chance of any potential Red Knights coming forward'. Richard Kurt throws some light on the misapprehension:

> *'David Bick, a tremendously entertaining chap who handled Keith Harris's media relations, would phone up from time to time to encourage us and swap gossip. Dave had a reputation as a street-wise Thatcherite but would nevertheless end up as an idealistic convert to fan ownership, showing that those behind the idea need not only be lentil-munching lefties!'*

But the message was always clear: Harris himself would not and could not get involved with 'the fans' until the Glazers made a formal move. Thus it was that the only time anyone at *Red Issue* had any direct contact with Keith Harris was on the night the Glazers launched their bid. Kurt recalls:

> *'Keith phoned me for a one-minute chat, agreed that it'd be a good idea for him to meet some fans, and took Andy Walsh's number from me. Within the week, he'd flown up to Manchester to meet Andy. SU and Harris thereafter enjoyed several months together to try to sort something out. Ultimately, SU took a perfectly respectable democratic decision not to proceed with the plan proposed, as was their right – but also their responsibility. The notion that Harris was somehow "kept from" SU was baffling. Not least as either party could have freely contacted the other at any point during the year preceding the bid, had they so wished. But these mistaken assumptions do happen in the fog of war, I suppose.'*

With all the suspicion breeding mutual mistrust, Adam Brown eventually stepped in as mediator and urged everyone to re-focus on the task in hand: stopping the takeover.

Members of the press made it clear to *Red Issue* that their sources believed Alex Ferguson held the key to Glazer's ability to finance the buy-out. It was thought that if Ferguson were to come out against the takeover, it would be sunk. It had already been seen in May 2001 how much store financial institutions placed on his continued presence, and there was little doubt that his son Mark would've appreciated how key to any deal he was. Given Ferguson's refusal to commit either way, *Red Issue* tried to influence the second most important factor in the deal: the financiers banking on fans' continued loyalty. After talking it through with a wide number of people over a period of about a month, I wrote a piece proposing a new breakaway club in the event Glazer got his hands on Old Trafford. This stated:

'FC United shall be based upon:
– An outright refusal to recognise Malcolm Glazer's franchise.
– Ownership of FC United being held by a supporters' trust.
– All profits being reinvested in the club.
– FC United will play in red, white and black.
– The club will never carry a sponsor on the front of its shirt, while tie-ups of any kind will only be accepted from reputable companies.
– Support amongst the youth of Manchester and Salford will be a priority and actively encouraged. Discounts will be available to all under-18s and OAPs.
– FC United will encourage local businesses whenever possible.
– The club will actively encourage local talent through its proposed Junior Athletic Club.'

The proposal was for the club to start in the bottom tier of the non-league pyramid, rent a ground in the Manchester area, and act as a vehicle for all those thousands who steadfastly refused to finance any

Glazer regime. Simon Mullock in the *Sunday Mirror* ran with the tale and an email address that was set up for people to volunteer their expertise was besieged with offers. However, on internet forums, fans were split – many thought it a great idea, but many others viewed it as an act of treachery. The arguments it caused would run and run.

By the end of February Keith Harris seemed to have grown increasingly exasperated with SU and emailed Jules Spencer:

> *'I feel that very little progress has been made by or with Shareholders United, despite having commenced discussions with Nomura some months ago. The threat of a takeover from Glazer still looms large and I do not feel that we currently have a clear corporate alternative.*
>
> *'All of that said, it is not possible for me to take any proposal forward without a mandate to represent an organisation. I am more than happy in any discussions I have with third parties to act on behalf of IMUSA. To do this I will need a form of words from you that provides such a mandate.'*

The mandate Harris sought was believed to be so he could open discussions with the ruling Emir of Qatar. Due to the adverse publicity that both Coolmore and Glazer had attracted, such a mandate from one of the supporter organisations had been requested to show that such a move would have fans' backing. In practice this meant Shareholders United agreeing to it. It later turned out that their reticence – and paranoia about *Red Issue* – was likely due to the fact that they had signed a confidentiality agreement to open their own secret talks following an approach to them by the Emir's lawyers. These ultimately led nowhere, with SU sources claiming the £3 per share price (which valued the club around £780 million) was deemed too much.

Some would have genuinely welcomed a Qatari takeover, given the presumed lack of debt, as well as the riches it might offer to counter Roman Abramovich at Chelsea; others saw drumming up a potential counterbid as nothing more than an obstructionary device. Richard Kurt explains:

> '*For the likes of me and Russ, for example, the aim was very basic, and was encouraged by a couple of newspapers' financial editors: get grouse-beating, to force a plausible competitor to the Glazers out into the open. This would have two effects: firstly, to raise the ultimate price of the club, thus possibly placing it beyond the heavily leveraged Glazers' means; secondly, to ensure the plc had a further valid legal reason to refuse recommending or accepting any Glazer bid. We did understand that the board had a fiduciary duty to act in the shareholder interest, and that this duty might ultimately dictate that they let their resistance to the Glazers drop. So having Qatar pop up promising a better alternative would have got everyone off the hook in the short term.*
>
> '*Frankly, at this stage, we were just looking for roadblocks to put up – anything to make it more difficult for Gill and Glazer to fall into each other's arms. I doubt many of us actively desired a Qatari takeover, no more so than any other. What we wanted was for the plc to survive the siege, and then continue to exist. Only then could we continue to have an ownership stake in the club of which we were members; only then would that slim avenue remain open leading towards fan ownership and control, in part or in whole.*'

Shareholders United appeared to be keeping as many irons in as many fires as possible. In March, Jonathan Northcroft, their favourite hack at the *Sunday Times*, reported on a cunning plan they'd formulated 'if, as expected, Glazer makes his long-awaited takeover attempt of United by the end of this week'. Northcroft had clearly been briefed to write:

> '*Fans currently control at least 10% and as much as 18% of United through the supporters trust, Shareholders United, and will need to raise a minimum of £50m to execute their plan to take their stake beyond 25%, the level they believe necessary to block the American tycoon.*

*'Advised by major mergers and acquisitions firm, Weil, Gotshal &
Manges, they say they are "highly confident" of pulling off a deal with a
leading City institution willing to lend them the money, which they propose to pay back by persuading thousands of their 26,500 members to
take out relatively small personal loans.*

*'Following talks with United, they hope to offer the carrot of five-year
fixed-price season tickets which could be purchased with part of these
loans.'*

In his book, *Manchester Disunited* (2007), Mihir Bose was scathing
about SU's conduct:

*'Did they indeed control 18%, albeit "loosely", and 10% "firmly"? And
had the United board agreed, as they told the* Sunday Times, *that part
of the personal loan could be used to buy season tickets and part to buy
shares? In reality both were wishes rather than the sort of hard reality
they had made out for the benefit of the newspaper's readers.*

*'I asked Nick Towle about how many shares SU could speak for. He
said, "Between us, with SU and members like me holding shares privately
and also through our share scheme, at that time probably just over 1%."
And of how much of this was held by the SU trust he said, "A small
amount. We never built it up. At the very end the Trust had about 0.3%."'*

This was a long, long way from the 18 per cent cited in the *Sunday
Times*. Jonathan Northcroft had written his report following a meeting
with Houston and Towle in a Wapping pub, and the latter's involvement came as a surprise to *Red Issue* and IMUSA. The day it was
published, Andy Walsh quickly pointed out that regulators at the
Takeover Panel would be very interested if United's board had indeed
been cooking up secret deals with SU. The attempts to play games
in the press had backfired spectacularly, and the normally impeccably
mannered Towle admitted to Jules Spencer, 'We will have to spend
all fucking Monday sorting this fucking mess out.'

The takeover saga dragged on into April with seemingly little action bar mounting speculation. Eventually, on 28 April, the Takeover Panel intervened, giving Glazer until midday on 17 May to signal his intention to issue a formal bid. Should none be forthcoming, he would be barred from making any other approach for six months. The plc's directors were extremely keen not to give fans any excuse to blame them for what might happen and said in a statement, 'The board has informed Glazer that it cannot provide a recommendation to shareholders to accept any offer made on the basis of the current proposal.'

On 1 May, in the *Sunday Times*, Northcroft had another article trumpeting SU's plans. Nomura had agreed to lend up to £100 million to 'a new fans' investment trust' on a pound-for-pound basis for every £1 of club shares or cash that was committed by supporters:

'Rather like a mortgage, the fans would then repay Nomura over a period of many years, using the annual dividends paid by United's board to shareholders. One of the beauties of the scheme is that units in the trust will be tradeable so that fans needing to sell up could. It is hoped several "Red Knights" – wealthy United supporters who have expressed an interest in saving the club from Glazer – will join in with significant funds. Fans are appealing to high-profile United lovers, such as actors and pop stars, and perhaps even football figures, such as Gary Neville and Ferguson himself, to come on board.'

To try and create a substantial, unified shareholding, SU planned to send letters out to the club's 30,000 individual shareholders who held around 18 per cent of the equity, asking them to join the trust. Towle was quoted in the article: 'This is the moment of truth. We want all United supporter-shareholders, small or large, rich or poor, to get behind the trust and help keep the club free from predators.'

Another moment of truth was imminent. On Saturday 7 May, United played West Brom, presenting one last chance for supporters to show the banks planning on lending Glazer the money that they could not be taken for granted. IMUSA and *Red Issue* advocated a full boycott of the match but SU refused to back the call saying, 'We canvassed our committee and saw the reaction from the forum – a fairly even split, even a majority against the boycott, basically because of the risk of failure harming the cause.' While many saw it as no excuse for not trying, it quickly became irrelevant. On Thursday 12 May, the fight was over – news broke that Glazer had bought out Coolmore's stake.

3

UNIVERSAL SUFFRAGE

Despite all the speculation and coverage, the timing of the takeover announcement still caught almost everyone cold. There was no real plan as to what should happen next. At Old Trafford supporters gathered to protest and the Glazer effigy that had originally appeared at the Arsenal game was set on fire. Amidst fans' anger and despair were calls for people to boycott season ticket renewals and stick to pledges not to give Glazer a penny, but some could already see the shapes of fans' divisions to come: boycotters vs. backtrackers; exiteers vs. remainers. There was no sense of anyone taking charge – it was almost as if the only plan had been to hope it wouldn't happen; there was no contingency. Shareholders United bizarrely continued to urge fans to carry on buying shares; advice which, if followed, could only possibly lose people money. Nick Towle would later admit, 'I knew it was gone. The game was over but we were still campaigning because the whole thing about this is keeping the continuity, keeping people's belief. It's a sort of religious exercise, absolutely.'

A 'religious exercise' it may have become, but there was a distinct lack of faith when it mattered. David Bick, Keith Harris's collaborator, was in no doubt that chances had been missed to stop Glazer. He told Mihir Bose:

'*There was clearly, initially, at Shareholders United a huge suspicion of Keith Harris. He'd been an adviser to the board on the Sky bid, he was a suited Manchester United supporter. The sheer ignorance that some of these people displayed was breathtaking. Because of having that suspicion they did not realise that when we said Keith was prepared to get behind their endeavours, he meant it. They then dallied for too long.*

'*After the Nomura letter went off [in October 2004], Keith waited for a response, essentially from Shareholders United, who were leading the charge on it. Nothing happened for months. In the end they came forward and said we accept that Keith is doing this for all the right reasons. It was too late by then. They spent too much time pursuing their own agenda, forgetting where the cause lay, suspecting people of things that never existed. In my opinion they effectively wasted six months that could have been put to use in finding a real solution to combat the invaders.*'

Russ Delaney blamed himself for the failure to help secure a deal for Coolmore's stake in the club. On the day of the takeover he was in hospital, once again stricken by the pulmonary sarcoidosis which had long left him in need of a lung transplant. From there he summoned up the energy to ring me to discuss how to proceed. Despite his condition and the emotional distress he felt at what had happened to his club, Russ suddenly perked up, mentioning FC United. 'It's too late to do that now,' I contested. 'Why's that?' Russ responded. Even from his hospital bed, there was no obstacle that Russ believed couldn't be overcome. Of course, it was all very well Russ saying so, but the question was where (*how?*) to start? And was it even worth it?

Though the current season was still to fully run its course, the traditional start of preseason training on 1 July was just seven short weeks away. Imagining an FC United was easy but the reality would be much harder to conjure up – there was no club, no structure, no money and no ground. Yes, there'd been plenty of vocal support for the idea since February, but so what? Talk was cheap; it needed action, and now.

Taking the blueprint of IMUSA's campaign against Sky, I realised that one thing was urgently required: a public meeting for people to thrash out where things would go from here. It seemed pretty clear that it was FC or nothing in terms of keeping any protest going. As far as its readers were concerned, *Red Issue* had promised there would be this option for anyone who boycotted. Few people realised it was only supposed to be a propaganda tool, and the easy thing would have been to turn round and say 'Oh, sorry. It was too hard to follow through with the plans.' But I felt we had a duty to deliver it to those prepared to stand by their principles.

If nothing else, steps had to be taken to make it as much of a viable proposition for as long as possible, until a decision on whether or not to proceed was determined one way or another. To that end Luc Zentar – a *Red Issue* contributor – and I set about registering 'FC United' as a limited company, while Mike Adams – a recruitment consultant who'd been involved in IMUSA since the very start – emailed the North West Counties Football League secretary requesting information on the scheduling of their AGM. This would give an indication of the deadline for any application to the NWCFL, as the AGM would be when the league's members voted on any new clubs being admitted for the following season.

The takeover's timing may have come as a shock, but it would prove very fortuitous for FC's history. The following evening had long since been earmarked as *Red Issue*'s traditional end of season curry night. All the magazine's contributors, sellers and elders (i.e. retired sellers/mascots simply out for a free night) would be expected to gather and gorge on poppadoms and Stella, talking nonsense until the early hours. But there'd be less nonsense than usual this time.

Writer Richard Kurt turned up having just got off the phone with a suitably dismayed United executive, who had told him that both he and David Gill were 'considering our positions'. Perhaps needless to say, both would end up choosing to stay with the invading occupier. For Kurt, a historian in a previous career, it was all too redolent of June 1940 to resist:

> *'Glazer's Panzers had suddenly smashed through the lines, and everyone was scattering, retreating in total disorder. Just as with the Allies that summer, the anti-Glazer forces' biggest weakness had always been their relative disunity. Several organisations and several big individuals, all trying to work in the same direction in good faith against a common enemy but necessarily having to operate within their own silos ... we already knew at the time that this was a problem, and in hindsight it's even more painfully obvious.'*

Now everyone was facing the choices that De Gaulle, Pétain, and others did in June 1940. Where do you go? Who do you choose to ally with? And what about your old allies who make different choices? It was no surprise that Reds soon started to read and hear allusions to the 'Resistance' and 'collaborators' once 2005/6 got underway. Says Kurt:

> *'I think a lot of those who ended up choosing FC would have identified with De Gaulle's flight to London, and recognised the unpleasantness of being branded "Judas scum" by some of those who'd chosen to stay behind with the occupier and their Vichy puppets.'*

David Gill would soon complete a very 1940 journey. From being a Glazer opponent 'on the barricades' with SU, to someone considering the revolver and whisky on 13 May, he would soon be transformed into the Glazer cheerleader-in-chief and de facto gauleiter. (At one point during the takeover battle, Gill had even insisted that the Glazers would find there were no revenue streams left to maximise, yet would now be responsible for doing just that. In January 2005, *Red Issue* had highlighted the absurdity of this claim simply by comparing the respective, and very similar, shirt sponsorship fees that United and Olympique Lyonnais were paid: 'Yes, you might well ask "who?" They barely sell a shirt outside the Rhone, let alone France.') In the pages of *Red Issue* and on its website, some would dub him 'Pétain'. The harshest and most factually au fait preferred the most sulphurous appellation of all: 'Laval'. The Frenchman was eventually executed; the Englishman would become a Vice-President of FIFA.

One of *Red Issue*'s newest recruits was Rob Brady. 'Beaten. Disaffected. Disenfranchised. Disillusioned,' is how he described feeling on May 13. Brady had only started writing for *Red Issue* that season, after giving up his legendary *Abbey Hey* column in *United We Stand. An Undividable Glow* (2006), Brady's brilliantly bonkers book on FC United's inaugural season, describes how the curry night unfolded:

Red Issue met on a regular basis for a curry and a parrot [chat]. This meant that there was an established political cadre in operation far in advance of anything I was used to. I just listened as things were talked about that I had no knowledge of. They talked about reprehensible acts of corruption and intrigue with alarming normality as they were past being shocked.

'The regular meeting of Red Issue Reds had definitely crystallised their clarity of the situation but it had also part forged them as a force for change. I can honestly say that if all the UWS lads had gone out for a beer to discuss the situation we were now in then we would have had a beer, discussed it, got another beer and probably not done anything about it. This meeting was beery but different. In fact I only had one beer all night as they all got whacked. The conclusion was that a meeting should be held the following Thursday. At this meeting the many strands of the intifada we were now in would be voiced. A football club of our own provisionally entitled "FC United"' would be a prominent element in the options Reds faced.

'When Jules Spencer and Andy Walsh dropped me back in Town that night they commented on my evening's quietness. I knew that the work

ahead was going to break up marriages with the commitment needed. Form a football club? Form a fucking football club? How? By going to the magic wand shop and wishing one? Excuse me, do you sell football clubs? Can I have one please? I found this football club outside on the pavement. Is it yours?

There was far from unanimity – even among *Red Issue*'s insiders, not all were convinced by the idea of FC. Bert Foulds, a *RI* stalwart from its earliest days, thought it all highly dubious; another contributor was openly hostile. The merits of the matter were debated until well gone 3 a.m.

After all the talk, it was time for action. The following lunchtime a small group of us turned up at Andy Walsh's house to decide tactics. It was the first chance most of us had had to see a newspaper, and the back-page headlines on the kitchen table screaming about the takeover really brought it home. I sought Walsh's counsel as to the best way to proceed, insisting a summit be called for the following week that brought together the fanzines, IMUSA and SU. This was agreed, but my further suggestion of a big public meeting on the Thursday was kiboshed. There was a desperate need for leadership but Walsh, for one, was uncertain how to proceed. He relayed how Michael Crick was lukewarm – at best – on the idea of FC United. Walsh himself wasn't overly willing to jump aboard, instead insisting that he'd be of better use helping to lead a proposed boycott of United's sponsors. (The only real manifestation of this boycott would come when Mani – bassist in the band Primal Scream and then a former Stone Rose – pulled out of a DJ appearance at that summer's Glastonbury festival due to the venue at which he'd been booked to appear being sponsored by Budweiser – one of Manchester United's commercial partners. Mani told BBC GMR, 'I'm not having anything to do with Budweiser or any of the other United sponsors until they stand up to Glazer and help get him out of our club. I love Glastonbury but there's no way I'm doing it if Budweiser are involved.')

The takeover still hadn't formally been completed, so it was proposed that Walsh speak with Alex Ferguson and find out exactly where he stood on it all. Ferguson had been silent since the autumn and, while it was almost inconceivable that Glazer hadn't already gained assurances of commitment from him, if there remained any possible way to scupper the deal, it lay in his resignation undermining the banks' confidence in lending the money for the deal. Word quickly came back that Walsh could ring Ferguson at home on the Sunday night following United's final league game of the season at Southampton.

On the early morning coach down to the game, plenty of people were talking of possible protests to oppose the takeover, most of which was far-fetched nonsense. Realistically, none was ever going to happen – at least none of those being spoken about. Most unrealistic of all was a piece in the *Sunday Times*, in which SU's Oliver Houston advocated disrupting games by 'throwing beach balls onto the pitch.' Down at St Mary's, a handful of United fans had a much more ambitious idea: to try to sabotage TV's coverage of the game by pulling the plug on the transmission vans outside the stadium. The idea was to highlight their ability to hit the club's revenue streams, as Glazer was coming for United's money, and a big portion of that came from Sky. The group waited outside the ground for an opportunity during the match, then set to the task, starting to remove all the leads that wired the vans into the mains supply. The feed began to be disrupted, prompting a technician to hare out to see what was going on. The would-be saboteurs had to flee, though some passing police officers apprehended one of the lads, on suspicion of criminal damage.

Back in Manchester after the game, a couple of us headed round to Walsh's house to find out the result of his discussions with Ferguson. Walsh reported that Ferguson had rejected any suggestion that he resign in solidarity with the protestors, citing the fact that he only had a couple of years left in management, and refusing to leave his colleagues and staff in the lurch by quitting now. It was a complete cop-out (especially as consideration for staff wasn't on Ferguson's agenda when he eventually did quit Old Trafford in 2013). While fully expected, the news was still a huge blow. I again stressed the need to hold a public meeting as a matter of urgency. Nothing could be done regarding FC or anything else until the strength of feeling was properly gauged and the viability of ideas for action tested. It was resolved to organise something for the coming Thursday.

On the Monday morning, I set to work trying to find a suitable venue in Manchester that would hold the public meeting at such short notice. There were not many available and even fewer that were afford-able. The Tyldesley Suite at the other Old Trafford – Lancashire County Cricket Club – was comfortably big enough but they refused to take the booking due to their relationship with neighbours United. A suggestion was made to try the Central Methodist Hall on Oldham Street, bang in the centre of Manchester. I didn't even know such a place existed. After making enquiries, its capacity was revealed to be a bit on the low side, at only 500, but they only wanted £150. In the absence of anything else suitable, it would have to do.

The same day, a call to boycott United's sponsors went out, aimed at targeting Vodafone in particular. Its effect was somewhat dubious with one *Red Issue* contributor saying, 'I cancelled a 600-user business contract with Vodaphone. They didn't even blink.' Despite this, in the echo chamber of the online forums, plenty of people convinced themselves of its merits. Another suggestion for mild rebellion began to be disseminated among the United support, with fans asked to wear black rather than red at Saturday's FA Cup final against Arsenal as part of an idea that the club was in mourning.

The *Manchester Evening News* provided those in favour of setting up FC United with an unexpected morale boost when Paul Hince, its unintentionally hilarious City correspondent, ridiculed the idea: 'Form your own breakaway club? Come on. Get real. This isn't Wimbledon we're talking about with more stewards than fans. The whole idea is ludicrous.' Jules Spencer emailed his comments round, adding, 'If you ever needed proof that FC United will work, Paul Hince says it won't.'

Some people were taking the prospect of a breakaway club far more seriously. That night, even the Northern Premier League's chief executive Duncan Bayley appeared on BBC Radio 5 to welcome it. It was a promising development. Jules Spencer subsequently contacted him to find out what steps a putative FC United would have to comply with to enter at Division 8 of the football pyramid (the NPL runs two divisions, respectively six and seven promotions below the Premier League), while I did the same with Geoff Wilkinson of the NWCFL (which fed into the NPL at Divisions 9 and 10 in the pyramid).

Hince's article wasn't to be wholly dismissed, however. He also gave voice to a line of opinion which, with United's season ticket renewal deadline fast approaching, already appeared to be gaining support. 'Those fans may detest the fact that the Old Trafford Empire is now being run by an American tycoon,' Hince wrote, 'but United is still their club. Surely what happens out there on the pitch is more important than who sits at the head of the boardroom table.' Only a few days after many people had pledged to do whatever it took to help force Glazer out, the attitude of a large proportion was already softening. Amidst growing talk of a 'fight from within' against Glazer's ownership, the *Red Issue* contributor Tony Jordan posted on the magazine's website lampooning the concept. He pointed out the reasons why, whatever fine words people spouted now, when it came down to it, no one would be invading the pitch, orchestrating walk outs, chanting protest songs, attacking the directors box or anything else that was being mentioned.

> '*You really are deluding yourselves massively if you think handing over a very large wedge of cash to this man, then trying to instigate any of the measures mentioned above when you are inside the ground, will make any difference. It won't: the ideas aren't practical, nor will they ever be acted upon by enough individuals to matter in the slightest.*
> '*For months now SU, IMUSA and the major fanzines have ALL campaigned against the backdrop of the very simple 'NO CUSTOMERS, NO*

PROFITS' tagline. They did this for a reason; it's the only nailed on, guaranteed, fool proof method of pissing all over Glazer's French fries. At no point, at any time previously, did I once hear anyone argue against this very simple and easily acted-upon premise. The only dissension in the ranks has once again come just at the point when the talking has to stop, and the action has to begin.

'What would be refreshing is for some people to simply say: "Deep down, if I stay, I know nothing I do will make a difference next season, but I just like watching United too much to knock it on the head for any-one." I can deal with honesty. I totally understand the dilemma, but please, don't delude yourselves that some mythical battle will be fought on a weekly basis inside Old Trafford next season 'cos, lads, it simply won't.'

By definition, the takeover rendered Shareholders United obsolete. But on the Tuesday, just five days after Glazer had bought out Coolmore's stake, they announced a solution that enabled their organisation to continue. A 'Phoenix Fund' would be set up using the money Glazer paid for its members' shareholdings, with the aim of building up a pot sufficient to ultimately buy the club. Those signing up to it didn't seem to have done the basic calculations: Manchester United was being sold for £780 million while SU had thirty thousand members, the vast majority of whom held less than £5 worth of shares.

The following night's meeting provided an indication of the divisions ahead. Adam Brown had spent the weekend on a fishing trip in the remote north of Scotland, where he'd drawn up an agenda detailing what he called 'a Battle Plan of activities and protests' against Glazer. However, to some eyes, many of his suggestions had already been undermined by Jordan's big dose of realism. Everything came back to whether or not people were willing to boycott, and whether the FC idea was feasible for those who were. On the first issue – even amongst the supposed anti-Glazer hardcore of IMUSA, SU and the fanzines – it was clear that a call not to renew season tickets would fail to garner overwhelming backing. On the second issue, Kris Stewart, chief executive of AFC Wimbledon, had travelled up to Manchester to provide invaluable advice about what setting up a new club would involve and how to go about it. While stressing the work involved, he also spoke of the pride and sense of unity that he and his fellow Wombles had felt in their achievement of bringing their club into being, against all the odds. To those receptive to the idea, his words were inspirational.

Also trying to inspire people was Shareholders United. By Thursday lunchtime, they had set up a 'roll of honour' for people to sign in order to publicly pledge not to give the Glazers a single penny. All their most notable representatives featured prominently. Meanwhile Alex Ferguson broke his public silence on the takeover ahead of United's trip to Cardiff for the FA Cup final. The BBC reported that he 'urged his players to put on a show for the Glazer family' and quoted him thus: 'I do not know if they will be there, but they will be watching from the States, I am sure of that. It will give them an idea what Manchester United is. And when, hopefully, they see our fans celebrating and see the atmosphere of that, it will be wonderful.' His stance couldn't have been more out of touch with that of most supporters.

On Thursday evening, 'wonderful' was the last word that would've been used to describe the situation by those who packed out Manchester's Methodist Hall. Representatives from IMUSA, SU and United's three fanzines comprised the top table and led a passionate meeting. Many United fans spoke of how they would carry on the fight against Glazer, pledging to give up their season tickets and not hand over the money that Glazer was after. One well-known *United We Stand* contributor said his opposition would be 'carrying out criminal damage in the ground' every match, the cost of which would exceed the price of his ticket. Perhaps he really believed it at the time. Yet there was definitely a sense of some people being swept along by the emotion. When Pete Boyle – a long-time *Red Issue* contributor and a familiar figure at Old Trafford – stepped forward to state he didn't feel able to give up his season ticket, he was barracked by some.

But his honesty was exactly what was required, as opposed to vainglorious pledges from some merely trying to impress.

On *Red Issue*'s website, a report of the meeting stated:

'A series of motions were voted on and passed unanimously as the way United supporters will carry on the Glazer fight. These were as follows:

1. *"Wear black" protest at FA Cup final*
2. *Build a public Rally, at the Apollo Theatre*
3. *Use customer power against Glazer: don't buy merchandise, cancel MUTV, boycott sponsors*
4. *Boycotting matches*
5. *Shareholder power: await orders from SU*
6. *Call on Gill/Board to resign*
7. *Make Glazer/Backers aware of anger*
8. *Write in protest, FA/PM/MP, Sports Minister etc'*

Many of those present had been eager to hear what was being done about FC United but the issue was only fleetingly addressed, instead being kicked back to the proposed rally at the Apollo, ensuring that the focus was kept on what people could do now. *Red Issue* assured people 'lots of work is being done behind the scenes on [FC United], the viability of which is dependent on the level of support the project would have. It is hoped that representatives of AFC Wimbledon will be present at the Apollo to explain their own situation and how they made it work.'

The public rally at the Apollo theatre in Ardwick was slated for the Bank Holiday on 30 May. Around £1,500 had been collected from those at the Methodist Hall towards the hire cost of £2,500. It wasn't clear what the rally was intended to achieve; people just thought it was 'a good idea'. Everyone still seemed to be looking to each other for leadership, but the schism that had already opened up around the subject of FC meant it was difficult for anyone to come out and admit that it was one of only two logical protests to make, alongside boycotting Old Trafford. At the time it seemed to some like a proper protest was building but the brutal reality was that the Apollo date served only to buy another eleven days' thinking time, as people wavered over committing one way or the other. United's renewal deadline was the day before the cup final and many had already decided not to renew, myself included. Glazer was buying the club with the sole intention of fleecing the fans for all he could get. Every leak of his plans over the previous seven or eight months had effectively said as much. The sums didn't add up without huge ticket price hikes. I simply wasn't prepared to be part of it, so in that regard there was no decision to make.

Down in Cardiff, the FA Cup final passed off without any major protests in an unusual atmosphere in front of a United end whose dark, black demeanour was only emphasised by the miserable, gloomy weather (the symbolic protest of wearing black had been taken up by large numbers of people). The game was just as strange, with United hammering Arsenal but simply unable to score. It went to extra-time and then penalties, Paul Scholes the only player to miss, allowing Arsenal to win 5–4. For Rob Brady in *An Undividable Glow*, the trip to South Wales signalled the end of an era, the effects of the takeover splitting the seventeen-strong group of mates on his minibus between boycotters and remainers:

> 'We don't know where we're going but we know what we are taking with us. Part of us will stay forever at Manchester United Football Club, it could be no other way. Part of us has gathered what we believe to be the soul and wrapped it in the softest of cotton and placed it gently into a treasure chest for its protection against hardship and arrogance, and deceit, and treachery, and slyness. And the lid was closed. For so many it could be no other way.'

The following week, United fans' collective mood plummeted even further following arch-rivals Liverpool's comeback against AC Milan

in the European Cup final, the scousers coming out on top in a penalty shootout. How was it possible that their band of useless journeymen
like Traore, Cisse and Baros could have come from nowhere to win
as many European Cups as United had managed under Ferguson
during the club's most successful ever period?

Preparations for the Apollo continued apace. Tony Lloyd, the MP for
Manchester Central, and David Conn, a campaigning journalist from *The
Guardian*, as well as relatives of James Gibson, the businessman who
saved United from bankruptcy in the 1930s, were all lined up to speak.
Kris Stewart agreed to return to talk about AFC Wimbledon's formation.
IMUSA arranged for a skip outside the venue, and called on fans to
throw into it any clothes and trainers made by Nike – the company who
sponsored United – as part of a wider plan to target the club's commercial partners. Whatever was collected was to be given to charity.

Come Monday afternoon, a crowd of about 1,600 gathered in the
Apollo to hear what people had to say and, collectively, try to decide
a way to move the protests forward. While many attendees were
impressed by some of the speeches, and the passion on show, the
consensus afterwards was that no new ideas had been promoted, and
that the meeting hadn't really gone anywhere. On *Red Issue*'s forum,
the verdicts tumbled uniformly: 'A lot of good speakers from the top
table, but the same old topics: boycott matches, merchandise etc;
nothing constructive came out of it,' and 'lots of good rallying calls
but what now?'

The exception was the topic of FC United, for which I had ended
up presenting the case. There wasn't exactly a rush of people to front
it and, given my role with *Red Issue*, I could hardly have been in any
worse position than to be seen advocating 'Let's all go and set up this
other team.' But in the absence of anyone else doing it, muggins here
had to step forward. I didn't have a clue what I was going to say.
Almost straight away, someone from the audience heckled me after I
mentioned it would create a club that was affordable for local kids.
'What's wrong with out-of-towners?' he demanded to know,

completely – or deliberately – missing the point. No one who'd read any United fanzine over the previous decade could've missed the arguments in favour of getting more youngsters through the turnstiles.

For some reason, the interruption really threw me and all I could think was: 'What a fucking *stupid* question'. Scrambling to get back on track, I said that if FC United had sufficient backing, then there were people willing to try to put it together. But we wanted 1,000 pledges of support signed up by the end of the meeting. Someone else then asked what would happen to the club if Glazer sold Manchester United. How the hell could anyone answer that? He'd only just bought it! Someone, Walsh I think, stepped in to say that the club's members would take whatever decisions were necessary as and when they needed to.

Kris Stewart followed this up with his impressive and emotional story of setting up Wimbledon, telling the audience that as and when any FC United team took the pitch, no matter what had gone before then, *that* would feel like your club, just as it had for him at AFC Wimbledon's first game. His words undoubtedly sold the dream to a number of those present but, as it turned out, not enough to meet my challenge. When the pledges had all been counted, there were only just over eight hundred. It was almost 200 short. In truth, the whole meeting had been a bit flat, and noticeably lacked the fire and defiance that had underpinned the evening at the Methodist Hall. Somewhere in the intervening eleven days, the feeling that supporters could make a difference had evaporated. The reality was nothing could be done.

Feeling somewhat depressed by the proceedings, we decamped to the nearby Park Inn to catch up with everyone. Outside in the beer garden, Kris Stewart asked what was up. 'The backing's not there, so that's the end of that,' I said. Stewart looked a bit puzzled. 'So what? Do you think you could still pull it off?' he asked. 'Yeah. Of course we could,' I replied. 'Well, there you go.' He knew what he was doing. The challenge had been set.

4

UTOPIAN SOCIALISM

Early the following morning, mere hours after Kris Stewart's words were spoken, I invited key colleagues to join what was to become the FC United Steering Committee. Step forward Rob Brady, Adam Brown, Russ Delaney, Peter Munday, Tony Pritchard, Vasco Wackrill, Andy Walsh, Julian Spencer and Luc Zentar. It might sound overly dramatic, but if I'd not taken that initial step, I'm pretty certain nothing would've come of the idea.

It's impossible to exaggerate how far-fetched the concept of an FC United seemed at the time. Without some sort of coordination, it was too easy for everyone to let it drift and for nothing to get done. Moreover, a lot of people were advocating putting everything on hold so that proper plans could be put in place for 2006/07, a whole year later. But I believed it was now or never. For something to happen, it just needed someone to pull it all together and say, 'Right, this is what we're doing!'

Some important preliminary work *had* already got under way. In the days leading up to the Apollo meeting, Pete Munday, an accountant by trade and *Red Issue* contributor, had drafted an outline three-year business plan. It was predicated on the club attracting 2,500 backers, from whom £125,000 working capital would be raised, and it forecast the club would turn a small loss on revenues of £300,000 in its first season. Sums set aside for expenditure included £70,000 on installing temporary seats, on the basis that the club might end up playing at a local ground, such as Trafford FC's Shawe View, Abbey Hey or even Sale rugby club's old ground. A quote for this had been obtained from a scaffolding firm, working out at around £40 per seat for the season.

Finding a ground was always going to be the biggest obstacle to overcome. The ideal option of sharing The Willows, home of Salford rugby league team, was increasingly looking like a non-starter after a request made to John Wilkinson, the club's owner, led nowhere. Approaches to the second favourite, Altrincham FC, were also rebuffed. Tony Jordan had suggested the Butchers Arms, Droylsden's ground, and also flagged up a new development just outside Ashton, where a stadium was due to be ready in time for the coming season. Following this tip, Russ Delaney was delegated the task of approaching Tameside Council.

There was another option too, following an offer from the Conference North football club Leigh RMI. During the week before the Apollo meeting, one of their directors, Stan Walker, had contacted IMUSA asking to be put in touch with the people behind FC United; his number was passed to Andy Walsh. After speaking with him, Walsh said that Leigh were offering a groundshare, or even a merger. 'No, absolutely not,' was my initial reaction. A merger was out of the question. We weren't taking over someone else's club, and FC would never take off if based in Leigh. The town's 14 miles outside Manchester and doesn't even have a train station – it may as well have been on the Moon as far as most people were concerned. Walsh was more open-minded and insisted the approach was at least worth listening to. He arranged to meet with Walker following the Apollo. Walshy came up to Jules Spencer and I and asked if we were going with him, but by that stage we were both pretty deflated, given how badly the meeting seemed to have gone. We made our excuses and left him to it, heading to the pub instead. Walshy was in his element doing that sort of networking thing, and he'd obviously report back if anything interesting cropped up.

Walsh had made the right call. The North West Counties' AGM was scheduled for 18 June and the cut-off date for any applications to join was 15 June. To even be considered for entry, the league demanded proof of a licensed ground or legally compliant groundsharing agreement. Suddenly, Leigh RMI's offer was looking extremely useful. I realised that if we could use their Hilton Park ground to satisfy the application requirements, then it would buy us another two months before the season started to find somewhere closer to civilisation. Leigh RMI's original motivation for suggesting a link-up had been their own financial predicament and, while FC's counter-offer was not ideal for them, they agreed to it in return for a guarantee that they would be the first opposition any FC United team faced. With the gate receipts to be split between the two clubs, it was a deal everyone could live with. Just so long as it went to plan.

Russ Delaney made quick progress with Tameside Council and reported back to say they were looking for another team to share the brand new 4,000-capacity stadium alongside Curzon Ashton. Unfortunately, the only person who could authorise it was on holiday for another ten days, so it looked like a non-starter. After discussions with Luc and me, Russ set about drafting an outline to be presented to Mike Appleby, the FA official overseeing the non-league game, who was meeting the NWCFL's Geoff Wilkinson on 2 June. Part of it read:

'Our proposal is to join either the North West Counties or the Unibond League; as far as ground location is concerned, we are currently looking into ground-sharing with a number of local clubs who have a sufficient licence from the FLA to accommodate our anticipated support. We already have two firm offers; realistically we would look to have an average home gate of between 2–5,000.'

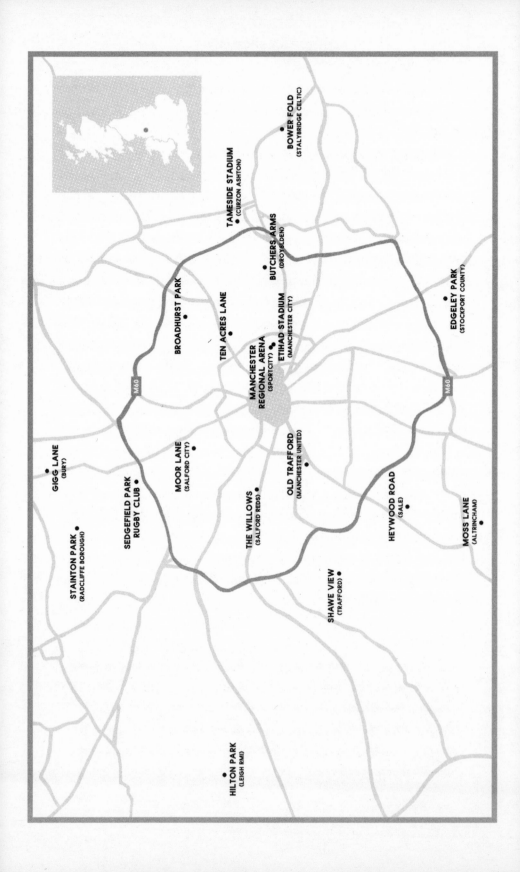

Although he wasn't even clear on what league FC United would apply to, Russ evidently had few doubts the club was going to attract a big following. Vas and Jules volunteered to attend the meeting and present FC United's case, while Pete Munday and Tony Pritchard set to work on a more in-depth business plan. Wimbledon provided some valuable insight, with their Finance Director Erik Samuelson kindly sending through their 2003/04 budget, along with an offer of any further assistance. Meanwhile Vas, something of a tech wizard (at least relative to everyone else), set up a webpage through which people could subscribe to an FC United mailing list and pledge help or support.

Many United fans were demanding updates on the forums and, while there remained little to report, it was obviously important to tap into whatever backing existed, rather than risk alienating people through silence. If the application to the league was successful, the club was going to need cash, and quickly, to pay for start-up costs like ground rental. With that in mind, on 3 June a statement was released announcing who was on the Steering Committee (Phil Bedford, Andrew Howse, Tony Jordan and Martin Morris had all been added in the previous couple of days) and providing an overview of where plans were up to. Though no mention was made of either Leigh or Tameside Council, the statement referred to 'two offers for ground-sharing agreements', along with an assurance that other avenues were also still being pursued. Supporters were encouraged to pledge financial backing at fc-utd.co.uk with a deadline of 13 June set for anyone who wanted to be recognised as a 'founder member'. As and when league membership was secured, people would be asked to make good on whatever amount they'd pledged.

Following the meeting with the FA and North West Counties, Vas reported back:

'Dave Tomlinson, the chairman, was by far the most positive, with his Vice Chair seemingly more keen to keep us well and truly down to earth. Basically, the FA has no problems with us being admitted to the league,

as long as we are approved by the clubs at their AGM on 18 June. There
are a number of hurdles that we need to jump through. If we succeed in
presenting evidence of our having done these things in good time before
the AGM, then our case will be strongly argued to the clubs by the league
committee.'

The scouser Tomlinson, brother of the actor Ricky of *Royle Family*
fame, gave the impression that clearing these 'hurdles' would be something of a formality but they appeared slightly more daunting to those
having to do the vaulting. As well as demanding proof of a ground,
the league required FC United to be affiliated to the local FA, and
also wanted to see details of the club's structure and constitution. It
was also made clear that an abstract name like 'FC United' would not
be acceptable – it had to contain some kind of geographical identity.
Vas stressed how vital it was that all these stipulations were met: 'If
we do not get the above presented and approved in time, then we
have no chance.' Despite Tomlinson's positivity, the chances of success
were regarded as slim. 'One person [NWCFL official] said he thought
it was doubtful/impossible,' warned Vas.

The other key point on which the league officials sought clarification would become something of a recurring theme. 'They were
concerned that we (i.e. us or the support) would walk away if FCU
had a bad season, or if Glazer dropped dead tomorrow,' Vas wrote,
'I think we managed to put a convincing case to them that this would
not happen, but this is definitely something we will have to be strong
on in anything we submit to them.'

The league officials' scepticism was shared by many. Tommy Baldwin, chairman of NWCFL member Blackpool Mechanics FC, was
quoted in the Blackpool Gazette: 'Does anyone seriously believe
people will stop watching Manchester United because of who's running the club? This is a candle in the wind and the flame will soon
blow out. It's a sad state of affairs for football if this is being used
as a gimmick.' Gimmick or not, many were already convinced. By

the afternoon of Saturday 4 June the website accepting pledges had been live for just 24 hours and yet already £35,000 had been promised by over 400 people. It was a fantastic response at a time when concepts such as crowdfunding and even Facebook were completely unknown, although it was important to keep in mind that none of those making pledges had yet actually parted with any money.

I coordinated matters as best I could over the phone from Spain, where I was away for a week, but it was clear that a proper meeting was required. This was arranged for the evening of Monday 6 June at the Seven Oaks pub in Manchester. That afternoon Dave Boyle, a Wimbledon fan who was chief executive of Supporters Direct, the government-funded body aimed at encouraging supporter ownership of football clubs, sent through a draft constitution along with details of the pros and cons of the club being set up as an industrial and provident society (IPS). 'I'd argue strongly against setting up a limited company,' he wrote, 'as it doesn't guarantee democratic ownership in the way an IPS can.'

At the meeting Russ relayed how he was hopeful for an agreement with Sale on a groundshare, with Ashton looking unlikely. The latest on pledges was that 1,400 people had promised about £50,000. Adam Brown contacted Manchester FA regarding the club's affiliation. This needed to be completed quickly so it was decided to press on with it immediately. To do so, the club's name had to be decided. That, in turn, meant having a vote, which was going to be tricky given there was still no club, let alone any members. A statement was issued informing people that everyone who had pledged support would help decide the club's name, with votes being accepted up until 5pm on Monday 13 June, just under a week hence. A list of twelve names was whittled down to leave three options – FC United of Manchester, FC Manchester Central and AFC Manchester 1878 – and a further update on progress issued:

'At the moment the Steering Committee is working on obtaining a ground and league registration. Once these, and other essential details,

are secured we will hold an Extraordinary General Meeting of mem-
bers. This will allow a democratic process in which members can stand
for and elect the board and ratify other matters such as the structure of
the club.'

Mike Adams and Phil Sheeran had been added to the Steering Committee, taking its numbers to 16. The sole qualifications for anyone
joining were that they had something to offer, and that they could
be trusted implicitly, but some people whose eagerness to help out
wasn't engaged were left feeling resentful. We had to get things done.
The last thing we needed was dealing with people in it for self-
aggrandisement, or those who couldn't be trusted to keep quiet.
Everyone was finding it hard enough making progress on a ground
without being hampered by leaks, as we were all acutely aware of the
reach of United's tentacles. We didn't need options to potentially be
closed down by them before we'd had chance to reach an agreement.
There were accusations from some quarters that I was operating a
closed shop, but so what? There wasn't time to worry about courting
popularity.

At the Seven Oaks meeting, it was reported that an approach to
Sale rugby club was looking promising. But by the following morning,
that hope had been dashed. The NWCFL had advised checking the
dimensions of any rugby ground's pitch to ensure it was big enough
to host football. Confirmation that Sale's was too small came through
at almost the same time as the news that their committee had rejected
the possibility of a groundshare arrangement anyway. As a result,
Droylsden was right back on the agenda, with Trafford FC's ground
also under consideration. Approaches were made to both, while Russ
had further contact with Tameside Council. Luc reported:

'Russ has secured an agreement in principle to use Curzon Ashton's new
ground. THIS MUST NOT BE LEAKED UNTIL WE HAVE

SIGNED THE PAPERS. We know that such things are not definite until signed, sealed and delivered. To this end, we need to keep chasing all other avenues.'

Those other avenues also included Radcliffe Borough, the athletics ground next to Manchester City's stadium, Stalybridge Celtic, and Sedgefield Park Rugby Club. Meanwhile, Tony Jordan had started canvassing options for the club's badge from designers who had volunteered their services, while Luc urged that consideration be given to the logistics of hosting the promised Extraordinary General Meeting (EGM). On the United fanzine forums, a huge stink blew up about the lack of options provided for the vote on the club's name – an unnecessary distraction, given everything else that was going on.

I reported in on the football side of things, which until then had barely been given any thought. I was supposed to be on a biking trip across northern Spain but along with my fellow cyclists – Dave Mitchell and Andy Mitten, *United We Stand* fanzine editor – we'd abandoned it halfway through in favour of a few days on the beach in Vigo. My two companions were well-informed about the local non-league football scene, and the pair were soon offering all sorts of advice and suggestions on possible grounds, players and managers. Mitten was a non-league geek of some repute and the idea of FC United tapped into his long-held ambition of taking a team up the divisions from the bottom rung of the ladder. His brother Jonathan ('Joz') was a decent semi-professional player and currently without a club; having realised FC was a serious proposition, he was so keen to play for them that he knocked back contract offers from established clubs.

None of us in the Steering Committee had the first clue about the non-league scene, so Joz's info rendered me the one-eyed king in the land of the blind. While sweltering on a beach in Vigo, I spent half an hour on the phone to him running through names of prospective players. Based on this I confidently assured the rest of the Steering

Committee that the likes of Mitten, Kirk Hilton, Brian Carey [both ex-MUFC], Simon Carden, Neil Hardy, Craig Fleury and Tony Coyne would all be gettable, and that we would have no worries about putting a team together.

As for a manager, despite not even knowing who these people were only hours earlier, I wrote, 'Woodley Sports recently sacked their manager Tony Woodcock. He comes well rated. A better bet supposedly is Karl Marginson. He's 34, ex Radcliffe and Rotherham. He's a United fan, from Stretford, lives in Urmston and is considered one of THE people to know at non-league level.'

Russ had a contact ring him to put the Manchester-born, ex-Portsmouth and Ireland player Alan McLaughlin in the frame for the manager's job and suggesting £500 a week would secure his services.

In the meantime, the priority remained a ground. Contact was made with Droylsden's manager and chairman Dave Pace, who seemed very keen to agree a groundshare, while the athletics stadium at Sports City also remained an option. On 9 June, Luc and Tony Pritchard visited both Tameside Council's new stadium at Ashton and Droylsden's Butchers Arms. Luc reported back:

'*Although Ashton was an impressive ground, there are many drawbacks to playing there. We are only allowed a 12 month lease, this means that we would have to sort another lease with a club before Wednesday for the following 2 seasons. Over 50% of it is uncovered terrace, which would make watching the match between mid Sept & mid March a pain in the arse. It is a long way from Ashton town centre, and there is nothing at all around the ground. It is also an expensive proposition.*

'*With Droylsden we were a lot happier. The ground is closer to town. We can have it for three years to satisfy the league. We have decided, having had no negative feedback from Wednesday's update, to go for it and Tony P is hammering out the details with Dave today to get a provisional deal agreed.*

'The reason it is provisional is this: Tameside council are worried about the traffic implications. Russ and I are working on a park and ride scheme in Ashton, expect more from that soon. Their noses may well be out of joint because we don't want to play at their brand new stadium, but FCUM.'

Notwithstanding the problems being faced, pledges were still pouring in and, after the £900m offered by an 'M. Glazer' had been discounted, along with a handful of other suspicious amounts, £95,000 had been provisionally committed. Martin emailed with news of promising commitments of friendly games from Macclesfield's manager Brian Horton (formerly of Manchester City), Stockport's Chris Turner and Ronnie Moore at Oldham. Martin also urged caution, given the influence that MUFC could exert: 'It goes without saying that the above have made no promises and we should expect some of the goodwill to be withdrawn.'

Clouds, as ever, were threatening to gather around Droylsden. Russ was told by a bigwig at Tameside Council that they were not, under any circumstance, going to allow FC United to use their ground – it was the new Tameside Stadium or nothing. Luc passed this news on to Dave Pace, who tried to reassure him. 'He tells us that he has sorted it out, and that on Monday we will have all the necessary papers to complete the agreement.' Luc was far from convinced, and urged the same caution that Martin had.

Through Joz Mitten, contact had been made with Karl Marginson, and on the afternoon of Saturday 11 June Luc and I went to the Bowling Green pub in Chorlton to sound him out. The meeting was probably as much to convince Marginson that FC was really happening as it was to give us a sense of what Karl was like. On the way down there, I said to Luc, 'How do you interview for a football manager?' Pretty much the only criteria we could base anything on was whether we liked him or not! Marginson had spent the previous season as assistant manager at Flixton, having recently retired from playing, his career having taken him around many non-league clubs, as well as a spell as a professional at Rotherham. His main job in 2005 was as a fruit-and-veg delivery driver.

Over the weekend there was a suggestion that Tommy Lawson should be in the running for the manager role. He'd resigned at Prescot Cables the previous season, having led them to the North West Counties championship and cup triumph over the past few seasons. With Dave Pace promising that the groundshare agreement would be ready on Monday, it was decided that Russ, Luc, Tony Pritchard and I would go to the Butchers Arms to sign it. Both Marginson and Lawson were also invited along to be interviewed for the manager role, with Dave Pace on hand to offer his thoughts and experience. The results of all this could then be taken back to the rest of the Steering Committee at the latest meeting that evening at the Town Hall Tavern.

Unfortunately, come Monday, the paperwork for the groundshare still wasn't ready, but Pace assured us it would be in hand the following day. Instead, the focus was on the interviews. Marginson turned up in a jumper and jeans, in contrast to Lawson who was suited and booted. No one had met Lawson before and, for some reason, it came as a surprise that he was a scouser. Pritchard was impressed with Marginson but, back at the Town Hall Tavern meeting, expressed doubts that the inexperienced Karl had the necessary steel should the FA place FC in the Northern Premier League rather than the North West Counties.

The business plan which Pete Munday and Tony Pritchard had drawn up conservatively estimated a £35,000 loss for 2005/06, albeit before any pledges were factored in. While it all seemed convincing enough, the truth was that there was nothing to measure it against. The rest of the meeting was spent arguing about which badge designs should be put to a membership vote, and over the contrasting merits of Marginson and Lawson. Tony Jordan won many people over when he stated there was absolutely no way they could appoint a scouser: 'If whoever we go for is a mistake, people will readily forgive us – after all, who knows any better? But they won't if we opt for a scouser.' It was a good point, although I argued that if Lawson was deemed the best man for the job, he should get it – although my personal choice of the two was Marginson. A decision on any appointment was held over. We needed to consult more widely for other managerial options before the next meeting on Thursday.

Later that night, Vas totted up the 1201 votes that had been cast for the club's name, and FC United of Manchester was declared the winner with 44.7 per cent. The following morning, a statement was released announcing the result, along with news that the number of pledges now topped 2,600. The scale of the backing made media outlets realise that there was genuinely something happening. Journalists, sceptic Paul Hince among them, suddenly started ringing up requesting more information – TalkSport radio even devoted an hour to the club that evening. Tony Pritchard and I headed back to Droylsden where Pace presented us with a 'pre-agreement' to sign for the ground, claiming that a full contract couldn't yet be issued due to ongoing issues with Tameside Council regarding the traffic impact. Pace insisted that he was in the process of sorting it all. He sounded far from convincing, so I tracked down the local MP David Heyes, who promised to help out where he could.

Russ, Luc and I worked late into the night, finalising the league application which had to be delivered first thing in the morning. It was looking like a lost cause at one point but Russ in particular made sure everything was in order. I still don't know how Russ managed it. He'd driven up from Surrey for the meeting on the Monday, which was held in the smoky upstairs room of a pub, with no thought for the fact that he was desperately ill and wired up to an oxygen tank. Of course, he wouldn't have wanted anyone to make a fuss but it was the last thing he needed. For him then to stay up in Manchester and put in the hours that he did was unbelievable. He must've spent 36 hours in that office working – I remember me and Luc both being dead on our feet by the time we finished at 3 a.m. on the Wednesday morning so the impact on him must've been much more severe. You wouldn't have known it. The craziest part is that once we'd finished, he got in his car and drove home.

Vas and Luc took the application to St Helens the following morning to present to Geoff Wilkinson of the NWCFL. Later that day, Vas shared his confidence that everything had gone well, but it still seemed that, due to safety concerns, the club might actually end up in the Northern Premier League instead, whose members had more stringent ground grading requirements. The potential size of FC's fanbase was on everyone's mind.

> '*I think that the NWC as it stands at the moment simply could not cope with us. However, in the meeting today this point was (sort of) broached and the consensus amongst their committee was that they would be looking to us to help out with some of the issues arising (eg. providing our own stewards on aways, liaising with police, etc).*
>
> '*The fact remains that many of the grounds there will simply not have enough turnstiles, enough toilets and enough bar staff to cope with gates of 1,000+.*'

Luc drafted a letter for Tony Pritchard, the club's acting chairman, to send to the local police chief superintendent, asking for advice on whether it was necessary to avoid fixture clashes with Manchester City in the event of a groundshare at nearby Droylsden, and also requesting that he make a recommendation on crowd safety issues:

> '*I would conservatively estimate that we will take 500–800 people to away matches next season (possibly a lot more) and wonder if this would cause a problem with event management at places that are used to attendances of under 100. The FA has asked us to seek your advice on this matter, and have indicated that should you have concerns over safety*

due to our participation at North West Counties level, they will enter us in the Unibond League.'

There was suddenly a much better prognosis from Tameside Council; it appeared that they were eager to help smooth things out, their traffic concerns seeming to have stemmed from some misinformation that four thousand extra vehicles were expected in Droylsden every match day. At that time, we received another boost – celebrated Manchester property developer Tom Bloxham, of Urban Splash fame, was cheekily approached to see if he had any offices going. We were promptly offered one rent-free for three months in Ducie House by Piccadilly train station. Word was that Bloxham had been a *Red Issue* reader for years, even using its occasional comedy cut-outs to bait his City mates.

There were numerous new names being thrown into contention for the manager's job, with Gus Wilson, Benny Phillips, Mike McKenzie, Dalton Steele and Peter Wragg all seemingly well respected on the local non-league scene. But by the time the following Steering Committee meeting came round, all had been ruled out for one reason or another. After a lengthy debate, the historic decision was made that Karl Marginson would be the club's manager, though it was agreed that the news was to be kept under wraps pending a proper announcement. The length of time that the decision took to reach reflected the importance many placed on getting it right, but there was no doubt that, other than his lack of prior managerial experience, Marginson was near unanimously regarded as an appropriate choice.

Following a suggestion by Wimbledon's Kris Stewart it was also agreed that an open trials day would be held to recruit players, while the EGM was pencilled in for Tuesday 5 July at the Methodist Hall. With over £132,000 now pledged, Russ volunteered to contact the 33 people who'd committed £500 or more and ask them to send in cheques to the PO Box. This would give the club immediate access to funds if the league placing was secured that weekend. Tony Jordan was given the task of finding a suitable training venue available from July onwards. Ground, league, manager, players . . . all simultaneously needing finding, all demanding urgency, all weighing on the committee's shoulders. But at least a flood of cheques would show FC had public support.

The day before the NWCFL AGM, Luc and I headed to Sports City at Manchester City's ground for a meeting to discuss the possibility of FC United playing at its athletics stadium. Officials there had initially fobbed off any approach, but that changed following a request to Tony Lloyd MP for his intervention. The prospects of coming to an arrangement looked more promising when it turned out the person we'd be dealing with was Eddie Flanagan who outside work, was also the manager of local amateur club Gregorians FC, with whom my younger brother and I regularly trained and played. Unfortunately, Flanagan explained that, while he'd be open to a deal from 2006 onwards, long-term problems with the pitch's drainage meant he'd want to see how it fared during the coming season before committing to its more frequent use. He agreed to reassess the situation in the new year, which of course was no help in the short term. As we departed, I noticed a sign by the entrance. It seemed a UEFA conference was currently taking place at Manchester City's stadium . . .

The following afternoon, stories started appearing online of a protest having taken place. Under the headline, 'Glazer protesters home in on UEFA' the *Sunday Telegraph* reported:

'*Manchester United fans protesting about Malcolm Glazer's takeover stormed a UEFA meeting yesterday and demanded that European football's governing body investigate the Premiership club's new American owners.*

'*UEFA officials had just wound up a routine press conference, at the home of rivals Manchester City, when chief executive Lars-Christer*

Olsson was suddenly surrounded by 30 angry fans who called for UEFA to bar the Glazer family from taking control and to stop the club from spiralling into debt.

'Security officials seemed powerless to prevent what appeared to be a planned protest.'

At the exact time that was going on, the NWCFL AGM was taking place at the Castle Green Hotel in Kendal, 75 miles north; 'Introduction of new clubs' was item 11 on the agenda. Geoff Wilkinson had invited two representatives from FC United along for the day's events, which included a formal dinner in the evening. Somewhat surprisingly, there weren't many takers, and Tony Pritchard and Luc ended up attending while most others on the Steering Committee took well-earned advantage of the sweltering weekend. I received the result of the vote in Salford Cathedral while attending a wedding, extricating myself from proceedings to ring round everyone with the good news. We had all been fairly confident about the outcome for the previous couple of days, yet what had actually been achieved still seemed scarcely believable.

With a league placing secured, any thoughts of entry into the higher Northern Premier League were set aside. Even so, the hard slog was only just beginning. The night of Monday 20 June brought another meeting at the Town Hall Tavern and a summary of the decisions taken was compiled by Luc afterwards. It included, 'Sorting out pre-season friendly fixtures, training pitches, training balls and equipment, organising the open trials day, arranging St John ambulance personnel to attend, further approaches to Salford rugby club and Bury FC about negotiating a groundshare, arranging a meeting with a kit supplier and sourcing samples, setting up an online payments account for the pledges, ringing round everyone who'd pledged £200 or more, finalising paperwork with the FA, a full report to present to the club's members, the organisation of the EGM and investigating the legal requirements for stewarding at football games.' At 2:24 a.m., Luc wearily signed off, only half-jokingly: 'That is all (I think).'

Hours later, the list had another item on it. There was a major issue with the groundsharing agreement. Following the initial meeting with the NWCFL on June 2, Vas had informed everyone, 'it is also vitally important that we get permission from whatever league the landlords play in' before the FA would sign off any groundshare agreement. Geoff Wilkinson now duly emailed to say:

> '*I have just been contacted by the FA, who have advised that the Nationwide Conference have NOT been approached by either Leigh RMI or Droylsden with regard to ground sharing. The indications are that Leigh RMI may not be granted, due to both rugby and football being played there.*'

This was a major blow; a press conference had been arranged for Wednesday morning to officially launch the club, yet now it seemed that there might not be any ground to play at and, therefore, no place in a league. It was no time to panic. I urged the immediate prioritisation of sourcing a ground: Russ was to deal with Leigh and also get in touch with Bury; I would get on to Stalybridge; Mike Adams was to chase up Salford; Luc would try and find out what was happening with Drolysden; and Martin was asked to give Altrincham one last shot.

As though that wasn't enough to be dealing with, Luc, Jules, Walshy and I also had to continue preparations for the press conference; Vas was setting up online registration for the coming weekend's players' trials; Tony Jordan was liaising with the kit supplier to see if they could produce a bespoke kit in the short time between the EGM and the Leigh friendly on 16 July; and Andrew Howse was still working his way through the minefield of the copyright registration. Adam Brown had injected a bit of caution around this, wisely highlighting the potential problem with using the name FC United of Manchester should anyone at Old Trafford object to its similarity. Legal opinion had been sought on the matter, with Howse despatched to report back on any issues that could arise. No, it was no time to panic. Primarily because everyone was too busy to do so.

All options had been exhausted trying to source grass pitches for the trials. Manchester council were no help, as most of their pitches had been decommissioned for the summer. Written requests to the likes of St Bede's College and Manchester Grammar offering to pay for the use of their playing fields were flatly rejected. The only option was to book the poor quality astroturf pitches at the Armitage Centre in Fallowfield.

Come 8 a.m. on the Wednesday morning, all the problems were temporarily forgotten as local TV and media assembled in a suite at the Midland Hotel. Russ had insisted on paying the £200 room hire to ensure the club got a fitting introduction, rather than having the launch take place in a dingy pub. The Midland location, where Charles Rolls had his fateful meeting with Henry Royce, lent a graceful nod to Mancunian history. The club's acceptance into the North West Counties League was formally announced, publicity was garnered for the upcoming trials day, and Karl Marginson was introduced as manager – and made available for interviews. Any questions about where the team would play were batted back with the response that it would be announced to the club's members at the EGM.

Margy, as he'd quickly come to be known, had met the press before he'd even been introduced to most of the Steering Committee, but this was put right the following night. At another meeting at the Seven Oaks pub, he and assistant Phil Power were invited to offer their input on things like the playing budget, training requirements and suggested opposition for preseason. Russ reported that he'd made good progress on groundsharing with Bury, indicating that they seemed keen to do a deal and had already begun seeking the necessary permission from the Football League. Droylsden remained the preferred option, due to the expense of renting Gigg Lane and the fact it was an all-seater stadium, but the suspicion was beginning to harden that Pace was messing everyone about.

Andy Walsh had got a lot more involved in proceedings over the previous few days since the press conference had been arranged, and it soon seemed apparent why this was. I was surprised when Luc announced that he and Walshy had agreed they would provisionally take the two staff roles, club secretary and chief executive, which would need filling once everything was formalised. It was the first I'd heard of this suggestion and I looked around the room for everyone else's reactions. There wasn't a flicker; no one looked surprised or raised any questions – it was as if everyone else already knew about it. I thought for a second I must've missed an email where it was discussed but that was impossible.

For some reason it really pissed me off. It was obvious that the roles had to be filled by people from the Steering Committee, at least in the short term – there was no one else who wanted them, for one thing. It just would've been nice to have been consulted rather than having it presented as a fait accompli; nothing else had been decided like that. I could understand it having slipped Luc's mind, given everything that had been going on but something just didn't sit right about the way Walsh seemed to have gone about it. Still, I decided not to make a fuss about it, as they were the obvious choices – it certainly didn't warrant falling out with anyone over it.

The other main point of discussion was the worryingly low amount of money which had come in since requests for pledges had been made the previous weekend. This was despite Martin reporting hugely positive feedback following a ring round by him, Phil Sheeran and Russ:

'I have to say that the response, both to being called and to the work that has been done so far, has been phenomenal, and I've been touched by

people's praise. Speaking to people has really brought home how much this means. It is clear that people like the fact that we have personalised the pledges by calling, and almost everyone I spoke to wanted to be delegated some sort of role. So we may have more stewards than fans come August!'

The following morning, any possible panic was definitively averted – there were over seven hundred cheques waiting in the PO Box.

With the trial day fast approaching, hundreds of applicants submitted their details. These were whittled down to about 200 on the not-wholly-scientific basis of their proximity to Manchester (for example, applicants from Australia were immediately ruled out) and how convincing their descriptions of previous football experience were. Anyone who'd been on the books of a professional club was looked on more favourably than those claiming to have always wanted to represent a club, and being willing to go out and buy some boots if they were invited down. The 200 who were successful were all given time slots to turn up, and we made attempts to sort out balanced teams, having requested applicants provide details of their ideal position. However, come the actual day, we would have had more success herding cats than trying to get 22 players on each pitch when they should have been.

Wimbledon had warned us not to expect much from the day other than it being a good PR move but a fair few trialists went on to play for the club, including Rob Nugent and Adie Orr, while 17 were initially invited to training. My own brother and a former United player's son both played but didn't get picked out, so there was no favouritism on display!

The following day, Brady, Walshy and I convened in Adam Brown's office at Manchester Metropolitan University to start preparing for the EGM. There was a lot to get through, as members would be asked to vote in the club's Board; vote on the club badge; be given a rundown of what work the Steering Committee had completed; and receive a run-through of the club's budget.

That same day, no one was overly shocked when word came through from Tameside Council that Droylsden's lease didn't allow them to share the Butchers Arms, but it piled more pressure on delivering one of the remaining hopes. A surprising story emerged in that afternoon's *Manchester Evening News*, claiming that a group of 15 City fans were looking enviously at what we were doing, with a view to creating their own breakaway called 'Fans' Football Club City'. One of them, Simon Cooper, claimed, 'We have had a meeting and we are all for building another option for City fans to go to. The framework is fragile at the moment, but the City fans we have approached have been 75% in favour.'

At that evening's Steering Committee meeting, Tony Jordan took centre stage and presented the final options for the club crest, following which there was much debate and argument before the shortlist was decided. He also delivered a mock-up of the team's proposed shirt. Tempest, the company which made Wimbledon's kit, had been chosen primarily on the basis that they promised to deliver a bespoke design in time for the first game, despite only having eleven days from when the badge was voted on at the EGM to complete it.

On Tuesday 28 June, the first preseason training session took place at Parrs Wood High School in East Didsbury. The excitement that was building was evident from the number of fans that turned up to watch. This giddiness was countered by the report that a lengthy conversation with John Wilkinson about a ground share at Salford Rugby League club had led nowhere. Wilkinson cited the toll on the pitch as precluding the possibility of any groundshare. Pritchard suspected it had as much to do with Salford not wishing to alienate people at MUFC – Wilkinson also owned an interest in a pub very close to Old Trafford. Meanwhile, Stalybridge announced that FC United would play them in a friendly at the end of July in a benefit match for a club 'stalwart' who was suffering from cancer. This came as a surprise, and put the club in an awkward position when it turned out that Stalybridge had seemed to confirm it on the basis of no more than a chat with Margy – no official approach had been made. It caused some resentment that FC was being backed into a corner but, given agreement with Bury was still in the balance, nothing was to be done to undermine Stalybridge. Not least because they might still be required as a last resort groundshare option.

Progress seemed slow going but, on Thursday 30 June, Tony Pritchard met with Bury FC officials and an arrangement was decided in principle, pending financial details being agreed. NWCFL officials were obviously getting nervous, as was everyone else, with FC United's inangural EGM just days away. Tony Pritchard was determined not to be rushed, and assured that it was better to get things right than do anything rash:

> '*I've asked [Bury] to inject some pace and urgency into [their] solicitors regarding them producing the relevant ground share document. Whilst I accept that solicitors are more inclined to "break into a walk" as opposed to get on a sprint, we must be careful that our tight deadline does not provide Bury's solicitors with the opportunity to put up "smoke & mirrors". We need to be 100% clear about what we are signing up to.*'

Dave Boyle, the chief executive of Supporters Direct, provided valuable assistance to Adam Brown, Russ and Mike Adams in finalising the club's constitution, while the rest of us worked on the documentation and voting forms needed for the EGM. Come Tuesday evening, everything was ready to go; everything, that was, except the announcement of a ground. Earlier in the day, the club had been asked to comment on a website report that FC's proposal to play at Droylsden had fallen through. The timing couldn't have been worse but I was confident the membership at that night's meeting would be happy to grant a few more days' blind trust and urged that, in the meantime, everyone stick to the agreed script:

> '*We currently have a viable ground share agreement in place, which we will be in a position to announce later in the week once the legalities are out of the way. Until that time we are not going to become involved in unhelpful speculation.*'

The Methodist Hall was packed out once again, with an unbelievable buzz in the air and goodwill towards the Steering Committee in abundance. Having seen what had been achieved thus far, there were no doubts raised by anyone about having to wait another few days for confirmation on where the ground would be. Twenty-three candidates stood for election to the Board, including ten of the sixteen who'd put the club together (only Mike Adams, Phil Bedford, Andrew Howse, Tony Jordan and I stood aside, while Luc Zentar as club secretary was ineligible). Nine of those ten were voted in, alongside lawyer Joe Tully and businessman Scott Fletcher, with Rob Brady narrowly missing out.

The NWCFL released the fixtures later that week, with FC United scheduled to open the season away at Leek CSOB on 13 August, their capacity of 5,000 allowing league officials to gauge what demand there would be ahead of games against clubs with much smaller grounds. Jules Spencer marked the Steering Committee's passing by summing up the previous six weeks in a light-hearted email:

> '*Big group hug. Ahhhh. The work has been outstanding. Commented last night, that when you see the lists of achievements written down, it doesn't do justice to what went on behind the scenes. Superb effort all round. Cat-fights, banter, democracy gone mad, emotional pleas, "FCUM just F*CKEM", long nights and longer days (especially Luc and JP). And a scouse Dwarf. Magic, the lot of it.*'

'And the last word (as always) should go to a certain inebriated Mr O'Neill at half 4 one morning in Spain ... "FC UNITED - I salute you all! Hasta la Victoria Siempre." Mint.

'Now how's that f*ckin ground doin?'

Tony Pritchard was still toiling away, trying to bring the agreement to a close and regularly updating on proceedings. The day after the EGM he wrote:

'Bury FC's legal people are currently working like crazy. We have now got the football league lawyer involved, and he is being very helpful also. At present, we are still working to a late afternoon / early evening deadline, but do be prepared for this to run to Thursday morning.

'I really must be getting on their nerves right now. In fact, I think I'm getting on my own nerves! I'll e-mail more news as I get it.'

Bury finally sent over the contract late on Thursday 7 July. After a few minor alterations were requested, it was eventually signed and sealed on Friday 15, a nervy full week later. The following day, Marginson's brand new team was due to take the field at Leigh's Hilton Park for FC United's first ever game. The seemingly impossible had been achieved. Even at that very moment of triumph, another major issue was already rising to the surface. In spite of Andrew Howse's best efforts to head off any trademark problems, the registration application for the club badge was rejected due to its grouping of 'Manchester' and 'United', and obvious similarity to existing trademarks. It was a sickener that, after all the hard work, the club in its current guise could still so easily be sunk on such a technicality. Manchester United hadn't actually raised any objection, so the only solution was to make a direct request to them, asking that they waive any potential claim. It was a pretty embarrassing position. In some ways we were like the stroppy teenager who makes a big fuss of leaving home and who, halfway out the door, has to go back, cap in hand, and request a loan off his parents. No one knew which way it would go: United would have been within their rights to tell us where to go, but, equally, they might have been keen to avoid the negative publicity such a move would attract.

Tony Pritchard wrote to David Gill and, to many people's surprise, in late August a reply came back from David Beswitherick, the official with responsibility for protecting Manchester United's intellectual property rights: 'I confirm that we have no objection to the badge nor do we have any objection to you registering the mark "Football Club United of Manchester."' It was a decision that, in time, some at Old Trafford may have come to regret.

5

THE PEOPLE'S CHARTER

The media's interest in FC United grew exponentially following the first announcement of the pledges in early June. By the time of the EGM, the club was big news. There'd been approaches from journalists around the globe, from Malaysia to Germany, while various companies were extremely keen to film a documentary on the club's formation. All such offers had been rejected. In the early days of the Steering Committee, information had been strictly controlled, in part to allow the focus to remain on the task in hand. Now, with the club set up, it would become a delicate balancing act: to manage the interest in what was happening while actually getting the work done.

An example of this quickly cropped up in the form of an unofficial online fan forum (called *The Soul Is One*) which, in the wake of the EGM, published a preview of the club's kit, as well as the premature story that the club would be playing at Gigg Lane. With issues ongoing around the club badge trademark and the final agreement with Bury, Board member Vas Wackrill aired his frustration: 'Personally, I'm not a fan of that site. Whilst I can see the benefits of a message board, I don't think half of what gets posted there does us any favours.'

Mike Adams was quick to pounce on what he saw as the potential for poachers to turn gamekeepers and warned, 'We can't, nor should we, seek to impose any kind of pressure on editorial or other content unless it transgresses the usual boundaries. We've got to be prepared to take the brickbats as well as the bouquets, and having an independent site with independent views is natural and healthy.' It was an early indication of problems to come.

During the week leading up to the game against Leigh, the press coverage became even more extensive: there was little need for any promotion of the game. Despite the interest – or maybe because of it – it was difficult for anyone to predict how many people might turn up. The consensus was that a crowd of 1,000 would be respectable, and provide something to build on. Some thought there'd be double that. The uncertainty only added to the excitement for those involved.

A couple of days before the game, Adam Brown drafted a leaflet that was to be distributed. It said:

'Seven core principles of how the club will operate are set out below which have been agreed by the membership. These principles will be protected by the elected Board:

1. The Board will be democratically elected by its members.
2. Decisions taken by the membership will be decided on a one member, one vote basis.
3. The club will develop strong links with the local community and strive to be accessible to all, discriminating against none.
4. The club will endeavour to make admission prices as affordable as possible, to as wide a constituency as possible.
5. The club will encourage young, local participation – playing and supporting – whenever possible.
6. The Board will strive wherever possible to avoid outright commercialism.
7. The club will remain a non-profit organisation.'

These weren't too dissimilar to what had been proposed in my original article that had appeared in *Red Issue*, and they formed what became FC United's manifesto to be displayed on the club's website.

Saturday 16 July was a sweltering day. While Luc and Walshy embarked on their new careers with much work to do, I met others at Victoria station in Manchester to board a train to the back of beyond, and from there a bus on to Leigh. We got off near the ground which was pretty much deserted, and so followed our nose to find the nearest pubs. We thought we were arriving fairly early but when we got there they were all already packed with Reds! The sun, booze and giddy expectancy combined to create a balmy cocktail on a barmy day. Stuart Brennan reported in the *Manchester Evening News*: 'It was not really about the football, rather a boisterous celebratory day out.' That mood was somehow summed up by the sight of a huge dinghy bouncing around the terrace behind one goal, part of a haul of inflatables liberated from a nearby shop and contributing to the joyous, holiday vibe.

The attendance was a whopping 2,552, of whom three were encouraged by the afternoon heat and lack of police to disrupt the game by streaking, although it was another pitch invasion at the end of the 0–0 draw that came to symbolise the day, when the players were chaired off the pitch by the crowd. Joz Mitten, one of that original FC United line-up, had never experienced anything like it. 'That was unbelievable,' he told the *Manchester Evening News*. 'I looked round the dressing room afterwards and all of the lads were just stunned into silence. We thought there might be 800 to a thousand, so to get so many was a shock. Most of the lads here have not played in crowds bigger than 400 or so.'

The following week, FC United headed south to play AFC Wimbledon, for a friendly arranged in recognition of the links that had sprung up between the clubs over the previous couple of months. Another bumper crowd of 3,301 watched the Dons win 1–0. Despite the defeat, the buzz was growing, adding to the attention the club was getting. The following day, *The Observer* did a full-page feature on the club's two games thus far.

On 30 July, FC played Stalybridge Celtic in another great day out, although the 'Red Rebels' – as the *Evening News* took to calling FC – failed to score yet again. The lightning-fast creation of the club was occasionally apparent in some of the quaintly slipshod details; on this particular day it was the fact that one player, Rory Patterson, took to the pitch in a shirt that didn't even have a number on the back. From the terraces resounded a hymn to 'The man with no name'; the song stuck and Rory would become a firm fans' favourite.

After three scoreless games for the fledgling club, by the time FC headed to Flixton in early August, some people were genuinely wondering if they'd ever see the team score. However, this was the first time they'd faced opposition from the level at which they'd soon be playing, and everything fell into place. Steve Torpey scored a cracking opener as FC United won 5–2. These four friendly fixtures set the tone for the season – pretty much everywhere FC played, the pubs were packed and the crowds buoyant. Stephen 'Swampy' Bennett, soon to become a match commentator on the club's internet-based radio station, describes it thus:

> *'The first season must be on a par with that very Madchester "second summer of love" – everyone off their heads and loving it, hoping it would last forever. For me, it felt right from the start, with my son James aged ten now standing beside me on the terracing – everything my father and his father had once been able to do at United, but what to the modern fan was an alien concept, due to the Taylor report.'*

Over the course of the coming season, more and more people would turn up, drawn in by whatever it was they thought a football experience should be. The mantra that quickly became widespread was 'Our club, our rules', the words being depicted alongside the classic Northern Soul 'clenched fist' symbol on numerous badges and T-shirts.

By the time of FC United's first league game on 13 August, a fanzine had already sprung up, its title *Under The Boardwalk* adopting the name of The Drifters' song that became an instant hit at FC games following its first airing at Wimbledon. The magazine quickly came to reflect the ethos of the club, the following edition's editorial describing those very early days:

> '*The buzzphrase of the moment appears to be "punk football", which seems to eloquently sum up the back to basics DIY ethic that permeates FCUM. Anyone who read Sean Ingle's recent article in* The Guardian *must have identified with his sentiments that:*
>
> *"Football, for all its fault, is still the best sport in the world. But it has become an increasingly ugly mix of Thatcherite greed and Gradgrindian inequality. It needs to be taken down a peg – and supporters are the best ones to do it."*
>
> '*And that, I reckon, is what we are doing, and it's that air of positivity as much as anything creating the great buzz around watching FCUM . . . we are kicking back against the corporate world of football that has oppressed and depressed us for so long [it] feels like the year zero attitude of 1976 . . .*'

In Leek, the vibe was more biblical than anything else. Torrential rain permeated everything and everyone yet somehow added to, rather than detracted from, the occasion. Once again, FC ran out 5–2 winners in front of another huge crowd of 2,590, and the team headed straight to the top of the league table. The following weekend brought the club's first game at Bury's Gigg Lane against Padiham, a small town just outside Burnley. FC won again, 3–2 in front of 2,498, but what truly stood out was the atmosphere the fans created: a deafening noise booming out for the entire match, with songs of defiance against Malcolm Glazer in amongst the usual Manchester United anthems, and the newly adopted – and adapted – FC United versions. Karl Marginson soon started referring to a '90–90' support – 90 per cent of the fans singing for 90 minutes long.

In early October, two successive home games just days apart saw a crowd of 3,110 for the visit of Oldham Town and then 3,808 against Daisy Hill. The North West Counties League had never known anything like it – many teams usually attracted under 100 paying punters. Almost every away game saw an all-time record set for the home club's attendance. While this provided a welcome cash injection for many of them, the crowds also brought logistical problems: that season, only three clubs would have the facilities to host FC's support at their usual home ground, with many matches having to be moved to much bigger venues.

One of the few whose facilities were deemed adequate was Darwen. However, when FC headed there in November, Darwen refused to grant their normal concessionary prices for children, forcing everyone to pay the full adult price. FC's Board decided to take a stand, and boycotted their boardroom hospitality, while Andy Walsh didn't hold back in his criticism, telling the *Manchester Evening News*:

'It's just greed. Darwen got new owners in the summer and they obviously have seen the opportunity to make a quick killing. It's very disappointing when a club does this because we want to encourage as many people as possible to go to games.'

One person who wasn't able to go to FC games any more was Russ Delaney. His health had deteriorated badly in October, following his epic exertions during the summer, and his battle with illness had come to an end. Russ had advocated supporter ownership of Manchester United since way back in December 1989. While those efforts to save United from predators were ultimately in vain, Russ had eventually played his part in delivering supporter ownership through FC United, even if it had likely played some part in shortening his life. Fans acknowledged Russ's contribution to the club with a minute's applause before a game against New Mills, and I wrote a tribute in the match programme, detailing Russ's United-supporting background and vital work for the Steering Committee. Stuart Brennan wrote a similar, admirably lengthy article in the *Evening News*.

Richard Kurt recalls often phoning Russ in hospital as the end approached, only to find his questions about Russ's health being dismissed if they went on too long:

> '*He couldn't wait to change the subject and talk football politics, and offer up his latest ideas for this 'n' that. He once said he "didn't have time to wallow", which was obviously painfully true. The only time he allowed himself to sound worked up was when he was apologising for the fact that those "shameless robbers" in charge of premium rate bedside telephones were charging us 50p a minute to ring him! He once thanked me for cheering him up with some salacious* Red Issue *gossip but, in fact, it was usually Russ who'd cheer us up: he was always looking for solutions and upsides, and refusing to be beaten by his burdens.*'

Delaney took the details of all his tireless behind-the-scenes activism with him but Kurt thinks he may have played a hitherto unknown role in encouraging Coolmore to hold fire for months:

> '*Russ was certainly speaking regularly to someone who'd then go off to talk to the Coolmore boys, and we used to discuss on a weekly basis what I should include in my* Irish Examiner *newspaper column, which I was told someone at Coolmore was reading closely. To be frank, I was quite happy to lay it on thick with every pleading argument available that they should not sell to the Glazers just yet. I still don't know what Russ was up to, or what he was telling them; but one day, he suddenly became very confident – and shortly thereafter, news did indeed break, to general surprise, that Coolmore weren't prepared to sell just yet. That bought months of time, and I'm sure Russ played some part in that.*'

In late November, *Red Issue* secured an interview with Eric Cantona, in which the former United star slammed the Glazer takeover, providing a morale boost for FC United.

'I don't like these kind of people, who are involved in the game, how could I be a manager for this kind of man? I don't think he knows the game, I don't think he [Glazer] is passionate about the game; I don't think he loves the game. I love Manchester United too much, the identity and philosophy of Manchester United. He could pay me a hundred million euros, I would not go there.

'I agree with the fans [setting up FC]. Because whose interest do the fans have in doing that? It's for the passion and the love of the game and their love for the club. So I have the same feeling as them. To develop this kind of thing, I think it's a bit of dreams. A bit of a utopia. But I like the dreams they have, because it means a lot. It means a lot. All about the love they have for the game and especially Manchester United.'

Another former Manchester United legend was in FC's sights the week of the New Mills game. In a move of which Russ would've undoubtedly approved, Andy Walsh and I drove down to Hale to try to track down Roy Keane. He'd departed Manchester United a few days earlier following his spectacular falling-out with Alex Ferguson and, as he was unable to play for another professional club until the January transfer window opened, I thought it would be an audacious move for FC to try and sign him. Keane had been linked in the press with a move to any one of Celtic, Juventus, Milan and Bayern Munich, as well as a number of English clubs including Nottingham Forest. There was also talk that he may retire. Just that morning, *The Mirror* had even reported that Stuart Pearce, Manchester City's manager, was attempting to lure him to Eastlands.

Obviously, we first ran the idea past Margy – after all, he might not have fancied adding a multiple-champion, international captain and trophy-winning machine to his squad, and the last thing anyone wanted to do was undermine a fledgling manager only a few months into his first job!

A mate of mine lived in Hale and had occasionally given Keane a lift home from the pub over the years, so he'd described to me roughly where he lived. We were driving down this leafy street, trying to find it from these sketchy details, as it's not like houses round there have numbers. All of a sudden, Keane drove past us and up the drive of one of them – problem solved. Sort of. As we parked up, Keane got out of the car and shot into the house, looking far from pleased.

'Oh well, we're here now,' I said to Walshy, and we headed up the drive to knock on the door. After a few moments, the door inched slightly open. Keane's head peered inquisitively round the side, his eyes darting from one of us to the other, weighing us up. 'Yeah?' he half growled. 'Erm, Roy, have you got a minute please?' 'Go on . . .' he replied, still only his head visible, with the door no more than a few inches ajar.

Walshy carried on: 'Obviously we've heard you're without a club at the moment, and we were wondering if you'd be interested in coming down to play at FC United before you sign for a new club in January. It'd be up to you if you just wanted to train. But we've spoken to the manager, and he's happy for you to play or even help out with coaching if you're looking to continue your badges.' Keane was still looking us up and down when a vague look of recognition seemed to come across him, and his demeanour warmed somewhat. He swung the door open and, with a smirk, asked, 'Would I have to do everything the manager tells me?'

He then asked for a second so he could go and grab a pen, before scribbling down Walshy's number, and promising to get in touch if he decided to take up the offer. As we were leaving I stopped and said, 'Just one more thing, Roy: we don't expect you to tell us your plans, but just reassure us that you're not going to sign for City.' He was obviously aware of that morning's reports and replied, 'You don't think I'm that mad do you?'

Unfortunately Keane's call never came and he eventually signed for Celtic, while FC United continued their romp through the North West Counties. At the end of November, a truly riotous affair took place at Stockport County's Edgeley Park, where Cheadle Town had moved their home game against FC. George Best had died the day before and, with Manchester United away at West Ham on the Sunday, many Reds turned up at FC intent on paying tribute, which they did as much through their alcohol intake as via paeans to his genius. A thrilling game saw FC equalise in the final minute to draw 3–3.

With 25 December fast approaching, many FC fans remembered the prediction of former Manchester United and Bolton player Alan Gowling, who months earlier had dismissively suggested the protest club would 'not last until Christmas'. As a reminder, many sent him what became a deluge of seasonal greetings cards, which Gowling accepted with good grace. There was a fantastic buzz around the club at the time, and players such as Simon Carden, Steve Spencer, David Chadwick, Adie Orr and Rory Patterson had all been quickly established as firm fan favourites, despite being unknown to them only a matter of months earlier.

FC United's only home game that December saw FC United win 10–2 against Castleton Gabriels, though the highlight for many was actually one of the Castleton goals. The scorer celebrated by running into the stand, taking a seat, and applauding his own strike. The new year saw Winsford United visit Gigg Lane for a top-of-the-table clash that attracted a gigantic 4,328 crowd. In another electric atmosphere, FC went a goal down before coming back to win 2–1, but the big day of the season was still to come: Blackpool Mechanics away.

As with Gowling, their chairman Tommy Baldwin had famously scoffed at the idea of FC United, so it was ironic that his club should benefit more than any other during the 2005/06 season. Sensibly, given the thousands of fans planning the trip to the coast that February weekend, Mechanics hired Blackpool FC's Bloomfield Road to stage the game. The crowd was officially 4,300, and the *Manchester Evening*

News reported that the travelling contingent comprised 'the biggest away support at Bloomfield Road for 20 years . . . Lancashire Police admitted they were caught off guard.' The day coincided with Manchester United's lunchtime televised FA Cup game against Liverpool, and so the seaside pubs were packed from early morning. The *Evening News* explained the inevitable result of this, noting that, 'five fans were arrested and a number of fixed penalty tickets were given out for drunkenness and drinking on the streets.' The only wonder to anyone present was that the tally was so low. Unusually, a police spokesman actually seemed to agree: 'Any trouble was only on the sort of scale you'd expect with a crowd of that size. The pubs were heaving.'

Off the pitch, so that everything could be seen to be above board, Walsh and Zentar's positions were advertised, and the pair were invited to apply for the paid roles they'd assumed the previous summer. Following a full recruitment process, both came out on top and were reappointed. Andy Walsh had to resign his elected position on the Board as a result. Although they were the only two paid staff members, there was no shortage of help from supporters. Scores volunteered their time and services to assist with anything that needed doing, be it in the office during the week or at Bury on a match day, from manning turnstiles to selling programmes.

What Swampy dubbed 'the second summer of love' continued towards its inevitable climax, with FC eventually promoted on 12 April following a 4–0 win against Chadderton. Three days later, FC were without a league fixture, but due to rivals dropping points, found out they'd won the league following a friendly game at Clitheroe. The stage was set for a bumper celebration at the final home fixture against Great Harwood Town and, with children allowed in for free, an enormous crowd of 6,023 turned up to see the championship trophy presented. The support provided another crackling atmosphere, but the players failed to rise to the occasion, putting in one of the worst performances of the season to lose 1–0. The players accepted the trophy in T-shirts bearing Russell Delaney's name, and an open top bus was brought in to take them and the trophy down Manchester Road to the nearby Swan and Cemetery – the pub which had acted as the club's unofficial post-match HQ for much of the season.

As a couple of thousand fans lined the few-hundred-yard route, the club's friendly police liaison officer desperately tried to smooth the bus's passage, as traffic backed up in both directions. I asked Walshy how he'd wangled permission for it all and Andy said he'd asked the copper, who'd assured him, 'Don't worry, just leave it to me.' No wonder he was looking stressed when he saw the crowds! It was symptomatic of the season; FC even managed to get the police embracing the 'Punk Football' philosophy.

On 12 May 2006, exactly one year on from the takeover, a few hundred FC fans watched in the Bruno-Plache-Stadion in Leipzig as the team fought out a 4–4 draw in a friendly game against Lokomotiv Leipzig before a crowd of 7,421. In 1987, Leipzig had played in the European Cup Winners' Cup final against Ajax Amsterdam before sliding down the divisions and being made bankrupt in 2004. The club was immediately reformed by a group of fans, and had just finished their second season working their way back up through Germany's lower tiers; the match was organised as Leipzig's way of acknowledging what had been achieved by Manchester's small band of idealists.

This sort of recognition and acclaim that FC United received abroad was in stark contrast to the mood that was actively being promoted by some back home, where Alex Ferguson was getting increasingly agitated by the club's achievements. When invited by one journalist to congratulate Karl Marginson on FC's promotion, Ferguson pretended not to know who he was, before replying, 'You're joking, right?' and storming out of the press conference. *The Guardian*'s Danny Taylor later described FC United as 'high on Ferguson's list of taboo subjects' and some senior staff at Old Trafford made their displeasure known to *Manchester Evening News* journalists about the amount of coverage the paper was granting the club.

In September 2006, Manchester's *Time Out* ran an article by Oliver Thompson introducing the city to visitors attending the Labour Party conference, being held in the city for the first time since 1917. It touched upon the differences of opinion FC United had garnered:

'Our dissent is not always explicitly political. When the US businessman Malcolm Glazer added Manchester United to his portfolio of sporting franchises, a group of disenchanted fans defiantly resolved to set up their own club. Variously described and derided as "brave rebels", "irrelevant outsiders" and "a right bunch of dicks", the group stuck to their guns and formed FC United of Manchester. Their inspiration was AFC Wimbledon, set up when Wimbledon moved north and became the Milton Keynes Dons, but FC United nonetheless stands as living testament to that peculiarly Mancunian talent for gazing at the world in all its wonder, thinking for a minute, and then muttering: "Nah, that's bollocks. This is how we'll do it . . ."'

While FC fans instantly adopted that 'right bunch of dicks' tag, Alex Ferguson was deadly serious when, the same month, he slammed the people behind the club as 'sad', and accused them of being 'attention seekers'. In contrast to his claim in 2004 to be 'the bridge between the club and the fans', he now scoffed at those who'd been protesting: 'They carried on to the degree where they actually thought they should have a say in the running of the football club.' But even his bitterness and animosity was as nothing compared to what was going on under the public radar . . .

6

SALFORD YEOMANRY

A few days after FC's first ever game at Leigh in July 2005, Manchester United headed to the Far East for three pre-season games in Hong Kong, Beijing and Tokyo. Although the games were only friendlies, a number of fans always went on such tours, being an excuse to make a holiday of watching the team in far-off lands. A couple of nights before the first game, a number of United's hardcore fans gathered in a bar in Hong Kong's Wan Chai district to watch the start of what would become a legendary Ashes series. I was there with them, while being interrogated by supporters and friends from Old Trafford, who wanted to know what FC United was all about. There was no antagonism, it was more a case of people just wanting to understand what was going on. They'd heard about it, maybe read a report or two in the press, and wanted an inside track into what was what.

Many of those present had travelled on a tour organised by Tony O'Neill (no relation), the self-styled 'Red Army General' and one-time hooligan leader who'd written a book on his exploits following the club, and who now worked as a travel agent, organising trips for supporters. Tony was fine, too – there was no reason why he wouldn't be. At one point, I went outside the bar, and he was stood there, looking like he was taking a breather – he still wasn't 100 per cent after being shot the year before. I remember he said something like, 'They're all doing your head in, right?' and basically told me not to bother too much about it. The only real issue was having to have the same conversation over and over as everyone got more drunk.

After the following game in Beijing, a handful of us headed into one of the executive areas, where what seemed like half the local police force lined a corridor under the stand. It was obviously where United's official delegation was enjoying whatever hospitality was laid on, so we thought we'd go in too. Inside were a collection of club directors, sponsors and officials, including one of the Glazer brothers.

Even though we were clearly out of place in there, wearing shorts when everyone else was suited, no one much gave us a second look, so we just tucked into the buffet and drinks that were laid on. Next thing, Andy Anson's stood next to me, so I asked him about one or two things that had been printed about him in *Red Issue* (Anson was the MUFC director whom the Glazers had sought to oust the previous November. He would go on to lead England's disastrous 2018 World Cup bid). He looked like he'd seen a ghost, and immediately went up to whisper something to David Gill, before all the United contingent were quickly ushered out of the room. It was bizarre.

The paranoia of all the club's top brass about any contact with supporters had clearly increased following the mini-riot that took place when the Glazers had turned up at Old Trafford in June. That they still didn't feel safe, with a huge squadron of Beijing's police only yards away, perhaps showed the impact that the MEC's threats had made.

Back in Manchester, United were drawn against Hungarian side Debrecen in the qualifiers for the Champions League. The first leg on 9 August was the first game at Old Trafford of the Glazer era, and Shareholders United were planning what they hoped would be a big demonstration. They'd spent the months since 12 May seemingly trying to convince people that they could still help block Glazer's ownership, bizarrely employing tactics used against Rupert Murdoch following Sky's bid in 1998, even though Glazer's takeover was complete.

On 3 June, they announced that they'd written to all 72,000 of the club's (former) shareholders, urging them to join their organisation 'in its continuing campaign'. They also wrote to the Premier League's chief executive Richard Scudamore and the sports minister Richard Caborn, as well as making a submission to the Office of Fair Trading, complaining about the potential effects of Glazer's leveraged buyout, and urging them to act. They suggested laying a wreath at the Stock Exchange on the day Manchester United was de-listed and, under the banner of 'No Customers = No Profits', proposed fans buy an alternative range of United merchandise in the club's original green and yellow colours to raise money for their 'Phoenix Fund'. This would be boosted, they said, by 'a series of "Phoenix Nights", beginning with a major fundraising benefit concert in Manchester to coincide with the beginning of the new football season'. Yet SU's time had passed: the fight had been lost. The only logical ongoing protest was FC United. Certainly, the proposed Debrecen march was badly misjudged, not least because everyone who'd be at the game was well aware what the issues were, and had already made their decisions one way or the other. Protesting 'from within' was as pointless as it was sure to alienate continuing match-goers.

Sure enough, SU's turnout was pitiful. Not only that, but as the eighty or so marchers made their way down Warwick Road, they were abused and spat at by United fans going to the match. A couple of us were stood at the top of Warwick Road as the SU march came past and, while I'd guessed it wouldn't be well received, I couldn't believe the vitriol being displayed towards them.

I'd just had some experience of it myself on the forecourt outside the ground. I heard a shout which I thought was directed towards me. I looked round and, sure enough, this guy was staring at me, despite having what I presumed was his young son in tow. He shouted over, 'Fuck off to FC, you Judas cunt.' I didn't have a clue who he was and, with a couple of police walking over, told him that if he wanted to discuss it, to leave his kid and walk up the road with us.

The next day, I got a call off someone who'd been in the Amblehurst pub in Sale post-match, who asked me what had gone on the previous evening. I couldn't think what he meant at first, until he said the son of United's 1960s star Paddy Crerand had turned up in there, boasting of how he'd 'put that fucking JP in his place' before the game.

The takeover had caused huge splits in the club's support. While some gave up their season tickets and boycotted Old Trafford completely in favour of attending FC United, others had stuck with SU and pledged 'not one penny', having also given up their season tickets. Others would have boycotted except for having already submitted their season ticket renewals before 12 May. Many of the remaining supporters deeply resented the takeover but just couldn't, or didn't want to, stop going to Old Trafford. Some were even happy to watch both Manchester United *and* FC, whenever fixtures allowed. Despite the protests the previous season, the largest proportion just didn't care who the owners were, with many having the same lack of interest in any other team, whoever they were or however they'd come about. However, of this final group, a sizeable number soon became very vocal, and were agitated by any suggestion of the dilution of anyone's support for the club – be it people watching FC or simply not wanting to finance the Glazers. To them, all such groups were lumped in together: you didn't question your football club and you certainly didn't change your allegiance – if you did you were 'Judas scum'.

One possible reason for this increasingly aggressive stance towards the Glazers' critics was perhaps linked to an incident before the away leg of the Debrecen tie. As the Manchester United squad arrived in Budapest, some fans also passed through the airport's arrivals area, and one of them took the chance to confront Alex Ferguson about his failure to speak out against the takeover. Within the hour, *Red Issue* had published the exchange online, after the quotes were phoned in by one of the fans involved:

'United fan: "You've fucked us over, you could've spoke out about it."
Ferguson: "I've got close mates who've been working with me here for
fifteen years. They come first in all this."
United fan: "So don't the fans come first?"
Ferguson: "Well I suppose they do come somewhere."
United fan: "You what? That's well out of order."
Ferguson: "Well if you don't like it go and watch Chelsea."
United fan: "The fans have been screwed right over. It costs me
£20-odd a game now as it is."
Ferguson: "It costs more than that at Chelsea, go and watch them."'

The fan subsequently explained his reasoning on *Red Issue*'s forum:

'He [Ferguson] could have helped us, he didn't – he protected himself
and his mates as he always does. Then he comes out with comments like
"No one was behind the fans more than me." Bollocks, he did nothing
when he could have made the difference. I've had my fill of his bullshit,
and when I got the chance to say it to his face I said it.'

The clash was splashed in all the tabloids the following morning, causing embarrassment for Ferguson which undoubtedly displeased United's ultra-loyalists. The irony was that, while it was someone very much against the takeover who'd harangued Ferguson, the fan who made sure news of it was fed to *Red Issue* was someone who would come to be seen by some as a Glazer mouthpiece.

Ferguson was feeling the pressure at home as well as abroad, with his team struggling badly on the pitch. *The Guardian*'s Danny Taylor described the malaise afflicting the club in his book *This Is The One* (2007), as United lost to Blackburn in late September:

'All the frustration comes to a head today. The crowd turn. Effing this.
Effing that. Thousands of them, in every part of the ground, but par-
ticularly around the dugout. Ferguson is a "disgrace". He is "fucking
clueless". He does not know what his tactics are. He is a "shambles". It is
time he "fucked off" and took Queiroz with him.

'*Towards the end, a big fat guy in a leather jacket to the right of the dugout is jabbing his finger at Ferguson, all pent-up anger. Nearby, on another row, there is a middle-aged bloke dressed all in black. Between them, they are giving Ferguson a terrible time, not even watching the game. It is spiteful, vicious, toxic stuff and Ferguson stirs. He half-turns, as if he is about to have a go back. But then something tells him to break the habit of a lifetime. He stares impassively at the pitch, trying to blank it out. But these guys are close enough for him to hear every word. Two stewards in fluorescent jackets move in but it doesn't make any difference. As soon as they move off, the supporters are back on their feet, yelling abuse. It is a savage, relentless tirade.*

'*Managers can suffer from losses of form, as players do, and Ferguson seems strangely out of sorts right now. There is a bad vibe about United and the fans are starting to wonder if this is the Ferguson of old: the guy who used to dismiss every "crisis" the way the rest of us would swat away a bothersome fly.*

'*Losing today leaves them ten points behind Chelsea. For some it is too much to bear. The outpouring of anger is astonishing.*

'*Old Trafford is half-empty at the final whistle and when Ferguson makes his way to the tunnel it is the longest walk of his life. Mark Hughes, manager of Blackburn, is in front and the fans stand respectfully to applaud one of their former players.*

'*Hughsey! Hughsey! Hughsey!*

'*Ferguson follows ten yards behind, his head bowed, shoulders hunched. When he flashes his eyes at the crowd, the hostility hits him like a mallet. There are V-signs, middle fingers raised and faces contorted with anger. There is nothing to prepare you for seeing and hearing Sir Alex Ferguson being jeered and abused by Manchester United's supporters. It is unthinkable.*'

The contrast with the exuberance and enjoyment of FC United's early games couldn't have been starker, and FC United suddenly filled the role of a very convenient scapegoat for everything that was wrong at

Old Trafford. Andy Walsh had heard of one supporter, wearing an FC shirt on a random weekday, being berated at a petrol station by the ex-hooligan leader Tony O'Neill, in what seemed like a complete reversal of his attitude in Hong Kong. Word started spreading that Tony was planning much more. The NWCFL cup draw had pitted FC against Cheadle Town – Tony O'Neill's local club – and he was rumoured to be encouraging his goon squad to attend. The fixture was subsequently postponed and moved to Curzon Ashton's new ground at short notice, officially on account of the inadequacy of Cheadle's facilities. It ultimately passed without incident.

Tony O'Neill had a regular column in the fanzine *United We Stand*, in which he expounded upon whatever topical issues tested his patience that month. In October's edition, he made clear that his targets now included FC United, while stating numerous lies about FC supposedly refusing to play at Cheadle as the reason for the game being moved. He wrote:

> *'All [Cheadle's] hard work getting ready for their big day and pay day was wasted because the Chelsea of grass roots gave it: "we're the big club and we don't like going to Cheadle so we're demanding a change of venue." . . . You arrogant bastards. Just who do you think you are? You left MUFC and took your dummies with you, with shouts of "we don't like the way football is going." YOU then turn round with your superior: "we're FC United and we dominate this league so do as we say and we're telling you to change the venue regardless because we're a massive club and we rule." The words "Chelsea", "Abramovich", money and "arrogance" all come to mind.'*

For whatever reason, FC United was now The Enemy and, although Tony O'Neill was then serving a lengthy ban from attending games following a conviction for hooliganism, his influence still extended deep within the club's support. All manner of acolytes immediately fell into line with his diktat, and it was noticeable that others who, until then, had been happily attending FC games suddenly stopped.

Coincidentally, at the same time Tony O'Neill was taking aim at FC, Manchester United's marketing director Peter Draper pointedly claimed in an interview with the *Manchester Evening News* that there was no difference between the two clubs:

'It's only a question of scale. The most interesting thing [about FC] is that they aren't letting anybody in for free. They will have a sponsor in due course. If they win promotion they will want to buy better players. In order to fulfil that wish they will start to sell nice butties rather than curly ones.'

In reply, Jules Spencer accused Draper of 'spectacularly missing the point,' adding, 'We have never had an issue with commercialism, only the nature of it and where the money is ending up.' Only two months after MUFC had helped FC by waiving the opportunity to exert their trademark, it was clear that FC United was now very much in the sights of those running Old Trafford.

At the start of November, FC were due to play Eccleshall in Stafford. A few days earlier, Manchester United were in Paris for a game against Lille. There, I was warned by one long-standing Red to 'be careful' if I was going to the FC game that weekend: 'This person said he'd been invited to go on a coach Tony O'Neill was planning to run to the game, and it wasn't for the purpose of making friends with anyone.' However, Fate had already intervened, as the Red Army General had been arrested at Manchester Airport while trying to make his way to Paris with a flight load of his travel company's customers. This breached the terms of his banning order, as he'd not been granted the dispensation to travel. He was briefly remanded in custody, thus scuppering any immediate plans he may have had for the weekend, and was convicted of breaching his ban the following February.

In spite of this, in early 2006 Tony O'Neill was involved in a series of meetings with Manchester United officials, as later relayed in an interview with *United-Supporteren*, the magazine of United's 40,000-strong

Scandinavian branch. He expressed surprise that 'somebody with my background' was able to talk to the club about the idea of building a supporters' social club close to Old Trafford. A website appeared, announcing that Paddy Crerand had agreed to be the putative club's patron, and calling for people to invest in bringing the idea to fruition. Around the same time, an official Old Trafford supporters branch of Manchester United suddenly sprouted up, its registered address being the same as Tony O'Neill's office. For a long time the club had given little encouragement to the creation of branches in the Manchester area, yet now here was one suddenly operating from the same street that the stadium was on, with branch status granting whoever ran it access to match tickets. It had once been almost inconceivable that the club would authorise such links to a convicted armed robber and banned hooligan. Not any more.

Following the Glazers' reception at Old Trafford the previous summer, I was made aware that a well-known Salford gangland figure had been approached by someone purporting to represent United's security company. This person had requested that the gangster act as unofficial protection on the street in a bid to ensure that no similar incidents happened to the Glazers in future. Though the gangster spurned the invitation, it wasn't clear whether the vacancy was subsequently touted out to anyone else. It also wasn't clear what the *quid pro quo* for any such arrangement might have been.

Tony O'Neill continued his campaign of trying to undermine FC. In March, a young, female journalist from the *Sunday Mirror* turned up at Gigg Lane eager to speak to several people about their role within the club, including my own. At this stage, I was editing the match programme, having been asked to fill in by Andy Walsh on an interim basis when the original appointee quit, but this wasn't widely known. While others at the club such as Luc, cooperated with her purportedly positive article about the club, I realised that there was no way my name should've come onto her radar. *Red Issue*'s vast network of contacts was put to work to find out what she was up to.

Very quickly, word came back that the journalist had been sent to Belfast in December to cover George Best's funeral and get some reactions from people on the street. It was alleged that she had come across Tony O'Neill there. *Red Issue* later learned that the journalist had filed a story to the *Sunday Mirror* attacking named FC United officials for alleged misdemeanours. A suspicious staffer checked the proposed story with those concerned; it was then promptly spiked.

With the *Sunday Mirror*'s big exposé not materialising, Tony O'Neill took it upon himself to publish and be damned. He turned up to FC's championship party against Great Harwood with a load of leaflets detailing the very same story the *Sunday Mirror* had declined, which he handed out on the stadium forecourt. These named 'Luc Zentar – Vasco Wackrill – J P O'Neill and others' as having been 'given permission to sell FC United T-Shirts using the name of your club so they could take the profit'. His leaflet also quoted a strangely unnamed Steering Committee member as supposedly having said, 'I wasn't spending 3 months of my time setting this up for nothing.' His allegations weren't taken as seriously as he might have hoped. The banal truth was that Vas and Phil Bedford had run a T-shirt business for years. After accounting for their company's sponsorship of FC, they had actually paid the club *more* than they'd turned over from any sales. Meanwhile, Luc, Tony Pritchard, Chris Robinson and I had started a similar business in late 2004 but, in part due to the time three of us devoted to setting FC up, had already taken the decision to close it down. So much for the 'mystery' of the *Sunday Mirror* spike; there simply wasn't a story to be had.

Despite this, the *Manchester Evening News* still thought the matter newsworthy, and followed up with an article by Stuart Brennan claiming 'unhappy' supporters were planning 'to press for a change at autumn's annual meeting to forbid any such dealings'. Two anonymous fans 'who feel strongly enough to do something about it' were quoted voicing their disgust. No such resolution was ever submitted.

The following season saw no let up in Tony O'Neill's campaign.

One Saturday in mid-September, he turned up to a game at Gigg Lane with a little band of brothers in tow. Police had been tracking them all the way from Manchester and, on arrival, they were refused admission, and given no option but to head to the pub. There they conspiracised about how their plan had been thwarted with most deciding that it was because *I* had somehow discovered what they were up to and informed the police. The following day Arsenal were playing United at Old Trafford, and that night graffiti was daubed around the ground declaring 'JP is a grass'.

I found out exactly who did it. I suspected she was also one of those quoted in the *Manchester Evening News* article. Obviously I couldn't let something like the 'grass' claims pass unchallenged, as it's the sort of thing that comes to be accepted as fact, and for which people then come a cropper. The only way to put a stop to it was to confront the main man himself, so on the Monday I turned up at Tony's office to ask him about it. He ended up going off on various tangents, rattling on for about an hour, and it was only when I left that I realised he'd not actually answered anything about the 'grass' bullshit.

A couple of weeks later, Salford City hosted FC United in a game which had been moved to The Willows rugby ground to cope with the expected demand. FC were looking for a 13th straight win from the start of the season. Someone had clearly been stirring the pot in the weeks leading up to it and trouble was expected.

I'd been getting texts for weeks off some unknown number threatening what was going to happen. When the night came round, I met up with Luc and Phil Sheeran at a bar in Manchester, and we got the tram down. On the way, Andy Walsh rang to ask if I was OK. He said that he'd just been informed by Greater Manchester Police that there was a big group out looking for trouble, and word had been passed on that there was a 'price' on both his and my heads. I knew the sort of people who were going to be out, but it's not like I was going to turn round and go home.

Salford won 2–1 with two goals in the final minutes, in front of a bumper crowd of 4,058. A good crowd for Salford City was normally 150, meaning many of those celebrating their win were also those who'd spent much of the previous year berating anyone for the idea of supporting two clubs. On the terraces, the mood was ugly all game, with Salford's new-found fans accusing FC's support of being 'Judases'. Outside afterwards, gangs attacked FC's supporters, including parents with kids. Luc and I headed round the ground to the main car park to get a lift off Board member Pete Munday.

We turned the corner onto the road outside the main stand, and Luc pointed ahead to a group about 30-strong coming our way. I instantly knew who it was, what they were doing and that they'd know who we were. We carried on walking, but Luc headed out of the road onto the pavement. I should've joined him, but in hindsight it probably helped us not being together. I just thought 'I'm not moving for these twats' and carried on walking. Although it was dark, we must've passed no more than two metres apart, and I was bracing myself for the first punch. But nothing happened. Somehow they'd not noticed me.

Just when I thought I was past them all, I glanced across, and some young kid at the back noticed me. By this stage, me and Luc were pretty much between the car park and the main entrance to the ground, and I heard the doorman call over, 'JP, get on the car park. I'll deal with these.' He was an old mate from United, and the sort of person you'd want turning up out of the blue in that situation. Luc and I headed off, trying to locate Pete Munday's motor. I could hear the group shouting after us, though for some reason they wouldn't enter the car park. Apparently, as they'd come back up the road after us, the doorman had warned them all not to do anything, saying it was all covered with CCTV cameras. We'd had a very narrow escape.

There's little doubt among many FC fans that events at The Willows adversely impacted on the club's attendances. It wasn't like the clubs even considered themselves rivals in any way; both teams were at the top of the table but all the hostility had been generated through people jumping on an anti-FC bandwagon, as stirred up by certain people at Old Trafford, and shown by the fact that Salford usually only played to crowds barely a couple of hundred strong.

Towards the end of October, there was more aggro, this time in the Potteries, where FC were playing Newcastle Town. Towards half-time, a group of 40 Stoke City hooligans turned up and started attacking FC fans. Stoke weren't quite the same prospect as Salford though, and within seconds a group of FC fans had got together and chased the wannabe hard men out of the ground. Police quickly arrived to save the locals from further embarrassment. The Stoke contingent had got a lot more than they bargained for, but the curious thing was why they'd thought to turn out in the first place. It was not like FC had a reputation for trouble, nor had anyone within their ranks arranged it.

Later that night, Tony O'Neill appeared on a programme on BBC Radio 5Live discussing football hooliganism. For some reason, he was determined to move the topic onto events at FC's game that afternoon, about which – despite his exaggerations – he seemed suspiciously well informed. 'One of the biggest riots ever seen in a football ground' had taken place, he claimed, before rattling on with syntactical originality:

'What's supposedly a family club which is FC United of Manchester – they were involved in serious, serious disorder today with riot police and everything turning up.

'It's a hooligan what's actually involved in setting up the club. You know, they're right into it. I'm just going off my experiences and off the people I know.

'Stoke City have got their football hooligans who are banned and it's pretty obvious to anybody who understands football hooliganism and violence – Manchester United's coming to town and Stoke hooligans come even though it's not Manchester United.

'So their banning order people and Class C people have seen the chance today to go right at it and they went steaming into that ground today and you've seen one of the biggest riots today, hundreds and hundreds of people. Police and helicopters, everything.'

The presenter was eventually forced to cut the Red Army General off, following several attempts by him to name people he was trying to allege were involved.

The following February, a similar thing happened when FC played Silsden in Keighley in Yorkshire. Unusually, a large group of hardcore Leeds hooligans turned up intent on violence, although the game was so heavily policed that very little trouble occurred. An FC fan from Yorkshire, who had been acquainted with a handful of Leeds hooligans at various points over the years, later found out that they had turned out after being assured – by someone with the credibility to have convinced them – that a large group of Manchester United hooligans would be in attendance and eager to fight them. Just who that person might have been was never definitively confirmed.

The week after Tony O'Neill's radio appearance, I had been attacked at Manchester United's game in Copenhagen on account of my connections to FC. That seemed to cross a line, which many of United's hardcore viewed as unacceptable, but it wasn't until the following spring that the hate campaign finally fizzled out. In the quarter-finals of the Champions League, Manchester United drew Roma where, in previous seasons, English clubs' fans had been injured in ambushes by local gangs. United's fans were determined the same wouldn't happen to them and, as a result, it was not the time for any factional in-fighting. Manchester United provided ticket holders with a list of 'no-go' areas, which certain groups used instead as a handy itinerary.

On the afternoon of the match, 250 United fans assembled in the city's Piazza Flaminio before embarking on the long walk to the Stadio Olimpico. By the time they arrived, a large group of Roma ultras were waiting, and it sparked off 40 minutes of running battles. *Red Issue* later reported on the initial clashes:

> '*These were quickly chased off, until a squadron of police near the ground intercepted the United fans, allowing the Roma group to regroup and return. A game of cat-and-mouse (otherwise known as a full scale riot) then followed, with United fans chasing off the Roma fans, followed by the police attempting to disperse the United fans, before both groups quickly reformed and the same occurred again.*
>
> '*This eventually ended with the police firing CS gas canisters at United, followed up by a baton charge, which finally managed to split the United group. And when Roma – by now seemingly armed to the teeth – then followed up behind the police, it was almost as if the police let them take over, whilst quickly exiting stage left.*
>
> '*Roma's arsenal – handed out from a nearby car – included knives, thunderflashes, coshes, an axe, and even a black widow catapult. The madness of events is beyond words, and can only really be appreciated by the sight of a set of stepladders(!) being added to the missiles hurled at the United contingent.*'

At one point, one of the Roma contingent's leaders called a brief ceasefire in the fighting and, incredibly, initiated a round of applause for the United group in recognition of the scale and ferocity of the fighting in which both sides had engaged. This included a handshake of acknowledgment for one of the United contingent, who also happened to be well-known as an FC supporter. This was highly symbolic in many respects; the events by the Tiber almost immediately passed into United hooligan legend, meaning it became nigh on impossible for the still-banned Red Army General to generate further agitation against those he'd long attempted to smear as 'traitors' to MUFC. Not only did it make no sense, but when his troops were under fire in places like Roma, the so-called 'Judas scum' were also some of the few who could be relied on.

After Rome, it was noticeable that no more openly anti-FC moves were undertaken. Of course, undermining the campaign Tony O'Neill had been waging was the fact that Ferguson's managerial genius had restored Manchester United to winning ways; the team ended the 2007 season as champions, and suddenly there was not the same need for a scapegoat. Besides, the Red Army General had other things to deal with. On 12 August 2007, a meeting of backers of his proposed Old Trafford Supporters Club were told that talks with the Glazers' officials at the club had resulted in their officials-promising to commit £750,000 to the project. One of the Manchester United officials present at a number of the meetings later denied to me that this was ever the case, though did admit that chief executive David Gill had been part of discussions with Tony O'Neill. Whether any promise of such a sum was made or not, it was ultimately never delivered. However, Tony O'Neill *was* later handed £100,000 by one leading figure at Old Trafford to carry on pursuing the OTSC idea. Later on, a consortium fronted by Gary Neville bought out Tony O'Neill's interest, and subsumed the supposedly *independent* supporters club into their Hotel Football development.

7

YOUR LOST COUNTRY BOUGHT AND SOLD

If all the drama around the Salford City game in October 2006 affected some supporters, there was no noticeable reaction from the team. It was just one of two defeats in the league all year as they romped to the title by 13 points. The season ended with more silverware, when FC won the League Cup Final against Curzon Ashton, the team who had also finished runners-up in the league.

Despite these successes, for many the highlight of the year was actually a defeat, one that came when the club was eliminated from the FA Vase – the national knockout competition for teams at step 4 of the non-league pyramid. FC had begun their bid for a Wembley appearance with a 3–1 win against Brodsworth Miners Welfare in South Yorkshire, and then beaten Padiham in the following round, before a fairly comfortable 3–2 win against Salford in November. As with the league game against them, it was staged at The Willows, but this time passed off with none of the violence witnessed the previous month – in large part due to Manchester United playing against Sheffield United the same day. In the following round, FC were drawn at home against a team called Quorn from Leicestershire. Perhaps unexpectedly, it would be a meaty tie.

On a horrible wintry December afternoon, FC had two players sent off in separate incidents early in the second half, with the score level at 1–1. In spite of this handicap, urged on by a storming atmosphere from the 1,858 crowd, FC managed to hang on until the final few minutes, when they hared forward and took the lead! Then, just as it was looking like FC might record the unlikeliest of wins, Quorn equalised to force extra-time. What remained of FC's team was dead on its feet but they hung on for the extra half hour, and were confident of their chances in a replay – only for Quorn to snatch a winner in the very last seconds. FC's players were devastated but every single one left the field to a hero's reception. Many fans later admitted to being surprised by just how much it had all meant to them.

FC's championship win meant promotion to the Northern Premier League Division One. The club was thus departing the North West Counties League a year ahead of the target that had been set in 2005. After just a few months of the 2007/08 season, FC's Board was doing battle with their new league's officials. On 12 December, it was announced that the club's away fixture to Curzon Ashton, scheduled for Saturday 29 December, was being moved to a 12 p.m. kick-off so that it could be televised on the league's internet TV channel. Both clubs objected to the decision but the league would not be swayed. As a result, FC United released a statement urging supporters to boycott the fixture:

> '*When our club representatives discussed the new NPL TV deal with League officials over the summer we received assurances that no game would be moved for TV without the agreement of both participating clubs. The League also circulated all clubs in November with reassurances that Saturday games would not be televised live.*
>
> '*As a result of these assurances not being maintained and that the League Management Committee have gone against the expressed wishes of both clubs, the board of FC United and club officials will not be present at the fixture. In line with that position the Board requests that supporters exercise their power to influence decisions, by also not attending.*'

The boycott was a resounding success. In contrast to the previous season, when 1,683 had turned out on a Monday night for the league game between the two sides, and 3,210 had watched the clubs' mid-week League Cup final, the attendance was only 297. The league didn't declare what the internet TV audience was but, realistically, it was unlikely to have been any bigger than the number watching in person. Certainly, that was the last time anyone heard of the channel, let alone any games being moved to accommodate it.

On the pitch, FC had got off to a mixed start, losing the first two games before better results took the team up the table. However, by the start of December, they found themselves out of both the FA Cup and FA Trophy, and having just lost three league games on the bounce. But fortune changed, and in the following 33 games FC lost just four times. This included a run in March and April of 13 games in 29 days that, for semi-professional players, represented a near super-human feat. FC eventually missed out on the championship by only a point to Bradford Park Avenue, all but blowing their chances with a draw against Woodley Sports in the penultimate match. Promotion was eventually secured via the play-offs, FC beating Skelmersdale 4–1 in the final. Three seasons in and FC had remarkably progressed up three divisions, and would begin the 2008/09 campaign just three levels below the Football League.

Off the pitch, the club appeared to be making good progress too, but the first canaries had already been dropping in the coalmine. Luc Zentar's resignation as club secretary in the summer of 2006 had come about, in large part, due to disagreements he'd had with Andy Walsh. Accompanying his resignation letter, he submitted a lengthy report to the Board, detailing what he believed were problems with the Board's strategic oversight of the club; the lack of accountability of Walsh to the Board; a failure to apply proper rigour around financial reporting; and Walsh's inherent unsuitability to running a company of FC United's size. This included specific concerns about his time management, overreliance on unqualified volunteers, prioritisation of press and public-speaking engagements over club business, and his appointment of two close friends to part-time paid positions. History would show how right Luc was to urge the Board to get a grip of these issues when he did.

Luc believed 'the amount of work that this job presents has swamped [Walsh], and that he doesn't have the experience, assistance of a strong and efficient Board or the overall vision to turn things around.' Luc insisted that he wanted to point this out due to 'being part of something that I feel is now in grave danger of letting down the thousands of people who have invested such energy and enthusiasm.' It was a brave move, given the personal relationships involved, and Luc was immediately ostracised. Two days later he emailed me, saying:

'I've been removed from the Board e-mail circular group, Andy has said that he doesn't intend to respond. Not one Board member has contacted me. Looks like I've become an enemy of the people. Better keep my head down in case an ice pick comes my way.'

The following week, a short statement was issued stating the club had accepted his resignation, adding, 'The Board wish to put on record our heartfelt and sincere thanks to Luc for all the hard work he has put into the club and the post.'

The following year, in November 2007, Pete Munday also stepped down from the Board, ahead of the AGM. The official reason given was that it was 'due to time commitments' but, as he would later explain, it was more to do with his concerns regarding Walsh's overbearing influence not being acted upon:

'Throughout my time on the Board, I had issues with the governance and regularly advocated improvements, including the re-introduction of the Chair role which had worked so well for the Steering Group. I was asked to get back involved and turned it down, largely because I felt that the Board, as a Board, was powerless and the General Manager [Walsh] was too powerful.'

With Zentar and Munday determined not to cause a scene, the membership was never informed of their concerns. Even if it had been, it would have been difficult for anyone to delve into the veracity of such isolated claims, given the majority of Board members didn't accept what was being said – everything could easily be dismissed as a clash of personalities. The only possible gauge for members of what was going on behind the scenes were the minutes of Board meetings, which started being issued in 2007 but weren't particularly revealing. The reality, as at most clubs, was that events on the pitch were the most tangible measure of progress, and three consecutive promotions provided convincing evidence that FC could hardly be doing any better.

That said, the club had not managed to expand on the first season's crowds, once the novelty had worn off. Average home attendances had dropped from 3,059 in 2005/06 to 2,581 the following year, and to 2,086 in 2007/08, though this was as much to do with people's increasing sense of ennui when facing the trek up to Bury as with any failing by the club. FC United needed a ground somewhere in Manchester and it was proving to be a long, slow process getting one. The thought amongst the Steering Committee in the club's early, heady days was that this might have been achievable within three years, all being well. In the summer of 2008, there was still barely a hint of a prospective ground, even though the club had previously shared with supporters its confidence that work with Manchester City Council, exploring possible sites and partnerships, would prove fruitful.

In September 2007, as a way of enlivening the prospect of a day in Bury, Rob Brady had dreamt up a novel concept for games at Gigg Lane – a 'club night' in the afternoon. Named 'Course You Can Malcolm', in ironic homage to the Glazers' progenitor, it was held in an 80-capacity room, and aimed to showcase one unsigned Manchester band before every Saturday home match. CYCM was introduced on the club's website thus:

'After two seasons, and football matters sorting themselves out accepta-
bly on the pitch, it's time to sort out the other important matters. Anyone
who knows anything about football knows that football is not about foot-
ball. Anyone who does not know that knows nothing about football. Your
loved ones, friends, beer, music and football should always go together.
We now have an opportunity to make it so.'

The event was staffed by volunteers, and every act played for free, helping to raise thousands of pounds for the club over the following seven years. 'Malcolms', as it soon became known, would feature live music, theatrical performances, talks, poets, comedians and even a harpist, with acts giving their time including Maxine Peake, James Quinn, Terry Christian and Cabbage.

FC United's profile was rising, and Sixteen Films, the production company of the Palme d'Or-winning director Ken Loach, took an interest. They contacted the club to talk about a project Loach and his scriptwriter Paul Laverty were working on and, in February 2008, the pair turned up to a game to research what would become the film *Looking For Eric*. In an interview with *Red Issue*, Loach explained how it all came about:

'We had this extraordinary message about two years ago [2007] through
a French producer called Pascale that Eric Cantona was interested in
working with us. We thought it was a joke really and that someone was
pulling our leg. We eventually met in Cannes one year and it was extra-
ordinary to be having dinner with this legendary figure. We talked
around the idea and how to make a film which reflected who Eric was
and what his presence meant in football. And also about making a film
which tried to show why football is so important in people's lives.'

The shoot was undertaken in and around Manchester over six weeks in May and June 2008, with the story based on a suicidal postman called Eric, whose life is in disarray. He hallucinates that he is being mentored by his hero Cantona, and thereafter is slowly coaxed out of his depression by friends and work colleagues as he gets his life back on track. A number of Manchester-based comedians landed leading roles, including Smug Roberts, Des Sharples, Mick Ferry, and Justin Moorhouse – an FC United founder member of *Peter Kay's Phoenix Nights* fame. Steve Evets, who played the main character, subsequently became a regular at FC games, whilst both MUFC and FCUM fans were roped in as extras. Cantona seemingly enjoyed working with them as much as they did with him. He later told *Red Issue*:

> *'When I read the script for the first time I thought it was great . . . when I watch the film it's special. What I am proud of is that the fans are really as I have known them – the same kind of energy. The humanity and solidarity, you can feel the same energy between them, it's very strong when you watch the film.'*

Surprisingly, perhaps, the Frenchman also explained that he kept in touch with how FC get on:

> *'Of course. It's great to get promoted each year and then to be close to the play-off. Do the fans still support all the time? I've seen them on the internet, you can sometimes see interviews. I don't follow football very much but sometimes I watch on the web. My brother Jean-Marie showed me, because I'm not very good with a computer.'*

Heading into the club's fourth season, FC United were now in the Northern Premier League's Premier Division where, inevitably, competition was slightly tougher. By the new year, there had been early exits from the FA Cup, FA Trophy and League Cup, and the team was anchored in mid-table, having won as many games as it had lost. Despite this, the players did not lose heart, nor fans' support. This was most notable when one late comeback, from 5–2 down to draw with Cammell Laird, was helped by particularly raucous backing. While there'd been some bad results and poor performances, it was encouraging that the team had recorded fine results against four of the top five sides in the division.

In January, just as in the previous season, the team embarked on a storming run of 13 wins in 20 games to climb the table and go level with Bradford Park Avenue, ahead of the season's finale against them at Gigg Lane. This would effectively be 'a play-off for the play-offs'. A win for either side would mean the chance of another promotion; a draw and both would miss out. A 3,719 crowd witnessed a thrilling game in which BPA equalised late on, allowing Kendal to sneak into fifth place.

Following the 2006 trip to Leipzig, FC were invited back to Germany twice in 2008: once for a prestigious indoor five-a-side tournament in Riesa that also involved FC Energie Cottbus, then of the Bundesliga; the second time for an end-of-season friendly in Marburg. In May 2009, another continental invitation arrived, this time to head to Sweden to play Djurgårdens in Stockholm's Olympiastadion. FC won the game 3–1. Even these exotic trips could scarcely have prepared the players for what came next. In South Korea, fans of Bucheon SK had set up a new club when their existing one was moved from just outside Seoul to the island of Jeju. The parallels with Wimbledon's move to Milton Keynes led the new club, Bucheon FC 1995, to invite AFC Wimbledon over for a friendly. Due to prior commitments, the Wombles had to decline; instead, FC United were approached. So it was that FC came to be in Seoul in July 2009, just six days before Manchester United stopped off there on their own preseason Asian tour. A very respectable crowd of 23,000 watched FC's 3–0 defeat, while 64,000 would later turn out for Rooney & co.

For the 2009/10 season FC United introduced something of a novel concept for football: fans could name their own price for a season ticket, being invited to 'pay what you can afford'. The recommended amount was a minimum of £90, with those who could afford to pay more than the previous set price of £140 being invited to do so. The initiative proved so successful that it was carried on year after year. On the pitch, the team had a mixed start, but the campaign briefly exploded into life in October when FC took a 3–1 lead against Stalybridge Celtic in the penultimate FA Cup qualifying round. Stalybridge pulled it back to 3–3, before FC won a thrilling replay 1–0 at Bower Fold. The club would now face Northwich Victoria, just one game from the tournament's big time; unfortunately, FC lost 3–0. Before Christmas, FC also exited the FA Trophy and League Cup. Moreover, this season there'd be no new-year rescue act in the league – indeed, at one stage Margy's team won only six of 24 games, with the embarrassment of heavy defeats by Bradford, Kendal and Boston only outdone by losing at home to lowly Durham in March. That was the first game all season Durham had even managed to avoid *defeat*.

Understandably perhaps, the first rumblings about Margy's ability were beginning to surface, and the average home attendance was down to 1,954 – 10 per cent below the previous season. Despite this, all worries were forgotten by those who went to watch the team play in Hamburg in May. St Pauli invited FC United over for a game as part of their centenary celebrations, partly in recognition of the clubs' shared sympathies for left-leaning politics and social activism. As FC fans partied off the city's Reeperbahn, one small group toasted the memory of Russ Delaney, who in June 2005 had told me and Luc of his ambition: to one day take what was then still a pipe dream of a club to play St Pauli. Five years on from the application to the North West Counties League being completed, the dream finally became reality.

In early January 2010, news broke that the Glazers were planning a £500 million bond issue. The aim was to generate part of the £699 million they needed to pay down part of the debt on the loans with which they'd saddled Manchester United. They'd previously pulled off a successful refinancing in July 2006, but the 2008 global financial crisis had made it increasingly difficult to negotiate further new agreements. Similar problems were also evident at Anfield, where Liverpool's own American owners Tom Hicks and George Gillett had not managed to refinance before the crash, with the result that their club was plunged into crisis, with Hicks and Gillett ultimately forced to cede ownership. While the situation at Old Trafford was not quite as desperate, Manchester United being placed at the mercy of the markets was exactly what all the dire warnings in 2004 and 2005 had predicted; unlike at Liverpool, the Glazers had just struck lucky with their timing.

Many in the press saw the development as vindication for those who'd opposed the takeover, which in turn led to a temporarily renewed focus on FC United. Andy Walsh said in a feature in the *Daily Mail*:

> *'We could see the dash for cash happening in English football and we knew ticket prices at Old Trafford would rise. The figures from Old Trafford are quite shocking. Most people were aware of a level of indebtedness but for it to be compounded by the Glazers cynically "dipping in" is bordering on the criminal.*
>
> *'Most people have shielded their eyes to what's going on but the general public are now more familiar with the "casino economy" after Northern Rock and all the rest of it. People understand more about it and it's happening in football. That has shocked them.'*

The 'dipping in' Walsh referred to alluded to the prospectus the Glazers had issued to potential investors. Alongside announcing that the club's Carrington training ground might be sold off, they were also duty-bound to reveal the extent of the club's liabilities and commitments. These included the staggering amount of payments which the Glazers could legitimately take out of the club, the details of which were so obfuscated by technical jargon that they could only be properly understood and interpreted by financial experts. One of these was Andy Green, a United-supporting analyst and investor, who subsequently did a sterling job exposing the Glazers' dealings and finances, and presenting it in layman's terms.

The outrage stirred up amongst United fans was on a level not seen since 2005, and led to renewed protests against the club's owners. On 16 January, MUST (Manchester United Supporters Trust – the new name for Shareholders United) staged a meeting before MUFC's game against Burnley to discuss their options, but the organisation had long since lost credibility. Despite its 'No Customers No Profit' stance, they had handed over thousands of pounds to the Glazers by staging a big supporters' dinner at Old Trafford, and some of its leading personalities had taken out season tickets, thereby going back on their 'not one penny' public pledges of May 2005. Having had years to prepare for the moment the Glazers ran into financial difficulties, it was nevertheless clear that there was no new impetus, nor any actual strategy. One attendee at the meeting, Justin Gill, described it as, 'depressing and frustrating. The ideas coming from the floor were nothing new compared to what was said five years ago. In summary, no one really knows what to do.'

In the absence of any leadership, the growing anger at the Glazers was instead funnelled through an idea posted on *Red Issue*'s website. Dave Holden suggested supporters should adopt the colours of the club's forerunner, Newton Heath, as a sign of rebellion and their discontent with the Glazers. The rapidity of its take-up was spectacular. Swagmen outside Old Trafford struggled to cope with demand for suddenly popular green-and-yellow scarves, while the club's security clamped down on any staff brandishing the colours. In late January, another meeting was called, and fans packed out the City Road Inn in Manchester. Rather than MUST or IMUSA being involved, this was arranged by individual supporters, and somewhat surprisingly Tony O'Neill took centre stage. It ended up being more of an anti-climax than the previous week's MUST meeting. The Red Army General urged a lid be kept on dissent and – ironically, given his background – advocated reasoned and solely lawful means of protest. His contribution so tempered what had been a burgeoning sense of outrage that some cynics present wondered if he was actually working for the Glazers' interests, rather than looking to harness any protest against them . . .

Despite the lack of any truly meaningful action, over the following two months the protest of wearing green and yellow colours flourished, causing great excitement in the media and no little embarrassment for the Glazers. This upset some people, with all the usual club mouthpieces reeled out to talk down the unrest. Former player Paddy Crerand insisted, 'There are only a few hundred United fans that are against the Glazers, it's the minority,' while Gary Neville rejected the idea that players might speak out: 'We're always very well protected and we never get involved in the financial side of things. It's nothing to do with us at all.'

Having advocated lawful and reasoned protest, Tony O'Neill apparently had another quick volte-face. From United's Champions League game in Italy against AC Milan there emerged several allegations of him and his goons physically harassing United fans who displayed the Newton Heath protest colours.

In contrast to the actions of those on United's payroll, big names in the financial world came out to criticise the Glazers, leading to hope that a 'Red Knights' group of investors might buy them out. Paul Marshall, a United fan and leading hedgefund manager, called on the 'club's supporters to combine forces to return the club to where it belongs'. Jim O'Neill, the club's former non-executive director and Goldman Sachs economist, insisted, 'There's too much leverage going on.' He later told *Red Issue* that the 'Red Knights' plan was a serious prospect: 'The money could've been got – the number of people who approached me from different parts of the world was just unbelievable. The amounts!'

Keith Harris of Seymour Pierce said much the same in February 2010 in another *Red Issue* interview, when asked whether a takeover package could've been put together: 'Yes. I'm always very cautious about saying anything until it's there and it's done. Believe me, I would not say this unless I was absolutely confident that that side of it can be looked after. That's different to saying that the Glazers will ever listen.' Harris was aware that the Glazers had already rejected a

£1.25 billion offer for the club in early 2008, and insisted that supporters could play their part in forcing them to sell:

'We need a collective, unified voice to make this happen. If there were people who were considering giving up their season tickets on account of what they've heard about the Glazers' plans from the bond issue prospectus, then in the event that our takeover was successful we're sure it could be worked out so that they regained their places.

'Our intention is to set aside 25.1% of the shareholding in a supporters trust so that any future takeover would become impossible. Season ticket holders would get their seats back at a lower price and become shareholders in the club. The supporters wouldn't be running the club but would definitely have a say in the running of the club.'

As in 2005, the key to forcing the Glazers out was starving them of cash. Once the bond issue was successfully completed, the only realistic way this could happen was through fans boycotting season ticket renewals. It seemed MUST preferred to put faith in fans waving colourful scarves and hoping for the best. *Red Issue* was scathing:

'"There go the people. I must follow them for I am their leader." The words, it is said, of Alexandre Ledru-Rollin, a French politician who saw himself as instigator of the February revolution of 1848 – a popular uprising which led to the government's downfall. The parallels one can draw to recent events at Old Trafford are so obvious it would probably be worth MUST's hierarchy checking their family trees for any Ledru-Rollin branches; one big difference being there seems little chance of a successful conclusion to events in 2010.

'Almost five years on from the Glazers' takeover, we approach the end of another season with an overwhelming sense of deja-vu. MUST have Nomura on board, as they did back then, and are again promising to put together the finance to secure fan ownership of the club, whilst urging supporters to sign up to their organisation. Back in 2005, the folly

lay in seeking huge numbers of individual shareholders (via their £10, one-share sign-ups), when an alliance of large blocks of shares held by existing supporter shareholders was what was required. This time round, MUST's quest [should be] targeting today's balance of power – season ticket holders wavering over whether to renew.'

Notwithstanding such criticisms, MUST's Duncan Drasdo still invited *Red Issue* to a meeting he set up between Jim O'Neill and various fans' groups in late March. In the absence of anywhere near enough support for taking the action Harris and others had called for, the discussions predictably came to nothing.

It was clear that FC United would remain the only meaningful resistance to the Glazers' regime, and in March 2010 the club announced exciting news: agreement had been secured with Manchester City Council to develop a site in Newton Heath, the original home of Manchester United. A 5,000-capacity stadium and renovated community sports facilities were planned to replace the existing Ten Acres Lane council-owned sports centre, at an estimated cost of £3.5 million, paid for by a combination of grant funding, £500,000 of donations to the club's development fund and over £1 million of supporters' money in the form of an innovative 'community shares' issue. Andy Walsh said in a press release:

> *'The announcement will be a big boost to the club and we also want the development to be of benefit to Newton Heath, the discussions with the council have been very positive and we are grateful for their support. The significance of this location is historical while it will also showcase a new model of facility development, based on football supporter ownership and community involvement.'*

The response from residents to the prospect of FC moving into the area was described by the club as 'really positive and encouraging', and work began behind the scenes putting a project team together and submitting a planning application. If progress was being made off the pitch, on it little seemed to have changed as the 2010/11 season got under way. Three consecutive wins were quickly followed by six defeats in the next seven games, leaving the team languishing narrowly above the relegation zone in 17th place. The one win during that period came at Burscough, albeit following another awful performance that led to Andy Walsh and Board member Jules Spencer discussing the possibility of a change in manager outside the clubhouse afterwards. It was perhaps understandable; come the end of September, the team had been largely woeful for almost a year, and there was little sign of any imminent improvement.

Despite this, hope remained following FA Cup victories against Radcliffe Borough and Gainsborough Trinity, which had set up a tie in the North-East against Norton & Stockton Ancients, one of the lowest ranked teams left in the competition. On paper, it looked as good as a bye for FC, but after an hour they trailed 2–1. Margy's reign as manager looked like it may have run its course. Half an hour later, FC had won 5–2, and the team was in the final qualifying round for the second year on the run. FC would have to beat the giants of Barrow, opponents from two divisions higher, to reach the FA Cup first round for the first time.

All of a sudden, the team's confidence was up. A 4–1 win in the league had preceded the Norton & Stockton game, and a 5–0 win in the FA Trophy followed the week after. By the time Barrow arrived, both players and fans alike believed in the possibility of what just a few weeks earlier might have seemed unfeasible. Another bouncing crowd of 3,263 at Gigg Lane cheered the team on, before Carlos Roca scored late on to send FC through. Rochdale would be the opposition in the next round, for a game that was scheduled for the Friday evening – Bonfire Night – and due to be broadcast live on TV. There would be fireworks aplenty.

Around 4,000 FC fans contributed to a crowd of 7,048, and the din they began making even before the teams came out made an impression on all those watching. Ray Stubbs, the ESPN presenter, later replied when asked to recall his favourite memories of the competition: 'The FC United fans nearly nicked the cup to take it on an impromptu lap of honour, purely out of exuberance.' The commentator Jon Champion concurred: 'That was a special night.' It was even better for FC fans. Incredibly, the team scored either side of half-time to go 2–0 up, but Rochdale hit back almost immediately, before equalising with 12 minutes to go. By then, FC's part-time players were flagging against the professionals, and it looked like there would only be one winner.

Somehow, FC's defence held on. Then, in the fourth minute of injury time, following what looked suspiciously like a foul that wasn't awarded, the team's striker Mike Norton nicked in past the goalkeeper to slot the ball home for the winning goal, sparking a mass celebratory pitch invasion by the jubilant Reds. Across the country, watching neutrals were united in their admiration, not least in a Manchester hotel where MUFC's players were staying ahead of a game against Wolverhampton. As *UWS*'s Andy Mitten later reported, many got caught up in the excitement, jumping around to celebrate the feat achieved by the local outsiders. Quite what Alex Ferguson made of it all wasn't recorded. Post-match, FC gained further respect in some quarters when, in spite of all the excitement, Andy Walsh remembered to stop players and management from giving interviews to the BBC, in solidarity with journalists striking in a battle over pension changes.

High-flying Brighton & Hove Albion were FC's opponents in the second round, with many in the media getting excited by the fact the club was just one win away from possibly drawing Manchester United in the next round. In fact, this was a nightmare scenario for most connected to FC, not least due to the divisions between sections of the two clubs' supports that it would re-open. Down south, Sussex police's reaction to FC United fans heading to their jurisdiction was ridiculous. The flares and pitch invasions enjoyed by most un-hysterical viewers of the victory over Rochdale seemed to have convinced them that Brighton was set to be sacked and pillaged. As a result, they made the match all-ticket, and limited FC fans to an allocation of just 845.

In spite of that disappointment for the club, FC's players again rose to the occasion and took the lead just before half-time. Although they then had a man sent off midway through the second half, FC looked set for another glorious victory – until Brighton equalised with just seven minutes remaining. When the Seagulls were awarded a penalty in the sixth minute of injury time, it looked set to be the cruellest of defeats. But goalkeeper Sam Ashton produced a stunning save to take the tie to a replay at Gigg Lane. For FC's delirious following it felt like another victory. With Portsmouth awaiting the winners in the third round, the game attracted FC's highest ever home attendance of 6,731. But the fairytale had run its course. After their shock in the first game, Brighton manager Gus Poyet decided to take no chances, and played his full first-choice side. They outclassed FC 4–0.

Heading into the new year, FC were in the relegation zone in the league. But perhaps rejuvenated by the cup run, 18 wins from 25 games carried the team to a play-off semi-final against Bradford Park Avenue. They'd long been regarded as FC's bogey side, FC having only notched a first win against them in January. The play-off game was fairly easily won by the same 2–0 score, and Colwyn Bay awaited in the final. The Welsh team had finished just three points ahead of FC but were far stronger, and sealed promotion more convincingly than the 1–0 scoreline suggested. Yet that bitter blow was nothing compared to the setback FC fans had received a couple of months earlier. The election of the Tory-dominated coalition government in May 2010 had resulted in austerity policies being enforced on local councils, and in March the club issued a statement:

'Manchester City Council has announced that the proposal to develop a football ground with community sports provision at Ten Acres Lane in partnership with FC United will be under review.

'As a result of the challenging local government settlement, the Council has to ensure that any available resources are optimised and deliver the very best for Manchester. The Council has therefore had to revisit its

spending plans and examine other opportunities for securing a football facility within the city.

'The Council is seeking to examine the most financially viable solution for a ground and community football facilities in the city, which makes the most use of Council resources. The City Council will carry out detailed feasibility work to enable a preferred option to be brought forward.

'Both parties are aware of the commitment and support shown for the Ten Acres Lane proposal by many thousands of people, not least the residents of Newton Heath and FC United's members and the partners are committed to bringing forward a proposal which will benefit both community football and the residents of Manchester, while making the most of available Council resources.'

The attempt to sugar coat the reality that the proposed lease and £650,000 funding had been withdrawn didn't disguise the fact that the statement didn't actually make much sense, especially given the council stated it remained committed to keeping the Ten Acres Lane centre in operation 'regardless of the outcome of the report'. If resources had been cut, then surely a partner like FC United, whose fans had already raised £1.4 million towards the development, was what was needed to make it viable? However, Ten Acres Lane is barely a mile from Manchester City's council-owned Eastlands stadium, and it hardly seemed a coincidence that the previous day's *Manchester Evening News* had announced a huge regeneration of the area, agreed by the Council with money provided by City's Abu Dhabi owners.

An article by Charles Sale in the *Daily Mail* headlined 'FC United rebels smell a rat over Manchester City stadium deal' spelled out what many fans believed had happened: the council was happy to screw FC in order to cosy up to City's sheikhs, not wanting a competitor – however small – on their doorstep. Even the council-friendly Andy Walsh conceded that 'our fans have suspicions about the council project with City.' The whole situation was made much worse by the fact that

Walsh and the club's Board had failed to sign any contract, or secure any guarantees from the council, before committing over £400,000 of members' funds to the now-abandoned development. Some of the expenditure on plans and designs would be transferable to a new site but a lot of it was unrecoverable. It was a devastating blow and, though no one realised at the time, a sign of things to come.

8

WINDMILL STREET

The fallout from the abandonment of the Ten Acres Lane development inflicted surprisingly little damage on either Andy Walsh or the
club's Board, even though it seemed incredible that experienced political operators like Walsh and Adam Brown, or a prominent local
businessman like the Board member Scott Fletcher, could be so naive
as to trust the nod and wink of council officials like Richard Leese
and Howard Bernstein. Almost as incredible was the general public's
lack of protest in the face of the council readily handing over swathes
of East Manchester to a regime which a leading human rights cam-
paigner described in *Red Issue* as 'deeply disturbing'. Abu Dhabi was,
he said, 'a hub for organized human exploitation' with 'one of the
world's richest countries' responsible for 'horrific abuse and exploitation of some of the poorest people on earth', the British media
seemingly being averse to 'linking City's owners to the appalling rights
violations in the country they govern'.

Notwithstanding Walsh's quote in Charles Sale's *Daily Mail* piece,
both he and Brown were desperate to maintain relations with the
council, not least as any new deal would help divert attention from
the appalling loss of funds FC had already incurred. By early April
2011, the council's review of the options for FC was already

completed, and it settled on a joint venture with an amateur football club in North Manchester. Moston Juniors FC held a lease until 2032 on the council-owned Ronald Johnson fields, which were bound by a covenant dictating that they could be used solely for recreational purposes. The council had earmarked £750,000 for improvements to the site, but MJFC had no money of their own to make up the difference on the total they'd require. As a result, the council planned to bundle FC's ambitions in with theirs, but only after deducting the £200,000 required for a feasibility study and other related expenses from the £750,000 grant.

It represented a highly unsatisfactory deal for both parties, and local opposition had already mobilised, as the *Manchester Evening News* reported:

'Hundreds of people have launched a campaign to block a bid to use playing fields for a new stadium for rebel football club FC United of Manchester.

'The club – formed in protest at the Glazer family's ownership of Manchester United – want to build a 5,000 capacity stadium on the council-owned Ronald Johnson playing fields, close to St Mary's Road and Lightbowne Road in New Moston. But people living close to the site – currently home to a junior football team – have vowed to fight the plans. Nearly 1,000 have signed a petition against the proposals, which they are to take to the town hall.

'Joanne Hilton, who lives on St Mary's Road, said: "The community does not want this. It's our local field and it has always been for us. There isn't much greenery in Moston and we don't want a stadium here.

'"It has nothing to do with football. This field was gifted to the public and nothing was ever meant to be built here. There will be crowds, cars and there will be alcohol and the problems that causes."'

Andy Walsh presented the new option to FC's membership as an improvement on the Ten Acres Lane plans, and praised the council's honesty in delivering on their promise to find an alternative: 'They have done what they told us they were going to do.' Walsh's eagerness to please the council was also evident in a story covered by the *Manchester Evening News*:

'*Graffiti wars have broken out over FC United's plans to build a new stadium.*

'*Slogans have been daubed on walls across Moston both opposing and supporting the 5,000 capacity stadium. Opposition to FC United's plans has been mounting from residents concerned it will create parking chaos outside their homes. But supporters of the site say it will create much-needed facilities for the area. Both sides have condemned the graffiti.*

'*One of the slogans daubed by people opposed to the scheme was "Love Glazer, Hate FC United". And supporters of the plans have been using "reverse graffiti" – blasting dirty walls with water using stencils – to write 'M40 4FC'. [M40 being the Manchester postcode district in question.]*

'*Moston Councillor Paul Murphy said: "Graffiti of any description is unacceptable."*

'*Andy Walsh, general manager of FC United, said: "We condemn any graffiti at all no matter what form it takes. There has been a great deal of deliberate misinformation from the No campaign which has heightened anxieties in the area. We want to rectify that misinformation but this is not the right way to go about it."'*

Walsh's condemnation seemed an unnecessarily authoritarian response to someone spraying a bit of water, and betrayed how far the essence of 'Punk Football' had been abandoned in favour of ingratiation with local politicians. The club's unofficial motto of 'doing things differently' was increasingly ringing hollow, and I picked up on it, voicing displeasure at what I described as 'meaningless platitudes in order to pander to hysterical *Daily Mail* types'. Around the same time, another fan, Anthony Edwards, aired his concern at the direction of the club in a well-received post on *Red Issue*'s forum:

'*In respect of Moston, I am far from comfortable with it and I strongly suspect that others may be feeling the same without currently understanding or recognising that. We are attempting to impose ourselves on a community where a section of that community do not want us and are making that viewpoint stridently clear.*

'*Now, as is the way of human beings whose desires are being thwarted, we are rationalising that away. There's only a few of them, they're Manchester City fans anyway, most people want us (whether or not that is, or is not, actually true) etc. They **should** want us (even worse).*

'*Except that we know where we came from. We know why we're here. We're here because we are a minority (as it turned out) who didn't want Malcolm Glazer but he imposed himself upon us (our club, Manchester United) anyway against our will. We are now ourselves, whether we like to admit it or not, trying to do the same thing to another group of people albeit in a different circumstance and in a different way.*

'*Except that we cannot escape our conscience. If we go against our conscience, even in a small way or without fully realising it, that grows. We begin to become less honest, less trustworthy, especially to ourselves. We rationalise away things that previously we would not have excused (and crucially, which we would not excuse in others).*

'*We have always been as a club up until very recently absolutely, scrupulously honest. We are losing that it seems as time goes on. We need to keep that honesty and integrity because actually it is all that we have, it is the shining light that has guided us and brought us our successes so far.*

'*We should, I think, walk away from Moston. I suspect that will be the eventual outcome anyway so the decision will be made for us. If we retain our integrity and honesty (which is all that we have), the right opportunity for the right permanent home will present itself to us when it is right for that to happen.*'

The question of integrity soon arose in relation to another matter. In September 2011, FC United were scheduled to play at Chorley the same day as MUFC were at Bolton, the two grounds being just ten miles apart. Chorley made a request to the league to change the kick-off time to 11:30 a.m., the reason for which FC announced to fans as being due to 'safety concerns'. It was also proposed that only 500 FC United season ticket holders be admitted to the game, by advance ticket purchases only, with each team's fans segregated. Despite rumours that Tony O'Neill was running a coach to Bolton and planning to stop off at Chorley beforehand, it was a draconian response even if there had been any genuine 'safety concerns'. In response, FC fans were almost certain to boycott, just as they had done at Curzon four years earlier. But, with the Board indulging in misleading talk of a 'duty of care', the club made the nannying decision to refuse any allocation of tickets, thereby withdrawing people's choice to decide for themselves whether to go or not.

The decision seemed to go against the club's very ethos, given it had been set up to give Manchester United fans an option when deciding whether to boycott Old Trafford under the Glazers – yet that option was now being withdrawn, without any consultation with the membership. It looked even more dubious once the club announced plans to broadcast a live stream of the match at The Miners Club in Moston. Furthermore, both Walsh and his wife showed no solidarity with the rank and file by turning up to the game in Chorley regard-less. I made my thoughts on it all known on The Soul Is One [TSIO] forum, leaving Walsh far from happy, and prompting Mike Adams to try to act as mediator. Having already spoken to Walsh, Adams asked me to tone down my criticisms: 'Listening to him, what worried me is how jaded he sounded . . . there was an exasperation in his voice and tone that worried me. Maybe I'm over-worrying, but behind it is a fear of the unthinkable, i.e. he walks away or steps down etc.'

This supposed 'doomsday scenario' of Walsh quitting the club didn't impress me, as I'd noticed for a while that, in spite of Walsh continually bemoaning his workload, my offers of assistance were never taken up. Yet there was no shortage of arguably unnecessary events Walsh would turn up to, or speeches that he'd give. On one day off that July, he'd driven to Harrogate to give a talk at the town's summer book festival. I noted to Adams 'the pointless right-on tasks he takes on' asking, 'What's the priority; who's he working for? When I hear Walshy's "jaded" I just think a lot of it is his own fault – for not accepting help, and for taking on things that are nothing to do with him or FC.' I also criticised the lack of questioning from the membership, saying, 'What we have now is a mass of support who are so in awe of the Board that any questioning of them borders on sacrilegious – and that cannot be at all healthy.' I pointed out that, in practice, the Board's approach to democracy amounted to 'little more than "We respect what you have to say, as long as it doesn't contradict what we do." Not exactly Voltaire is it?'

At the AGM that October, I submitted a resolution aimed at ensuring the Board couldn't withdraw fans' right to choose to attend a game in future. It seemed to have widespread backing amongst the membership. Before the voting commenced, Andy Walsh took the mic to give a rambling, hour-long speech in which he spoke of overcoming any funding shortfalls in the Moston stadium build by saying, 'We'll wing it – we're FC United, that's what we do.' These words were lapped up by the audience, as were those uttered when Walsh addressed the issue of the club's former player Scott McManus. He'd been convicted of assaulting his girlfriend while an FC player, though he had transferred to Halifax Town before he pleaded guilty. Walsh told the meeting that it was just as well, as 'We would've sacked him anyway'.

This stance suggested a disconnection with the club's heralding of its community work, as well as seeming a touch hypocritical, given that the club had still banked the transfer fee they'd received for him. When I was invited to present the resolution, I chose instead to highlight some of these points, while also accusing Board members of misleading the membership over the Chorley issue. Sixty-one per cent voted in favour of my motion – slightly short of the two thirds necessary for it to carry – with many members later admitting they voted against it on account of my *lèse-majesté* in questioning Walsh. The membership's focus on the personalities, rather than the issues, would become more pronounced in the years to come.

On the pitch, the 2011/12 season was solid, if rather flat. The team was eliminated from both FA competitions early but, in the league, FC again qualified for the play-offs. Only a pair of 5–2 victories over Bradford Park Avenue were particularly noteworthy, as Chester won the championship at a canter, leaving everyone else fighting for a play-off spot from very early on. FC United actually ended up finishing sixth, following a mini collapse in April, but because runners-up Northwich Victoria were punished with relegation for breaches of the league's financial rules, the play-offs were contested by the teams finishing between third place and sixth. This meant FC were away to Chorley in the semi-finals, but with no segregation or limits on FC supporters this time round. FC won 2–0, with the game passing off with no hint of crowd trouble, and would face Bradford in the final. The game went to extra-time before Tom Greaves – who would join FC the following January – scored a last minute winner for Bradford.

Progress on the Moston ground was slow. Planning permission had been granted by the council in late October 2011 and, in January 2012, FC's website published a news story headlined, 'Council Executive approves extra funding for Moston site', but it could scarcely have been more misleading. The council wasn't providing any more funding, it had merely given final approval to the remaining £550,000 of the £750,000 that had long been allocated to Moston Juniors, while the executive committee had also allowed a facility for FC to *borrow* up to £500,000, as required. What wasn't mentioned was that this loan was to be repaid by the club at around 6 per cent interest; the council was set to benefit every which way from the £1.1 million increase in projected costs caused by their withdrawal of the offer of Ten Acres Lane. Worse was to come.

In April 2012, the club informed members of its expectation of a legal challenge by the group of Moston residents opposed to the ground proposals. In August, it was confirmed that they had obtained legal aid to issue Judicial Review Pre-Action Protocol in order to challenge the awarding of planning permission. The notice of judicial review was eventually issued in late November. In January 2013, judgment was passed in the High Court in London dismissing the objections, 15 long months after planning permission had been granted. Even then, the process wasn't over. The protestors applied to the Court of Appeal, requesting the right to a further challenge. Their case was rejected. Building work could finally go ahead, but the whole process had cost the club more than £60,000, even though the case was actually the council's to fight. More worrying was the fact that, with all the delays, the build costs kept rocketing. The total was now estimated at over £5.7 million, including £93,000 allocated to 'highways' costs, and a further £115,000 to 'contaminated land', which included dealing with an unexpected outbreak of Japanese knotweed.

Andy Walsh told the press, 'It has been a long, drawn-out process and we look forward to beginning building as soon as possible and bringing the benefits of this development to the area.' The widespread expectation was that preliminary work would begin on the site sometime in April. Even though Dave Payne, a former town planner for Manchester City Council, had been in place as the club's project manager since January, it wasn't until 1 December that the club finally undertook a ceremonial ground-breaking. With a 44-week build timetable, Broadhurst Park was due to be completed by mid-September 2014.

That seemed a reasonable target, even though neither Walsh nor Payne had any prior experience of such matters. It was clear that the club would need help and support, but the problem was that Walsh had increasingly alienated and ostracised former key allies; instead preferring to surround himself with his former associates from Militant Tendency, the radical entryist group which had tried to take over the Labour Party in the 1980s. One of them, Phil Frampton, was one of the appointments in 2006 that Luc Zentar had highlighted in his resignation letter and, since then, Robin Pye had been recruited in 2007 as a contractor undertaking the club's community work. More recently, someone called Andy Walker had taken over the volunteer communications role and been appointed to the club's management committee. To the members, he was unknown; within 18 months, his name would become notorious.

Rob Brady had been quick to spot what was happening and, in a Brighton pub the night before the FA Cup game in December 2010, had a frank discussion with Walsh. Brady questioned what he saw as Walsh's slipping principles, as well as a willingness to surround himself with, and be influenced by, old political allies, rather than by those friends and colleagues who had the club's interests at heart. Walsh immediately left the pub and proceeded to tell people that he did so in fear for his safety, due to Brady having 'threatened' him. The accusation was completely at odds with what the group of 20 or so FC fans present had witnessed. Needless to say, Brady was quickly excommunicated by Walsh and, post-Chorleygate, I joined him on the growing list of *personae non gratae*. Brady's fiercely principled political ideology was reflected in his writing, and his columns in *Red Issue* and *UWS* had made him Walsh's favourite United writer. Brady was also one of the very first pioneers to take up the idea for forming a new club in opposition to the Glazers. The fact that the pair of us were now ostracised by Walsh, ostensibly on account of us sticking to points of principle, was telling.

Following this incident, Walsh began pushing the Board to generate more revenue from *Course You Can Malcolm* – the match-day event that Brady had set up – on the basis that its beer prices had not increased since it started. Board member Mike Sherrard was deputed to visit '*Malcolms*' and ensure compliance. Unsurprisingly, the volunteers who ran it to help raise funds for the club objected to being dictated to, not least as the latest deal that the club had secured with Holts brewery had resulted in a reduction in the price paid for stock.

Despite the fact that those who ran '*Malcolms*' freely gave their own time to do so, even paying for and cooking at home the food that was sold there, the Board demanded they now 'recognise the budget and work towards targets', rather than simply carry on with what they'd been doing for the previous four years. One volunteer, Chris Cheetham, who spent up to eight hours each home game organising the event and setting it up, was so disgusted with the Board's attempts to monetise their collective efforts that he quit, never to return while the club was still run by Walsh. Another, Mike Turton, had been a Board member from 2007/08, and was left similarly disillusioned. Such alienation of a successfully run volunteer operation seemed a very strange way to go about increasing revenue and profitability.

The strength of feeling on the issue amongst a large, disparate group of supporters who enjoyed '*Malcolms*' was highlighted in *A Fine Lung*, a magazine sold at FC games and founded by Brady, Tony Howard and others in 2008. Scott Taylor, a '*Malcolms*' regular and contributor to *AFL*, summed it up for many when he wrote: "*Malcolms*" is a unique, independent pre-match social run by volunteers and should be free to set its own beer prices without interference.' Opinion was stridently against the moves Walsh was trying to impose but the web of relationships involved was complicated – for example, Tony Howard, a journalist by trade, was the editor of *A Fine Lung* and also volunteered in '*Malcolms*'. However, Howard had also taken over the editorship of the club's programme, meaning he needed to maintain a good relationship with Andy Walsh, not least given the fact that his partner Lindsey Robertson was the club secretary. Walsh would surely not forget his insubordination.

During 2012/13, the team achieved its highest ever finish to a season, finishing third and once again contesting the promotion play-offs. Witton Albion were overcome, sending FC through to face Hednesford in the final. The Staffordshire team, which had finished the season level with champions North Ferriby, missed out on the title by goal difference. Thousands of FC supporters headed south for the game, making up a big proportion of the 4,412 crowd. Unfortunately, the team was unable to recover from a two-goal deficit after half an hour, and lost 2–1. It was an agonising third successive play-off final defeat.

Notwithstanding a successful season, which included another run to the final FA Cup qualifying round and defeat to non-league giants Hereford, overall crowds were down. That Hereford game drew in only 2,212, while the home league average was down to 1,849. The ever-decreasing appeal of schlepping to Bury was clearly having an impact, but other factors such as the 'Malcolms' dispute were increasingly coming into play. At the November 2012 AGM, another major flare-up would occur, one that would leave many members stunned.

In the lead-up to the meeting, Alison Watt, who had been on the Board since 2006, had been her usual busy self, quietly briefing certain groups of members as to what she saw as the Board's deficiencies. She also posted on both the TSIO forum and the club's new official forum, where she claimed, 'the culture of the Board makes me feel unable to stick my head above the parapet to make a formal objection to . . . decisions'. This claim of reticence came as a surprise to many who knew her. Nevertheless, her sudden decision to portray herself as a staunch defender of the club's democracy was a decent pitch in the battle for re-election. At the AGM, she went much further, making alarming claims that she had been bullied during her time on the Board. John Taylor, a member who was in attendance, summed up how it all played out:

> '*A member asked Alison a justifiable and understandable question as to why she'd said on one of our forums that she'd not voted the way she*

would have liked when faced with a large majority the other way. Alison,
put on the spot somewhat, was then forced to tell the membership that
she'd been subject to continued disparaging remarks that she was always
the dissenter, and over time this had dramatically affected her.

'*She had therefore adopted a policy that when going against a large*
majority she would just go with the flow, as the culture of the Board
meant she would get an easier ride. Alison mentioned two specific cases
of abuse, which were quite frankly unacceptable behaviour from the
Board. A couple of Board members stated something along the lines of
"we're not aware of any problem."'

Many members were aghast, with Watt hoovering up sympathy as a
number of long-standing Board members – including Jules Spencer
and Phil Sheeran, the last two remaining from the Steering Committee –
were vilified by some. It had the desired effect: Jules Spencer, Paul
Farrell and Alan Hargrave all resigned their positions the following
day. Spencer issued a robust defence of both his and past and present
Board members' integrity, adding:

'*For the past decade, including the time as the Chair of IMUSA, I've*
had to listen to disingenuous bullshit about a "Stretford Boys Club" or a
"board within a board". Given how hard I personally try to build con-
sensus, it's frustrating to hear, but you learn to accept it as par for the
course.'

The references to both the 'Stretford Boys Club' and 'board within
a board' tags will have met with a knowing acknowledgment from the
many at FC who had regularly heard them from Watt over the years.
In spite of the implicit allegation of sexism, if not misogyny, in Watt's
claims, it was noticeable that Helen Goldsmith was one of the first to
note her appreciation for Spencer and Hargrave's efforts, having served
alongside them on the Board from 2009–11. An independent review
was commissioned and found no evidence of the bullying that had

been alleged, but did make recommendations for the future conduct of Board meetings, with specific ones regarding the way decisions should be reached in future. These included 'recognising that some decisions should go to a vote' and stressing that the status quo of 'consensus decision making is time consuming, so should be reserved only for really significant decisions.' Both were recommendations members had already been calling for in order to bring more account-ability to the club's democratic processes.

The review clearly stated of the Board's current approach that 'trying to arrive at consensus and moving to a vote if it's not possible – is not recommended.' Yet little seemed to change. The whole incident would have deep and far-reaching implications for the club, not least because it unexpectedly opened up three slots on the Board, to be filled at the April 2013 General Meeting. Voted in from a small field of very weak candidates were the volunteer Tom Stott, the unknown John Nicholson, and Kate Ramsey, who'd admitted in her candidate statement that, until very recently, she'd not even been into football. To many observers, it was staggering that she got the required nomi-nations, let alone backing. But it was a sign of where the club was headed under Walsh. The desperate need for cash to develop the ground required ever more courting of grant and funding bodies, resulting in the dilution of what the club originally stood for. A fan base of raggy-arsed, former Old Trafford match-goers was not one that 'ticked' many different 'boxes', but by broadening the club's 'community', whether it detracted from what it had been set up as or not, could be financially beneficial. Thus FC United began to appeal to the non-football-supporting likes of Ramsey, while those who'd been at FC from the start lamented the slow decline of the match-day experience, just as had happened at Old Trafford in the early 1990s.

Walsh emerged the clear winner from the AGM, as a much weak-ened and inexperienced Board now oversaw the club. Many members' thoughts were reflected in the words of Stephen Heywood on the club's forum: 'There's only one saving grace from this whole sorry affair – thank God that it's actually AW [Andy Walsh] running the club and not the Board.' That such an inversion of the club's democracy should be welcomed, even jokingly, was alarming. Back in 2005, Walsh had given an interview on BBC Radio 4, in which he compared the experience of Premier League football fans hit by incremental ticket price increases to that of a frog which, if thrown into a pan of scalding water, would immediately jump out. However, if the frog was placed in cold water and the heat was slowly turned up, it would sit there and boil to death. At FC the water was starting to bubble away . . .

In early 2013, Cobbetts, the law firm the club had retained to advise on the ground build and hold the £1.7 million that had been raised in community shares, suddenly collapsed. After the Ten Acres Lane calamity it might have been expected that the club would have ensured relevant precautions were taken – and that it would now have full knowledge of the status of its members' money. But official confirmation of this was painfully slow in coming. I wrote at the time:

> '*Club officials should know exactly what the status is – and long before any fear of administration was raised, given the palaver with TAL – and be able to relay it instantly without having to go to Cobbetts for a nod of reassurance. After all, these sorts of details would've been checked in advance, wouldn't they?*'

Former Steering Committee member Mike Adams again got in touch, unhappy with my despondency:

> '*Your points about communication and transparency are for the most part valid and need addressing. For better or for worse I don't scrutinise club affairs to the extent I should and you and others do, that's more a criticism of myself than anything. I just feel since Chorleygate there has been a relentless, unmitigating volley of doom and negativity from you*

about anything and everything FC and because it's you, more than any-one, it depresses me.

'There have been times at certain home games this season where it's been crushingly downbeat with the lack of crowds and I've hated that, the irony of playing the ostrich over certain aspects of club affairs and the politics of it is not lost on me given where I've come from but it just goes to show how corrosive the last 18 months have been.'

I replied:

'The most corrosive things about the club are i) still being in Bury, and ii) the cult of personality that exists. How ironic that FC should now virtually have its own equivalent of Fergie, and one who is seemingly as averse to criticism or questioning, and which meets just as much internal opposition for anyone daring to do so.

'After all, it's the growing apparent disdain – by design or omission – for the membership and the democratic process that initiated the Chorley situation, that has so upset the CYCM volunteers, and which is evident in the lack of communication over the Cobbetts issue. If that's the FC we created, then so be it: if not, then I'm not going to stand by.'

At least once the build was underway in December 2013, fans could concentrate on the football and enjoy the club's final season at Gigg Lane, safe in the knowledge that September 2014 would usher in a glorious new era. Indeed, the 2013/14 season was going well enough to have fans thinking promotional glory might eventually arrive. Despite first round exits in each of the FA Cup, FA Trophy and Manchester Premier Cup, the team was going well in the league, and even though Chorley were well ahead by late January, there were plenty of games to go. FC started chalking off the wins, racking up four in a row before heading to Chorley at the start of March, Tom Greaves making it five victories with the game's only goal deep in stoppage time.

By the time Chorley headed to Gigg Lane in April, FC were

looking for a 13th straight win and a real battle for the championship was on. In a tumultuous game and atmosphere before a crowd of 4,152, FC were behind for most of the proceedings, before hitting back with two goals in the closing minutes to make it 2–2, and earn a richly deserved point. FC lost the following game, at home to mid-table Buxton, to all but gift Chorley the title. But another three consecutive victories – one memorably against Ashton United from two goals down, sealed with a last minute winner – ensured the race went to the final day. While FC beat Barwell, Chorley also won away at Buxton, to win the league by a point. The play-offs beckoned once again but Ashton returned to Gigg Lane to wreak revenge. With FC winning 1–0, Ashton scored an injury time equaliser to take the tie to extra-time, before adding a winner in time added-on, with penalties beckoning. It was another cruel finale to what had been a thrilling season.

Throughout the first half of 2014, supporters were led to believe that the club would be moving into Broadhurst Park near enough on schedule, some time in September. In his monthly reports to the Board, Andy Walsh updated on the progress. In February, he claimed everything was going so well that there was a possibility the ground could be completed early. A month later, 'high winds' had knocked this back to 'three to four days' behind target, while in April the delay was up to eight days. However, in May, there was positive news once again: 'The works are currently 6 days behind the contract programme; the contractor remains confident that they can recover the lost days and hit the 21st September handover date.'

At the start of June, the stadium project manager Dave Payne's hours were increased by an extra two days a week to help deal with the workload, but no indication was given of any problems or setbacks. Yet come the July Board meeting, the intervening lack of progress had resulted in such delays that handover was now 'currently expected to be the end of October'. In order to try to save costs, the club had bought a large terraced stand from Northwich Victoria when their ground had been closed down – but the company that was due to reconstruct it had gone bust. This led to a lengthy wait while a new contractor was found, at great expense. It was a classic case of 'buying cheap, paying twice' as, together with other increases, the overall cost of the build had shot up another £300,000 to £6 million. The club wrote to supporters, playing it all down: 'We would like to stress that we are only looking at a delay of a few weeks, and an increase in costs of 5–6%.'

In September, the Board was informed that the steel structure 'is expected on site by the end of September'. A month later, Walsh reported that the completion target had now been put back to just before Christmas:

> '*This new date is in recognition of the current reported delays to main contract of three weeks and the delays to the St Marys Road stand and electric power, both of which are under the control of FC United. We are therefore targeting a first game on December 20th.*'

This admission showed that, despite many members subsequently being led to believe that the delays were caused by the contractors Thomas Barnes, the reality was that Walsh and Payne's project-management was at least partly responsible. Walsh's seemingly shaky grasp of the logistics and time frames was revealed in the very same report of 22 October. While he stated 20 December was now the target, in the very next paragraph it was shown to be an impossibility:

> '*The steel is now on site and erection began last week. We have a six week construction programme for the stand with eight weeks of TBS [various works by Thomas Barnes] to follow. We have agreed that TBS works will commence once the stand is 50% complete.*'

The timings involved meant completion was still at least 11 weeks away, well into the new year. In November, Walsh was forced to recognise this reality: 'The delays to the east stand are our current biggest outstanding problem. The possibility of a first game on 31 January are looking remote.' The constant delays added to the construction costs, while the continual false hope sapped supporters' morale.

There were other reasons some fans were losing heart. A schism had opened up between two sections of the club's support, which neither Walsh nor the Board had done anything to address. At Gigg Lane, in addition to 'Malcolms' in the Manchester Road End, another group of fans ran what became known as the 'Main Stand Inn'. This was organised by people close to Walsh who were employed by the club, and in the summer of 2014 both they and 'Malcolms' volunteers submitted competing proposals to run a bar at Broadhurst Park, under what would become the St Marys Road End. There was no reason that the two proposals should be in competition with each other, but nothing was done to cultivate cooperation. The 'Malcolms' volunteers believed it was part of a deliberate attempt to sideline them, following Walsh's fall out with Brady and the subsequent spat over beer price increases.

In addition, some of those who'd frequented the 'Main Stand Inn' gradually became openly hostile to what they saw as the 'Malcolms' crowd, and its supposed imposition of 'lefty' politics on the club. While it was true that many of the 'Malcolms' people espoused a socialist outlook, the 'inclusive' attitude being objected to was more due to policies led by the likes of Walsh, Adam Brown and the club's community team, which adopted causes and agendas that might help open doors to grant funding. (For example, an anti-homophobia initiative in September 2014 met with resistance from a small minority who were increasingly of the mind that, in the words of one contributor on TSIO, 'FC is a football club not a political organisation. If you want to spout politics fuck off to a political party.') This split became more pronounced as time went on, with the 'no politics' brigade adopting an increasingly right-wing stance.

By the time of the November 2014 AGM, ill feeling had built up to the extent that people believed it would all come to a head. Phil Sheeran chaired the meeting and opened with an appeal for everyone to behave respectfully. Fearing deliberate marginalisation, 'Malcolms' stalwarts had submitted a resolution calling on the club to provide them with the space to host future events at Broadhurst Park. Although Sheeran's initial address had seemed ridiculously over the top and unnecessary, when Lynette Cawthra – a petite librarian – stepped up to introduce the 'Malcolms' motion she was literally shaking, fearing more of the animosity which she'd encountered over previous months. The Board requested people vote to remit the resolution pending the move into the new ground, which seemed the sensible option to a majority unaware of the issues, and the vote was passed accordingly. 'Malcolms' volunteers felt betrayed by the Board, and their event would not appear again for as long as Walsh remained CEO.

Given that the move to Broadhurst Park was supposedly imminent at the start of the 2014/15 campaign, FC arranged to play the club's first few home games at Stalybridge's Bower Fold rather than Gigg Lane. By the new year, the team was again well placed for promotion, after just four defeats from 23 league games, despite a disappointing early FA Cup exit to Lancaster. Most impressive was the progress in the FA Trophy. Padiham, Buxton, Barwell and Conference North side Harrogate Town had all been beaten as FC moved into the last 32, being drawn away to Chorley. A thrilling game saw the home side go 2–0 up, before FC took a 3–2 lead in the last ten minutes, only for Chorley to equalise and force a replay. By then, FC had moved all their remaining home games to Curzon Ashton, a ground on which the team had never lost. Chorley weren't about to threaten that record, and FC deservedly won 1–0.

That same week, *Red Issue* brought out its final print edition, railing against what it called 'football's Bullshit Industry' and, in particular, against the latest revenue-obsessed personnel running the Glazers' empire, with their 'ludicrous boasts of Twitter, Facebook and Google statistics' being prioritised ahead of sporting considerations. The final editorial noted:

> *'History will mark the Glazers' leveraged takeover down as genius, even though the case of Liverpool is testament to the fact it was one refinancing away from the disaster we all warned about.*
>
> *'Ten years on, and with every aspect of the game run by bullshitters, imposters and chancers, it serves no purpose us still raging against it all. Especially when are we not just part of this very same Bullshit Industry, doing our bit to prop it up by way of another 25,000 words every issue? Even by undermining and ridiculing it there exists an implicit validation.'*

Almost a decade on from the takeover, *Red Issue* exited the stage. Whereas once the Glazers and their ilk had widely been viewed as leeching off the game, football had changed so much that the Glazers were now accepted – instead it could be said that it was *Red Issue* which was clinging on, eking out a living. The hypocrisy in continuing felt too great. (Adam Brown was just one of many who lamented the end of the magazine's vitriolic disdain for the ills of modern football, heralding *Red Issue*'s 'major contribution to the politics of United fans and football more broadly.') However, *Red Issue* would maintain an online presence, re-entering the fray as and when it deemed it necessary.

In the FA Trophy, FC United faced a side from the Conference North for the third successive round, with high-flying Fylde the visitors in the last 16. FC put in a barnstorming performance to wallop them 3–1, the performance as good as any the club had produced in its history. A trip to Torquay awaited in the quarter-finals, with a big contingent of FC fans heading down to the English Riviera. The two-division gap to the full-time professionals proved too great and Torquay won comfortably, albeit only 1–0. Despite that disappointment, the team's five match unbeaten league run was gradually extended to 21, as FC closed in on the championship and another promotion. With a visit to second place Workington in the offing on the final day, FC sealed the title four days earlier with a nervy 1–0 win against Stourbridge. Promotion to the Conference North had been secured at last, just in time for the new Broadhurst Park era.

While fans celebrated, they also wondered when the ground would actually be ready. A prestige friendly had been arranged against Benfica for Friday 29 May – the anniversary of Matt Busby's Manchester United finally winning the European Cup at Wembley against the same opponents – and the club stood to lose a fortune if it had to be called off. On 12 May 2015 – ten years to the day since the Glazer takeover – FC United finally announced they had permission to hold a 'test event' at Broadhurst Park. The club was to stage a friendly game between current and former players, serving as a practice run to enable the council to sign the ground off as ready to host the Benfica game.

The following Saturday, 3,000 fans turned up in glorious sunshine on an emotional afternoon for all those who'd long dreamt of the club having its own ground. However, that ground was still very much a work in progress. That evening, I met Phil Sheeran in Chorlton. Sheeran confided that Andy Walsh was storing the £25,000 takings at his house, due to the lack of a safe at the ground. I couldn't believe that the Board would sanction such a risk, especially given the financial pressure the club was under, due to the escalating costs and eight-month delay with the ground. I promptly offered the use of a bank's deposit box so that the money could be kept securely over the weekend. Inexplicably, this was rejected. It was a further sign that, under Walsh, the management of the club was becoming increasingly dysfunctional.

In February, Walsh had reported to the Board:

'Russell Brand has been in touch to express his admiration for our stand against the evils of the "bastards running football and ruining the

*experience for working class fans". He wants to try and spread the activ-
ism that he has seen at FC United and I am due to speak with him
again in the coming weeks.'*

I wasn't alone in believing that instead of trying to hobnob with
bandwagon-jumping celebrities, Walsh's time might have been better
spent overseeing his responsibilities. Benfica had agreed to send over
their youth team to play FC as a result of a relationship developed
by the club's academy manager, Paul Bright. He'd been appointed to
the role in 2014 after eight years coaching at Manchester United, two
of them while also working in a voluntary capacity for FC. Despite
giving an impressive presentation to the AGM in November 2014,
detailing the club's ambitions for its youth system, by April 2015 he'd
already resigned his position, having been overloaded with work and
left disillusioned by conflicting instructions from Walsh and Marginson.
The lack of management around his departure was indicative of that
which he'd experienced during his time at the club:

> *'I had prepared a full handover document and nobody ever sat down
> with me to go through it and plan out the best way forward for the acad-
> emy. It could have run for the next ten years on the documents I put
> together but ultimately they would have had to employ someone in a
> senior capacity to oversee the delivery of the programme; instead, they
> gave responsibility to Margy, and he put in place his mates and a young
> lad.'*

What was equally baffling was a story published on the club's website,
announcing a commercial partnership for Wi-Fi provision at Broadhurst
Park. Walsh was quoted:

> *'Good communications are vital for a supporter-owned club like ours
> and we wanted to give our fans, and the club's owners, the opportunity
> to participate in real time on social media when they come to matches.*

'Our Facebook page already has over 734,000 likes and we have 55,000 Twitter followers, so social media is a really effective way for our supporters to engage with each other and the club.'

Puffing 'social media engagement' was *exactly* the sort of corporate clap-trap people had come to expect from those in charge at Old Trafford, and one of the things *Red Issue* had highlighted in its final editorial. Yet now here was the person running FC doing just the same. I believed that this was symptomatic of other issues that clearly needed addressing but, as Benfica's historic visit finally came around, it was recognised that they could all be dealt with further down the line. For now, supporters simply wanted to enjoy the moment of the inaugural game at Broadhurst Park. Many headed out into the pubs of Manchester city centre where, early that morning, a couple of fans had been round, decking out many of the city's statues in homemade FC United scarves. It made for a wonderful sight, and added to the building atmosphere of euphoria.

Come the evening, Broadhurst Park was packed, with a crowd of 4,232 revelling in the excitement of finally being in the club's own home. Benfica's manager Helder Cristovao, a former professional who had played in Portugal, England and France, was amazed by the reception, marvelling, 'We have never seen anything like this.' Andy Walsh lapped up the acclaim on the pitch, addressing the crowd and comparing FC's ascent to the slow motion downfall of Sepp Blatter in the wake of numerous FIFA executives' arrests two days earlier. 'You have all seen what has happened at FIFA this week,' he said. 'You are part of the change. Supporter-ownership is the future.' But who knew then what the future would hold? That night, no one much cared. Benfica won the game 1–0 but it did little to dampen the party spirit. The sense of joy would be short lived.

9

A SENSE AWAKENING

The Benfica game had an extraordinary effect. Even Mr Spleen, *Red Issue*'s legendarily curmudgeonly columnist wrote, when describing his first experience of Broadhurst Park, 'I have no shame in telling you that I wept like a fucking baby. Those who weren't having a quiet weep were grinning like lunatics. Everyone was happy. And that's the FC effect.' Little did Mr Spleen or anybody else realise, but such positivity wasn't to last. Bubbling away under the surface was a dispute that would tear the club apart over the next 12 months.

The argument centred on a decision to increase the price of the Benfica match programme by 50p. A trifling issue, on the face of it. However, it immediately resonated with supporters who had long backed IMUSA's stance against clubs using 'match grading' to cash in with higher ticket prices whenever Manchester United came to town. Now that these same supporters were running their own club, it seemed unjustifiable that this should be done in their name (and effectively against themselves!). Some also argued it was in breach of the club's founding principle that the club 'will strive wherever possible to avoid outright commercialism'.

The dispute began in the days leading up to the match. An email to supporters detailing ticketing information was signed off, 'Andy

Walker, FC United Benfica Ticket Team'. At the time, most people would have been unaware of who Walker was. A friend of Andy Walsh, he'd started out volunteering for the club, helping with the press and PR, before being employed as a fundraiser. Suddenly he had a much higher profile, after being handed a temporary executive role to oversee administrative arrangements for the showpiece Benfica match, while Andy Walsh was preoccupied ensuring the ground was ready in time.

On the club's online forum Walker responded to a query about the Benfica match programme. '[It] will be a special souvenir edition, larger than normal size, and will have extra pages and some quite excellent features and articles,' he excitedly informed people. 'It will cost £2.50 and we will be printing extra copies to cope with the anticipated high demand.' The very first response was not so embracing of the prospect, and homed straight in on the price issue: 'I wait with bated breath to see the reaction on that little gem Andy. Not our club's greatest decision.' The following day, Tony Howard, the programme editor, pointed out that he'd 'argued vociferously' against any increase, insisting 'the decision was not mine'.

It seemed the support – or at least those aware of the argument – immediately split down the middle between those who saw it as a nothing issue, and those who regarded it as a short-sighted move. Mike Turton, a former Board member, summed up the thoughts of many in this latter group by asking, 'Is this a taste of things to come?' and stated that he would not be buying it. Only two months earlier, FC United had taken a stand against Ramsbottom increasing their usual admission price by £1: 'FC United believes that it is unfair for Ramsbottom to penalise supporters by charging them more than their usual admission price. It is a matter of great regret and disappointment that Ramsbottom have not responded positively to our requests to review this last-minute decision.' This led to inevitable calls for a boycott and, facing a big loss of revenue from the large numbers of FC fans who were otherwise expected to attend, Ramsbottom backed down. Another small victory against football's profiteers for FC, yet now it was doing the same. The hypocrisy was stark.

'But, but, *this* is different!' seemed to be the basis of the argument put forward by those defending the decision. One, Kevin Taylor, argued, 'Well if it's a bit bigger and has more pages it must have cost a bit more to produce. I don't think you can compare it to other clubs fleecing us as away fans simply because at this match there won't be any away fans!' As the dispute rumbled on, it was brought to a Board meeting on the Tuesday night. The game was just three days away. The following morning, a club statement was issued.

'The pricing of programmes is not determined by the Board but is an operational decision routinely delegated to the relevant individuals. On this occasion, there are increased design, editing, production and print-ing costs associated with a one-off celebratory issue. These costs equate to double the usual costs.

'The cost of the programme was agreed in writing by all parties including Tony Howard at £2.50 in recognition of these increased costs. This is in keeping with previous "lite" programmes produced at short notice for e.g. cup ties when the sale price has been lowered from £2 in reflection of the reduced production costs and content.

'The Board fully supports the pricing decision.'

If it was expected that this would quell the growing rumblings of discontent then the hope was badly misjudged. It served only to pose many more questions. Who were the relevant individuals? Why weren't they named when Tony Howard was? To what extent did Tony Howard agree to the decision when he had already gone on record stating his objection?

Alongside the programme debate was another move by the club that caused unease. The last remaining tickets for the Benfica game had been put on sale, but only at full price; no concessions were offered for juniors or OAPS. Historically, this was another contentious issue, and one on which FC United had a history of kicking up a fuss – notably with Darwin in 2005. Again, the Board backed the decision. In conjunction with the programme pricing, it appeared doubly damning; the club was simply seeking to maximise profits at the expense of supporters, and was happy to do so even if it was viewed as breaching the club's founding principles.

Having had his integrity called into question, Tony Howard posted the contents of emails that detailed his objections to the 50 pence increase. 'I have finally looked at figures,' he wrote, advocating a £2 cover price, after calculations showed the planned 3,000 print run would realise a profit of £3,500 – higher than the programme typically generated in an entire season. This suggested that the Board's statement was inaccurate at best, and deliberately misleading at worst. I spoke to Tony Howard at length to find out exactly what had gone on. It seemed that Andy Walker had not only driven the decision over the programme price but also the commission of its new and completely redesigned format, presumably as a way of justifying it being a glossy 'souvenir' edition.

Following this, I entered the forum discussion that was already running to over 150 posts, and slammed the Board's 'snivelling statement . . . clearly intended to protect the identities of the people who did make this unpopular decision, whilst simultaneously and quite unjustifiably singling out and implicating Tony Howard in the process.' The requested programme redesign was nothing but a 'vanity project' involving time and expense that was 'completely unnecessary'. A normal-sized programme would already amount to a bumper edition 'given the 10–12 pages of compulsory league adverts which are not required.' Citing an alleged £5,000 profit target, I went on, 'Once the club/board starts viewing supporters as figures rather than people then we're on the slippery slope to MUFC plc circa 1997.' I also revealed, 'Apparently free speech is not allowed at FC these days: I'm led to believe the club has called [Tony Howard] into a meeting tomorrow to "explain himself".'

This was incredible, not least given how busy everyone supposedly was ahead of the upcoming match. Why were club officials wasting time calling Howard to account, simply for stating his position? And there's no way Walker would've had the authority to haul Tony in. Walsh had to be involved too. Walsh's displeasure at being questioned by me became evident the day before the match. There was an end-of-season *Red Issue* curry do organised to coincide with the Benfica game, and Walsh had previously confirmed he'd be attending. In the end he didn't show – despite his workload it was obvious this was because he was sulking over me backing Howard. He later conceded as much to a mutual friend.

In an echo of the fallout over the Chorley tickets issue, I'd also had a phone call from Phil Sheeran, Walsh's consigliere. 'You're a right busy bollocks aren't ya?' was his opening line, citing my criticisms on the forum. We had a long discussion in which I suggested that the print run was too small, and that the club would make more money from selling 4,000 at £2, something they'd easily do. Sheeran started spouting on about the usual programme-sales-to-match-attendance ratio being only 30 per cent, that I'd moan whatever they did, and that I didn't know what I was on about. He perhaps had a point about me moaning but to claim I didn't have a clue about the matter, well, I'd only worked in print for 20 years . . .

The decision went unchanged and, in the days following the match, the matter was set to be left to lie. That was, until Andy Walker went back on the club's online forum with a post preening at those who'd advocated a boycott. 'The programme was totally sold out. 3,000 copies sold. We are looking at a reprint,' he wrote. (Despite Sheeran's claims, it seems I had been right about the demand.) As the discussion moved on, a couple of Board members interjected, providing some enlightening insights. Adam Brown said:

'*As part of our business plan forecast, we anticipated and included sig-*
nificant additional revenue from this match (well before it was going to

be the "first game") as one of the ways in which we might offset some of the significant forecast losses for this year . . . resulting from all the problems we have had with the build.'

This contradicted the 'production costs' reasoning that the Board had previously given for the increased cost. Alison Watt added:

'Adam [Brown] has seriously downplayed the budgetary implications of the Benfica game becoming also the first game . . . the finances depended on significant income from both a first game, and the Benfica game. When that became one event it put a large hole in the anticipated income on top of the ever increasing cost of the build delay.'

Suddenly, members were feeling misled as well as taken for granted, though the matter would still likely have been dropped, but for another badly judged intervention, this time by Kate Ramsey. She didn't so much stoke the fire as detonate a napalm bomb, dismissing the dissent as merely coming from 'a small number of individuals'. To many, Ramsey's words echoed Alex Ferguson's infamous 'They carried on to the degree where they actually thought they should have a say in the running of the football club' comment. From being merely a heated discussion about the application of FC United's principles alongside fiscal pragmatism, it suddenly seemed to dawn on many fans that those running the club were now completely detached from the membership.

This wasn't the first time Ramsey had come to people's attention. In October 2014, she'd issued a 'put up or shut up' challenge to fans on TSIO ahead of the deadline for Board election nominations. At the time, she'd only been on the Board just over a year, having been elected following the resignations that came in the wake of Alison Watt's intervention at the AGM in November 2012. Ramsey's initial pitch for votes had openly stated: 'I wasn't even into football until I discovered FC. I was sceptical to start with, and didn't get how somebody could be a Manchester United fan but support FC.'

The broad sunlit uplands, clearly visible just a couple of weeks earlier, were already obscured by clouds of acrimony. Adam Brown re-entered the fray, and, in doing so, made the first accusation of 'abuse' which would come to be parroted so often. Disagreements should not be raised 'by targeting individuals,' he said. 'Whilst a debate is part of democratic organisations, some of the comments, particularly against individuals, are not being done in a civil manner.' This position didn't exactly appear consistent, given the Board statement that had specifically named Tony Howard.

Even at this stage, ten days after the Benfica game, all most people wanted was a simple acknowledgment from the Board that they had messed up, and an apology for their insinuation that Howard was a liar. None came. As the days passed, more and more questions started to be asked. Most prominent was just how each Board member had viewed the issue of the 50p. A resolution passed at the 2012 AGM held that all future Board votes 'that do not meet with a unanimous response from those board members present shall require a full voting list to be recorded.' In the three years since then, this had never happened. Why was the Board ignoring this direct instruction from the membership? Was the whole 'Our club, our rules' thing just for show?

Two weeks after the Benfica match, Board members Mike Sherrard and Des Lynch held a meeting with Tony Howard 'to discuss issues surrounding the Benfica programme.' Sherrard blandly stated: 'Views and information were exchanged and we will now report the facts of that meeting back to the full Board.' Before that could happen, Howard resigned. He'd discovered ahead of the meeting that Andy Walker had been soliciting quotes to print the programme, despite this being one of the duties listed in Howard's contract. Howard claimed Sherrard and Lynch were more interested in why he had turned up to their meeting with a union representative than in any resolution to the dispute, as well as in his justification for passing information to me. 'I have resigned. Can't be arsed with it any more. It is clear from last night that I see the club differently to "them",' Howard told me.

As the fallout continued, the Board eventually made a statement on Wednesday 24 June, almost four weeks after the Benfica game. They insisted that they stood by the decisions taken, and invoked the 'civil debate' line against their detractors, saying, 'personal insult and attacks are unacceptable and unnecessary'. It then declared:

> *'This will be the final statement from the Board on the forum on this matter. If any member remains unsatisfied with the outcome of the board decision, then the club constitution gives members the opportunity for the calling of a General Meeting.'*

Its tone and wording outraged many members. Mike Adams, the former Steering Committee member, referred to it as 'Orwellian'.

In the further absence of any apology, Tony Howard posted a series of emails revealing his conversations with Andy Walker regarding the 50p price increase. These showed that, despite Howard's protestations, Walker *informed* him in four separate missives that the price would be increased. The fact that the Board had misled the membership was there in black and white. Despite this, a sizeable number of people still backed them over Howard.

For me, the issue in all this wasn't the 50p. It was essentially about the direction of the club, the place of the membership within its democratic structure, and how quickly and easily the founding principles could be set aside when it suited. I commented at the time: 'What is the point of a nice shiny new ground if everything it was supposedly built upon is sacrificed the moment we get there simply to finance its upkeep?' The saga made people realise how quickly the club could be taken over by the self-interested likes of Walker and Ramsey, who seemingly had no real interest in FC or what it stood for, beyond using it as a stepping stone for their careers.

The most alarming thing was the ruthlessness with which Tony Howard was treated simply for questioning things. Of course, I'd experienced similar over the boycotted Chorley game four years earlier.

But bear in mind that Tony's wife remained the club secretary, and would have to work alongside Andy Walker and Andy Walsh on her return from maternity leave. She would be placed in a near-impossible situation, but it was clear there was no thought given to that – all that mattered was that any dissent should be stamped on.

Andy Walsh texted me on 14 June, simply saying, 'Your criticisms of Andy Walker are very cheap.' It was the first contact of any sort I'd had with him on the matter. The following week I had a missed call from him and then an email. Walsh requested I refrain from 'any more personal attacks on the members forum' and insisted that I wasn't 'in full possession of all the facts'. Apparently time was needed for 'the Board to complete its processes on the serious allegations being made by Tony Howard'. Tony hadn't actually made any allegations; he'd merely given his opinion on the 50p increase. Walsh again played the 'abuse' line by insisting that my 'comments on the members forum have left me sick and depressed. The viciousness and unwarranted attacks on individuals is making me consider if I wish to continue.'

I'd not made any attacks, vicious or otherwise, and asked Walsh to cite any. I told him, 'From your reactions to these current issues and others in the past, it would appear that you have no respect for my or other members' democratic views as to the running of the club where it clashes with your own. In light of that, perhaps it might be better if you did resign.'

Walsh had referred to me being 'wedded' to a narrative but, if anything, it was him and the Board who were wedded to one, continually associating any form of questioning with abuse and unjustified targeting of individuals.

Ahead of the Board's statement, I had pointed out the conflict of interest inherent in them reviewing their own decision at a meeting Walsh would attend, but from which Howard was excluded. Neil Boothman, who would be voted onto the Board later in the year, pinned the club's problems solely on Andy Walker, and called for his resignation: 'It looks like the majority of problems arising recently all have one common thread . . . he doesn't actually get "us" . . . long-standing volunteers are terminating their services and all for one individual.'

Andy Walsh's exchanges with me revealed that he viewed Tony Howard's behaviour as an attempt to undermine his authority. Despite all the talk about 'attacks' he had been carefully preparing his own. On Friday 26 June, Walsh made a lengthy post on the club's forum, titled, 'Personal statement in response to member concerns & comments.' It was a stunning, excoriating attack on Tony Howard's personal and professional integrity. Walsh referred to him 'challenging the legitimacy of my position as general manager' and, after highlighting Howard's supposed treachery, he wrote:

> *'It is simply not true that either Andy Walker or I have tried to undermine Tony Howard's position as programme editor, or diminish his role.*
> *'I have done everything in my power to uphold the club's core values and manifesto commitments, and I have absolute faith in all our club staff and elected Board to deliver a strong and stable football club.'*

Many amongst the membership were reassured – it was simply a fuss over nothing; a gigantic overreaction. Others saw through it. Adrian Naylor wrote: 'This is public bullying and it has to stop. Somebody is lying here, making it all the more important we get to the bottom of it.' I acknowledged the genius of Walsh's piece, pointing out how Walsh 'has turned this from a side issue about his good pal Walker to a central one about Tony Howard. [It] should be a lesson to any aspiring Machiavelli, and shows our favourite Stretford ex-Trotskyist has learned well the lesson of his old hero's demonization at Stalin's Show Trials.' I proceeded to dissect Walsh's post line-by-line, high-lighting 15 different parts that I believed were misleading, false or didn't stand up to scrutiny.

I now considered Andy Walsh fair game and compiled a 3000-word

'*J'Accuse*' post, directly accusing Walsh of mismanaging the club, risk-ing its assets by hoarding cash at home and subverting the club's democratic processes. Decrying 'the cult-of-personality adoration of Walsh', I pointed out, 'It's become increasingly clear in recent weeks as to the true extent of the General Manager's undemocratic hold over this club.' The post also compared Walsh's control to Alex Fer-guson's under the Glazers ('whilst his deluded acolytes could point to the shiny baubles in the trophy room as proof all was well, so FC fans do likewise with the shiny new ground') and called for 'the imme-diate resignation of Walsh, and a vote of no confidence in the Board'. In the event that it didn't happen, I was prepared to let my member-ship expire and walk away, stating, 'I have no desire to be part of a club or membership that has no courage and doesn't want to hear the truth, however uncomfortable it may be.'

With the increased scrutiny on the club's administration, it tran-spired that the minutes of Board meetings hadn't been published all year, meaning members could not keep abreast of what was being done in their name. Board members increasingly refused to engage with members or answer questions on the forum. As a result, fans started discussing taking up the challenge of forcing an EGM. With it increasingly looking a possibility, the Board seized the initiative. On Sunday 28 June, they announced that a meeting would be held: 'to discuss the issues associated with the Benfica game'. This was a humili-ating U-turn in the wake of their 'final statement' on the matter just days earlier, but was a wise move given the circumstances. The announcement included a *mea culpa* for 'the way the Board has han-dled communication,' which 'could have been done differently, and better'. The Board also acknowledged being 'slow to respond to members,' saying 'we misjudged the strength of feeling among the membership'. The conciliatory tone gained them some respite from the growing hostility.

Following all the debate and argument, the meeting was largely a damp squib. Most of those in attendance were always going to be supportive of the Board, while I was away and unable to front the arguments. Tony Howard tried to do so, but his address was too emotional and rambling, and did little to get to the nub of the issues. He actually drew flak from some quarters, and his wife, the club secretary, exited in tears. For many, the conclusion was highly unsatisfactory. One fan in attendance, Chris Leighton, commented, 'Any optimistic idea that Sunday's meeting would have cleared the air ahead of the new season seems wishful at this stage. Instead it's further highlighted the gulf between those we elect and the direction the club is heading.'

The notice of the meeting sent out by the club had asked 'that participants (including Board members and employees) come to the meeting to work towards a positive outcome for the future of our club.' Some on the Board seemingly hadn't got thier own message. Their approach to having to answer to the membership was summed up by Tom Stott's stunning declaration that the 50p dissenters had picked 'the wrong war, at the wrong place, at the wrong time, and with the wrong enemy.' Little did he realise, but the Board's battles had only just begun.

10

I AM GOD, AND KING, AND LAW!

By the time the Members' meeting was attempting to draw a line under the previous season's events, preparations for the new one were already well under way. There was no hiding the desperation. The club put out an 'urgent' appeal for volunteers – assistance was needed with concreting walkways inside the ground, which had not been finished to the FA's ground grading standards. A failure to get the work done would leave Broadhurst Park without the requisite license, which posed an obvious risk of cancellation to the club's first preseason friendly. 'This task comes with both financial and time constraints,' ran the announcement. 'Employing contractors is obviously an option but this will cost funds that we can ill afford at this time.'

The ever-growing financial pressures led to supporters raising questions about the lack of urgency in marketing the ground's facilities. The new function room was budgeted to bring in over £300,000 in its first year, yet was not even being advertised on the club's website. The club had appointed a full-time business development manager in March 2014, yet she had not produced a brochure showcasing what the club could offer potential clients – there seemed to be no strategy in place to generate bookings. The Board didn't seem concerned by such oversights. When Rick Simpson, an FC fan who had volunteered his professional input to help the club's catering operation, asked why promotion of the ground hadn't been in place for six months prior to its opening, he was referred to a blog post by Andy Walsh from June: 'There will be a period of settling in and setting up of our operational systems. There are a number of items for us to complete as part of the ground development and these will be progressed over the course of the next few weeks.' Adam Brown tried to provide reassurance that all was in hand: 'I am sure marketing/advertising will be made available once things settle down.'

For those who'd had their eyes opened by 50p-gate, such concerns were still largely off the radar. It wasn't so much a matter of what marketing wasn't being done, as what marketing *was* occurring. Towards the end of June, a commercial tie-up meant the club's Twitter account (operated by Andy Walker) had disseminated an advert for something called 'Honda winning Wednesdays'. Around the same time, one of the club's players involved in a promotions company started advertising 'FCUM Experience' packages to tourists, which included a 'Stadium tour of Broadhurst Park' and 'after match beers with first team players'. Both ventures were akin to something straight out of the Glazer handbook, leaving many fans outraged that a club with FC's ethos should have any part in them. The Board claimed not to have authorised the 'FCUM Experience', and blamed the player for pre-empting any decision on it. Board meeting minutes revealed that the player had submitted his company's proposal way back in March, and Andy Walsh had been delegated responsibility for reporting back on it but had still not done so. Supporters began to realise that the club's operations moved at a glacial pace and oversight of them was dysfunctional. One, Roger Hayes, addressed the issue on the club's forum:

'We have a structure where the Board is so tightly entwined with operations that there is no discernible distinction between them. The Board should be setting policy and providing scrutiny of club operations, and the operations should be implementing policy.

'This clearly isn't the case. You have Board members running parts of the operation, and staff members deciding on policy. Hence situations arise where somebody makes a decision and they all have to back each other up, and in doing so, members haven't got a clue who is representing them effectively and who isn't.'

Relations between the members and the Board had deteriorated so much that some started to discuss setting up an independent supporters association. The irony of this was stark – the whole point of FC United had been to give fans a direct say in the running of their club. The mood wasn't helped when Andy Walker immediately declared an interest in joining this quest for greater transparency and communication, and was joined by Board member Alison Watt.

The football side of the club was also under pressure, even though the concreting works had been completed, and the friendly against Wrexham went ahead. Greater Manchester Police used the game as a trial run for Broadhurst Park's first league match against FC's local rivals Stockport County. The size of the followings both Wrexham and Stockport could attract meant both encounters were made all-ticket affairs. This resulted in a lower capacity, due to both segregation and ongoing ground licensing issues, which in turn meant a loss of revenue. With the accompanying large police presence at both fixtures, the club was liable for costs that ran into thousands of pounds. It was another financial blow the club could ill afford.

A longer-lasting impact of these all-ticket games largely went unnoticed at the time. FC had pitched up in Moston amidst promises by Andy Walsh and Adam Brown of engagement with the community, but local residents who'd excitedly anticipated the club's arrival had seen the whole 2014/15 season pass without a single game being played at Broadhurst Park. Lance Manock, a United fan living just a short walk from the ground had bought several season tickets, intending friends and kids from the area to use them, so they could see 'what all the fuss we'd been making over FC for the previous nine years was about.' He described it as being like a 'series of body blows' when first the ground was delayed, then the Benfica game was made all-ticket and only available to club members, followed by the Wrexham and Stockport matches too: 'The perception spread around Moston that Broadhurst Park was some sort of private members' club and locals couldn't get in.'

The actions of Andy Walker were also having an adverse impact on community relations. After the Stockport game, in his role as 'Press and Communications Officer', he took to the club's Twitter account to boast: 'Great programme tonight. Supporters clearly thought so as we've sold out of all the copies despite printing 1000+'. Although the message might have appeared innocent enough, many who were party to the tumultuous events of the summer interpreted it differently. 'I'd be quite happy to see the head of whoever tweeted that stuck on a spike,' one said. 'There's no point preaching the gospel of unity and "moving on" if you're going to indulge in that kind of sly factional scab-ripping.' Amidst a barrage of similar sentiments, the tweet was quietly deleted.

In his paid fundraising role Walker was faring little better. Andy Walsh had intended staging a gala dinner at Broadhurst Park in June, but the delays to the ground meant the plan was eventually abandoned, blowing a £20,000 hole in the club's 2014/15 budget. As a result, the Board aimed to stage two such events during 2015/16 to make up the shortfall. The first was slated for Friday 9 October, with ex-MUFC and Scotland player Gordon McQueen booked as the guest speaker. A club announcement described it as 'an important fund-raiser . . . part of a range of different events and initiatives that are helping to generate the funds to enable the club to sustainably finance the continuing development of our new ground.' A profit of £20,000 was targeted based on two previous dinners in 2011 and 2012, which had raised around £40,000. These had been organised by volunteers, and advertised several months in advance to provide time to pitch them to the sort of businesses they were intended to attract, yet Andy

Walker gave himself fewer than four weeks to make his a success. '£1,000 + VAT for a table of 9. Space is limited and we expect tickets to sell quickly so those interested are encouraged to contact us as soon as possible,' prospective punters were confidently warned. Two weeks later, it was called off without Walker having sold a single place.

It caused embarrassment to Ray Vaughan, whose company was a long-term sponsor of the club's youth team. He had booked McQueen and a compere for the event on Andy Walker's behalf, only to then be asked if he could quietly cancel the arrangements. Vaughan happened to mention the matter to me, wondering why the dinner wasn't going ahead. From there the news was posted on TSIO and, in the absence of any confirmation from the club, the information was doubted and I was accused of waging a vendetta. Few FC fans seemed willing to see the connection between the club's finances and Walker being paid a hefty wage while failing to deliver on ventures intended to underpin them.

This latest incident renewed my determination to expose Walsh and Walker. Given Walker's track record, I'd been certain he'd carry on making a complete hash of everything, akin to some King-Midas-in-reverse. It was just a case of sitting it out, and letting him take Walsh down with him – the Gala dinner shambles was typical of what I'd expected. During the events of the summer, I'd been in contact with numerous people about how FC was run, and was convinced the club needed a complete overhaul. Walsh had to go, and the Board needed revamping with fresh input, ideas and genuine expertise.

The finances were clearly a complete mess, and the legacy of the ground build was liable to render the club unsustainable very quickly. To me, this was all blatantly obvious, but the membership just wasn't prepared to see it, mainly due to the backing and loyalty Walsh had built up – and, of course, the shiny new stadium which was there for all to see. In challenging the prevailing consensus, I'd naively thought my voice and 'status' as the erstwhile architect of the club might have been enough to make people listen. In reality, it seemed most had no idea who I was, and cared even less. And frankly, why should they? They had the ground that everyone had dreamt about for so long. This allowed Walsh to spread the idea amongst his followers that I was jealous of him having delivered it, and that I was simply looking for a way back in now the hard work had been completed.

One late-September morning, I arranged to meet Rob Brady in Manchester. I wanted to sound out where he stood on it all. Brady was at the centre of a big group of FC fans which included Tony Howard and many of his circle. I wanted to know if he thought FC was still worth the bother or should we all just forget it?

I pointed out that, with proper preparation, all the issues could be put before the membership via resolutions at November's AGM. This would need people to stand up and back them; to actually take on Walsh and the Board, rather than cowering like many had done at the meeting in July. I'd misjudged things in the summer and ended up badly burned by taking on a battle that, with hindsight, could never have been won. However, I was due to be away in November as well, so I'd need people willing to support any motions I put forward.

Brady's response was typical Brady. What I interpreted from it all was that he considered the club to have been lost to the new influx like Kate Ramsey, but that he still wasn't prepared to fully abandon it – he'd kept up his season ticket and membership. He told me, 'If anyone is potty enough to take them on and turn things round then it's you.' As with the conversation with Kris Stewart all those years earlier, it sounded too much like a challenge to not take on.

Andy Walsh was making moves to shore up his position. Following his earlier attempts to discredit questioning of his decisions through accusations of bullying and abuse, Walsh complained to the Board that there was no mechanism in place to deal with what he described as 'misconduct'. He called for:

'A code of conduct for co-owners that affords some protection to staff and volunteers subject to abuse or threats of violence from fellow

co-owners . . . Any co-owner found guilty of abusing a member of staff or a fellow co-owner should face sanctions including potential exclusion from membership of the club. Over the course of the last few months members of staff have had to endure personal abuse and threats of violence [yet] abusive co-owners are free to continue in membership with full benefits.'

No examples were publicly revealed, but the Board took Walsh's claims seriously and Kate Ramsey ordered that a code of conduct should be drawn up. Over the next few months, the lack of detail provided on these unsubstantiated claims of threats and abuse would lead many members to infer that they were associated with me, particularly given the next item of discussion in the same Board meeting: '[Adam Brown] is to speak with lawyer Kevin Jaquiss [formerly Alex Ferguson's lawyer] as regards the status of any expelled member and those who resign their membership and who also hold community shares.' In time, it became clear that there weren't many people to whom the membership item could relate.

My criticisms of Walker on TSIO led Andy Walsh to contact its moderators to complain about my posts. Kate Ramsey also sent them a message insisting allegations being made were 'potentially libellous' and called for a discussion 'regarding the appropriate moderation of comments in the best interests of all parties'. The idea that the people running a democratic, fan-owned football club were looking to silence its critics indicated how far FC had moved from its founding ethos. 'I can only imagine Walsh's outrage if Martin Edwards had attempted to gag him in a similar manner during his IMUSA days,' I wrote. Still no one much cared about what was generally regarded a trifling issue – but that was to change. First, the membership got upset about something different altogether.

On the afternoon of Wednesday 7 October, FC's Twitter account retweeted a message by Damian Hinds, a little-known Conservative MP: 'Great to visit @FCUnitedMcr to meet @andykwalsh at their incredible new stadium – financed through #SITR and #SocInv.' Alongside it was a photo of him, Andy Walsh, Adam Brown and Andy Walker. Later that evening, a news item on FC's website explained the visit: as exchequer secretary to the Treasury, Hinds had 'wanted to find out more about the impact social investment tax relief has had on the club'. Other photos emerged of Walsh laughing and joking with Hinds, while the Treasury posted a story online that cited FC United's example in justification of government policy. Members were outraged as, only three days earlier, ahead of the Conservative party conference in the city, many FC supporters – Walsh included – had joined a march in Manchester, protesting against swingeing government funding cuts. 'I honestly can't believe we even entertained this', 'An absolute disgrace', and 'What the fuck are you doing???' were just some of the reactions on the club's online forum.

Adam Brown attempted to quell the growing storm: 'The supporters' movement has always spoken to those in power to try and get its concerns addressed. At FC we have ALWAYS lobbied Government, and hosted them, regardless of who they are.' It was a reasonable enough argument but the club had previously boasted it was adopting a policy that neither it, nor Broadhurst Park, could be used for party political promotional purposes. Brown argued this was different, as Hinds was present as 'a representative of Government'. It didn't wash, even amongst some of the Board's staunchest backers. Mike Adams called it 'a PR gaffe of Ratner-esque proportions', pointing out the club had handed Hinds 'a gift-wrapped opportunity to grandstand his "friend of the working class" credentials.' Roy Williamson, a commentator on FCUMTV, said, 'Dramatic maybe, but this is for me the worst thing we have done and I want the people responsible to sort it out. Throughout the whole shenanigans in the summer I supported people at the club – I can't do so at this point.'

The consensus was that there would be nothing wrong with meeting Hinds per se, but why pose for pictures with him? And then tweet about it? It was just another example of club officials setting aside rules and principles by which they were supposed to abide, and of them being completely out of touch with a sizeable proportion of the club's owners. And, of course, just another example of the haplessness of the club's PR operation under Andy Walker.

The following day, the Board apologised for the furore, again pinning blame on an individual: 'The meeting itself was agreed to by board member Adam Brown, not the rest of the Board ... Adam accepts his responsibility for not ensuring that club policy on the political use of visits was upheld on this occasion.'

The deadline for submissions to the AGM was approaching, and I began to trawl the club's accounts for information on which to base my submissions. The club had employed Andy Walker as a full-time fundraiser the previous December but, despite this, and the publicity FC had attracted through their championship win and Broadhurst Park's opening, the figures to June 30 2015 showed sponsorship income was merely 1 per cent up. Every other budget line into which Walker had input had performed below expectations: club event income was 20 per cent down; donations 35 per cent down; development fund event income 22 per cent down; community coaching income 45 per cent down; education and training income 18 per cent down; community events income 32 per cent down; grant income 66 per cent down. Meanwhile, £24,000 had been spent on something referred to as 'development fund management salary'.

Regardless of the figures, Walker's overall influence within the club was in little doubt. He had not only been accused of contributing to the resignation of Tony Howard and the schisms that followed, but the exit of John Manning too. A former Board member, Manning had volunteered his expertise to help sort out the club's IT systems, but walked away after being overruled and undermined by Walker. 'Any enthusiasm I had for the club, and zest for sorting out the IT mess, was drained out of me by him,' Manning said.

Richard Kurt, for whom Andy Walsh had acted as best man at his wedding, provided a typically succinct analysis. He suggested that the only sensible move was for Walsh and the club to let Walker go: 'I think a way should be found for Walker to be sacrificed for the common good. After all, his prime raison d'être is to make FC appealing, whether he's engaging in PR, press, communications or fundraising. Given that he seems to annoy people with his every emission, he actually appears to be more damaging to the FC atmosphere than a fleet of dodgy Volkswagens.'

Given how obvious this move seemed to almost everyone but those who could enact it, I began wondering why it wasn't just sorted immediately. If Walker was Walsh's mate then fair enough, to some degree – even though Walsh had little problem excommunicating plenty of others who'd regarded themselves as friends. But why did the Board not act, unless they were simply beholden to Walsh? Thinking about this, it suddenly occurred to me just how many of Walsh's mates had been elevated to nice, cushy roles within the club.

Walker had joined Phil Frampton, Robin Pye and Helen Walker, amongst others, whose involvement in the club seemed to be solely due to their friendship with Walsh. In some instances it wasn't clear where volunteering ended and paid employment began. The lack of clarity begat a lack of scrutiny that seemed to suit all parties.

Questions about the role of Andy Walker and Robin Pye, and whether they were contractors or volunteers, had first surfaced on the club's online forum in December 2012. Gary Selvidge, himself a long-term volunteer, had helped raise thousands of pounds for the club since its earliest days back in 2005. He asked for information on the extent of their involvement and it resulted in a ferocious response from Andy Walsh. 'I am not going to allow a situation to develop where the name of every volunteer within the club is posted with the challenge of "have we made a payment to xxx?" We do not have the time,' Walsh insisted, in the course of a 2,180-word response. Defending Walker, Walsh accused Selvidge of having 'an agenda' that amounted to a 'pernicious pursuit of volunteers' which was 'draining and demoralising'. He claimed Selvidge 'deliberately [sought] to sow maximum suspicion and imply that there is some kind of self-appointed clique running the club . . . more akin to the McCarthy era, and is not in the spirit of our football club.' Walsh conceded, 'some members have expressed their disquiet at the way in which the Board appointed Andy Walker as the Club Press Officer [but] what is not in doubt are Andy's skills and outstanding ability to do the job.'

It was a stunning outburst. To the increasing number of those who'd been excommunicated, there was little doubt Walsh had changed since the club's early days. In June 2015, three days before he had similarly slapped down Tony Howard on the forum, a club announcement boasted, 'The EY [Ernst & Young] Entrepreneur of the Year Awards has shortlisted FC United general manager Andy Walsh as a regional finalist for the North area'. The winner was announced at a swanky dinner in Manchester, attended by Walsh and Walker. The latter tweeted, '@andykwalsh a worthy finalist', alongside a photo of Walsh's picture on the big screen as the nominations were read out. I wondered, 'At what stage did it all go so badly wrong that a club founded on FC's principles is even acknowledging Ernst and Young, let alone craving their awards and hospitality and effectively helping do their PR?' The point seemed to be appreciated better by outsiders than within FC's membership. One onlooker wrote:

'One of the winners of the entrepreneur award was Simon Cooper, of a company called On The Beach. For those of you who aren't familiar with Simon Cooper or the company, they received external investment from Inflexion in 2013. This buyout was facilitated by a significant amount of debt that was placed into the company so that the external investor could put as little of their own money into the business as possible. Once invested in the business, the investor did everything in their power to exploit the asset and grow its revenue and profit, with the ultimate aim of maximising their return on investment, which they did in September this year by listing the business on the stock exchange.

Top: Manchester United's Martin Edwards (left) and BSkyB's Mark Booth (right) hold a joint press conference to try and win the early PR battle to help force through the sale of the club, September 1998

Bottom: United fans show their opposition to the proposed BSkyB deal at Old Trafford, September 1998

Left: Andy Walsh and Adam Brown show their appreciation in my copy of Not For Sale, their account of the campaign against the BSkyB takeover, September 1999

Right: A pantomime horse hired by United fans attempts to kick in the door at Kroll's offices, in protest at Coolmore's toying with Manchester United, 11th February 2004

Alex Ferguson with John and Sue Magnier before the falling-out over Rock Of Gibraltar

Top: Malcolm Glazer, the American tycoon whose attempts to take over Manchester United attracted widespread protests by the club's supporters in 2004/05

Bottom: Alex Ferguson shares a joke with the Glazers after meeting them in Portugal, 30th June 2005

Website: www.blackpooltoday.co.uk

The Gazette Tuesda

Rebel United club won't last, fear Mechs

By MIKE YOUNG

THE team hurriedly formed by angry Manchester United fans has been dismissed as a potential one-season wonder by North-West Counties League rivals Blackpool Mechanics.

Set up in protest at American Malcolm Glazer's takeover, FC United of Manchester will play alongside Mechs in division two.

Organisers are talking of taking 1,500 to 2,000 fans to the likes of Common Edge – where gates rarely reach 100 – but Mechs chairman Tommy Baldwin has shot down all the big talk as a pipedream.

Conference North club Droylsden have agreed to house the fledgling club at their 3,000-capacity Butcher's Arms ground, which FC United reckon they will fill every time.

A NWCL spokesman said the club have shown they are serious by lodging a four-figure bond and have produced a 16-page business plan. 2,600 registered supporters have put up or pledged money. Non-League journeyman Ex-Droylsden player Karl Marginson will manage the team after Brian Kidd, Asa Hartford and Sammy McIlroy weren't tempted.

Baldwin, though, doubts that the anti-Glazer movement can convert the big talk into action.

"If it has been thoroughly thought through and provided the money is available, there shouldn't be a problem. But it's a sad state of affairs for football if this is being used as a gimmick," said Baldwin. "The league will be letting themselves down badly if they haven't done their research.

"Does anyone seriously believe people will stop watching Manchester United because of who's running the club? This is a candle in the wind and the flame will soon blow out.

"I would love having 1,500 at Mechanics but there's not a chance."

Baldwin believes there might be big crowds at the beginning but numbers will drop off, particularly if results aren't right. And he felt a bond merely amounted to £1 a head.

The new season kicks off on August 13 – the same weekend as the Premiership starts.

■ FLEETWOOD Town manager Tony Greenwood has earned £250 by walking off with the NWCL division one manager of the year prize.

Greenwood picked up the cheque and a plaque after Fleetwood won the championship to go into the Unibond League.

Opposite page top: Members of the M.E.C. interrupt the Reserves game at Altrincham to protest against Glazer's plans for Manchester United, 7th October 2004

Opposite page bottom: An effigy of Malcolm Glazer is hanged from the Stretford End during a game between Manchester United and Arsenal, 24th October 2004

Top: Rally at the Apollo in Ardwick, 30th May 2005

Bottom: The Blackpool Gazette reports on doubts from the chairman of Blackpool Mechanics that FC United would last, June 2005

Top: Options for the club badge that were voted on at the club's first EGM, 5th July 2005

Bottom: The crowds turned up for FC United's first ever game vs Leigh RMI, 15th July 2005

Opposite page top: Joz Mitten is chaired off the pitch at Leigh following a pitch invasion by jubilant supporters, 15th July 2005

Opposite page bottom: The players come out for the championship trophy presentation, wearing t-shirts dedicated to Russell Delaney, 22nd April 2006

Top: The team's post-match, open-top bus parade from Gigg Lane to the nearby
Swan & Cemetery pub causes traffic chaos, 22nd April 2006

Bottom: FC United fans boycott a game at Curzon Ashton in protest at the league moving the
game to a 12 p.m. kick-off against both clubs' wishes, 29th December 2007

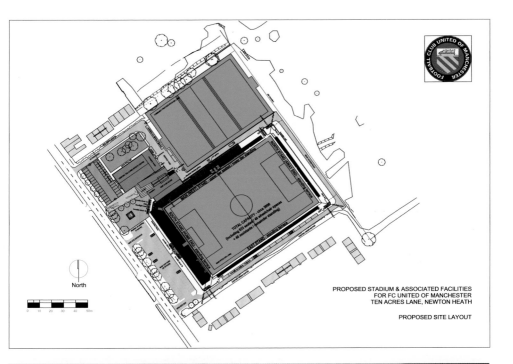

Top: Architects' plans for the abandoned Ten Acres Lane development in Newton Heath, August 2010

Bottom: Mike Norton celebrates his injury time winner against Rochdale in the FA Cup First Round, 5th November 2010

Top: Some are more equal than others: Andy Walsh stands head and shoulders above FC United supporters in a Co-operative Group advert, March 2011

Bottom: Striker Tom Greaves celebrates a 2-0 win for FC at AFC Fylde, 14th December 2013

Top: FC fans acknowledge Red Issue's role in the club's history after the magazine's final issue, 24th January 2015

Bottom: The players and coaching staff celebrate in the dressing room, 21st April 2015

Top: Broadhurst Park remains under construction, seven months after it was originally scheduled to be completed, April 2015

Bottom: Abraham Lincoln, one of numerous statues in Manchester city centre adorned with FC United's colours, 29th May 2015

Top: The infamous Benfica programme, 29th May 2015

Bottom: 'Our club, our rules', 29th May 2015

Top: Damian Hinds (far right) visits Broadhurst Park, posing for a photo with (left to right) Andy Walker, Christine Cottrell, Andy Walsh and Adam Brown, 7th October 2015

Bottom: Fans react to Damian Hinds' visit, 11th October 2015

Top: Fans display their opposition to the Board's "authoritarian" proposals for a Code of Conduct, 12th March 2016

Bottom: The FC United-Solihull game is interrupted by a pitch invasion and calls for the Board to quit, 29th April 2016

Top: The St Mary's Road End at Broadhurst Park, 25th March 2017

Bottom: FC fans at the Manchester Premier Cup final, 4th May 2017

> '*My point here is that FC United and the EY Entrepreneur of the Year award should in theory be like oil and water – they should never mix. Had I made the ultimate sacrifice and left MUFC behind because of the Glazers, I would have been raging at Andy Walsh, the FCUM Board, and whoever else sanctioned FCUM being involved in that event. They put their personal egos before FCUM's ideology, and shared the limelight with the very people whose business principles they fought against in 2005.*'

It contributed to a growing sense that the club had moved away from being for people whose primary interest had been Manchester United, to being for others like Ramsey who weren't even into football, but who saw the club as a high-profile, political vehicle, onto which they could hitch their own bandwagon and jump aboard. An example came at that September's Board meeting. John Nicholson, a Manchester-based barrister, inveigled something called 'Greater Manchester Law Centre' onto the agenda, and the Board approved their support for it. A fine and noble cause, no doubt, but surely irrelevant to support-ers and representatives of a non-league football club.

Over the previous few years, Walsh and Adam Brown had increas-ingly pushed the idea that FC had been set up as some revolutionary social force as much as a football club. In his rant against Selvidge, Walsh had insisted, 'In 2005 we set out to change the game', even though such an intention was never once raised by anyone on the Steering Committee. This slow hijacking of FC's ethos had largely gone unnoticed – it was akin to Walsh's 'boiling frog' analogy – and had likely come about as a way of tapping into various public bodies' funding packages to pay for Broadhurst Park. That was fine in itself, but alongside founding principles being set aside when it suited, it was clear that a reassertion of what the club was supposed to represent was desperately required.

I aimed to provide it. I wrote up 23 resolutions and eight members' votes aimed at protecting the club's democracy, and ensuring transparency and accountability. At the previous year's AGM, members voted on only five resolutions and three members' votes – which itself was more than usual. My submissions intended to address everything from the appointment of Andy Walker and his competency, to the management of the ground build; and from the composition of the Board and reassertion of its authority over senior employees, to Andy Walsh's call for a code of conduct and attempts to censor dissenters. Each Board member who wasn't up for re-election would be subjected to an unprecedented vote of confidence. It was enough for me just to have the issues on the ballot sheet, with the club compelled to circulate explanations of them to the entire membership. To submit them, I first had to renew my membership.

Two days before the deadline, Lindsey Howard, the club secretary, emailed me to say my membership application had not been processed:

> '*Due to your abuse of staff and individual club members the application has been referred to the club Board for further consideration. You may make a written submission to the Board explaining why you believe your application should be accepted.*'

However, that next Board meeting was on Monday 26 October – after the deadline had passed.

There was no constitutional basis for my membership application to be blocked like this; a referral for 'approval' was unprecedented. Adam Brown had touched on how controversial such a move would be earlier in the year: 'The FCA [Financial Conduct Authority] would probably take a dim view of any organisation that started to only allow in people who agreed with those in charge.'

The club's rules stated:

> '*10. Membership is open to any person, firm or corporate body who or which: a. is a supporter of the Club; or b. has an interest in the game of*

football in the Area and is in sympathy with the objects of the Club; and
c. agrees to be bound by these Rules and Rule 6 and 113 in particular.
d. agrees to be bound by the Club's equality statements, child protection
policy and codes of conduct.
    '11. The Club Board shall have power to refuse membership to any
person who does not in the opinion of the Club Board meet these
requirements.'

Rules 6 and 113 related to technicalities regarding the club's finances
and so were irrelevant to my situation, while – as Andy Walsh had
desperately highlighted – the club had no code of conduct for members. I emailed the Board stating that I would be taking up the club's
unconstitutional behaviour and dissent-silencing attempts with the
FCA. Phil Sheeran was the only one to reply: 'Proper little cry baby
aren't we?'

It all created an interesting legal situation, not least given that I
had £3,000 invested in the club's community share scheme. A condition of the shareholding was maintaining club membership, yet the
Board's decision now put me in breach of the rules. Even if the club
could prove any alleged 'abuse', there was nothing which precluded
membership on that basis. With no sign of the impasse being bridged,
I sought support on the forums for others to submit the resolutions
and votes on my behalf.

The news of the Board's action proved incendiary. Sam Mullock
commented, 'If the Club were trying to wage war on dissenters then
this is the biggest own goal I can imagine.' On the club's forum, John
Simpson wrote, 'If true, then it's pathetic and whoever at the club
made this decision should hang their heads in shame. How dare you
try to stifle democracy at our club?' Not everyone was outraged though.
Roy Williamson, who'd been so animated over Damian Hinds' appearance at Broadhurst Park, was clearly less concerned about the club's
constitution being overturned: 'Maybe it's time for people who feel
strongly about the last few months' events to put themselves forward

for the Board and change things?' But how could someone change things if they weren't allowed to be a member?

Mullock's 'own goal' comment was prescient; support for me flooded in, and lapsed members rejoined simply to back my votes onto the ballot paper. Eventually 58 people were named as co-signatories to each, indicating both the weight of backing and the level of outrage at Walsh and the Board. Post-Benfica, the Board's apologists had continually berated the agitators: 'If you don't like it you can submit a resolution to the AGM.' Their challenge had been met; the AGM would be drowning in democracy.

On the pitch, FC United had won through to the FA Cup first round, and the Board grabbed the opportunity to reassert its fan-friendly principles. The draw pitched FC at home against Chesterfield, in what was viewed as one of the ties of the round. BT Sport chose the match for one of its televised fixtures, which meant moving the kick-off to Monday evening. Both clubs would receive a whopping £67,500 fee – a much-needed boost to FC's depleted coffers. Despite this, the Board released a statement that implied the TV money was not welcome, yet refused to reject it. The club had 'contacted the FA to inform them of our views' and 'referred the FA to resolutions passed by FC United members and [the] following guiding principles, when deciding whether to accept an invitation to move a game to be shown on TV:

'1. The time of kick off proposed.

2. The travelling times involved for the fans.

3. The impact of a no decision on the other club.

4. The benefits to our club to be derived from this exposure.

5. The impact of any additional money in helping the club achieve its aims.'

None of these five principles appeared relevant to the situation, but the Board still refused to agree with the game being moved to the Monday evening: 'On this issue we believe that we need to make a stand.'

The statement was pure grandstanding. If the Board genuinely didn't want to accept the decision they could have declined what was only an 'invitation' for it to be televised. If they were then compelled to play on the Monday, they could have refused to do so, and genuinely 'made a stand' on the matter. They were 'protesting' having effectively been instructed not to by the members' resolution; 'protesting' yet still happily pocketing the cash.

The Board had also seemingly not factored in the membership's vote, in 2007, to accept both entrance into FA competitions and the consequences of any games being moved for television. As a result of this, there had been no similar dissent in 2010 ahead of the Friday night game at Rochdale that was broadcast on ESPN. Therefore, there now seemed no logical interpretation of those guiding principles that could lead the Board to take this stance.

To some, the statement seemed a transparent attempt to try and persuade the club's support that the Board could still be relied upon to defend the club's ethos, given what was going on with my membership. If so, attention wasn't deflected for long, especially once Chesterfield ended the club's cup run via a 4–1 pummelling. The Board informed me that my 'membership remains deferred', and I was summoned to a meeting at Broadhurst Park before a panel of three of them to discuss it. No such meeting was ever going to happen. For one thing, they knew full well I was abroad at the time, so any meeting was an impossibility. Even if I'd been in the country, there was absolutely no way I was going to submit myself to being 'vetted' by that bunch of clowns, seeking approval from some sort of North Korean 're-education' committee. As my resolutions had been submitted regardless, what was even the point of it?

In order to prevent the Board claiming that I wouldn't comply with what could be presented as a reasonable request, I didn't reject the offer of a meeting outright. Instead, I asked to be provided with the constitutional justification for it, as well as details of the supposed 'charges' against me. None were forthcoming. On the day of the

AGM, Thursday 26 November, after weeks of emails to-and-fro, the club informed me that my membership application had been refused, and that I would be refunded my community share money. I was banned from the club I created. It was baffling to neutral observers; even if Walsh wanted rid of me, just how had the Board come to act so unconstitutionally? None of it made much sense. Perhaps they thought I would finally walk away once I had my money back. I might well have done, but for what Walsh did next.

11

THE PROSTRATE MULTITUDE

The decision to formalise my membership rejection appeared to have been deliberately timed. In keeping with the club's election cycle, six of the eleven Board members' two-year terms had completed. Of those six, only Kate Ramsey sought re-election. Tom Stott, John Nicholson, Alan Hargrave, Phil Sheeran and Steve Pagnam had all announced they would stand down, while Andy Davies also resigned, only one year into his term. This meant a clear majority of the Board would soon be made up of entirely new candidates – the last act of the out-going Board was to deal with my membership issue while they knew it could still be forced through.

The Board had also attempted to influence the voting on my motions too. The notice of the AGM informed all members:

'Due to the large number of resolutions and members votes received, it has been necessary to take legal advice to ensure that all submissions are governed within the rules. A number of resolutions were not deemed to be legitimate i.e. in accordance with club rules. The Board have taken the decision that most resolutions deemed not to be legitimate will be put forward as members' votes.

> *'The Board deplore the use of individuals' names in any resolutions or members' votes and have taken legal advice on their use . . . Any resolutions submitted that contained names have been changed to members' votes or excluded. Whilst not legally unsound, the Board would not expect individuals to be named in members' votes either.'*

Inevitably, the association that people would make was that my resolutions and votes were in some way not 'legitimate', while the Board's reference to the 'deplorable' use of people's names was again in contrast to their own previous naming of the likes of Tony Howard.

The Board inserted their own recommendation following the explanation of each of the 46 votes. For 20 of those that I had submitted, this read, 'The Board recommends you vote against.' This virtually ensured they would be defeated; despite FC being founded on rebellion and protest, no vote had ever been passed against a Board recommendation. (Similarly, no sitting Board member had ever lost a bid for re-election.)

The tone of the meeting was set from the start. During the Q&A session for the Board candidates, a question was asked about my membership status. One of the nominees, Richard Searle, immediately branded me 'misogynistic'. Kate Ramsey then weighed in:

> *'[JP] applied for membership, that membership has been refused. That refusal was an issue that the old Board had to resolve . . . it wasn't something that could be carried over for a different group of people to then start getting involved in. Obviously I agree with that decision as part of the Board. I was part of it. I don't know him. His personal attacks on me have been painful and they have on other people as well.'*

The 'attacks' claim was all part of a piece, and Walsh soon took it up. The meeting's established running order was altered, allowing him to interject to make an address ahead of the evening's voting. Walsh made an emotional speech, during which some believed he almost came to tears, in which he drew a clear link between my challenges to his authority and the 'threats' he had complained about to the Board. 'Even one dissenting voice in 5,000 deserves a voice,' he conceded, 'but abuse and threats cannot be tolerated.'

The day after the AGM, with the results of the votes still pending, my membership ban became the main topic of discussion. The Board released a statement setting out their justification:

> '*In June this year JP stated that he wanted nothing further to do with the club and that he would not renew his membership.*
>
> *JP placed in public online forums statements that the Board considered to be aggressive, bullying and potentially defamatory to FC United's elected Board members and workers for whom the Board and members have a duty of care.*
>
> *The request for a meeting was turned down by JP on a number of occasions . . . he refused any meaningful engagement with the Board in this process.*'

This, they claimed, left them 'no alternative'. 'Mr Spleen' decided enough was enough: 'If it isn't sorted, then I'm out. With a heavy heart, but out. Membership, investment – the lot. And I'm sure I'm not the only one thinking this way.' The former Board member John Manning agreed, equating the Board's stifling of democracy with the events of 2005:

> '*I clearly remember that day I threw in the towel at United – as with many of us it was tough. Never thought I'd see another day like it. Many of us have put our hearts, souls, health and marriages into the club. For what? So that Ramsey can schoolma'am us? So that Walker can force long standing volunteers and contractors out of their positions? So that a bunch of dullards can tell me that any sign of perceived dissent cannot be tolerated?*'

FC member Stuart Rogers was just as outraged:

'*It is an absolutely disgraceful decision that smacks of Stalinist Russia. Somebody's opinion differs from the Board so that person is conveniently "disappeared" in this case by being refused membership on what appears to be no legal, moral or democratic grounds whatsoever. Cowardly, undemocratic and totally twattish behaviour from all concerned with the running of OUR club. I really hope that this decision does not split the club right down the middle but I fear it might.*'

Others voiced their unease at Walsh's tactics the previous night, concerned that he had subverted the club's democratic process. Adrian Seddon posted:

'*I am a bit uncomfortable at the way the schedule was changed. I can understand that [Walsh] would want to put his side across ... The financial report was not the place to do this though. It is also questionable to allow such a rallying call just before we have the resolutions, some of which are critical of him.*'

Although there were plenty of members who continued to reject any criticism of either Walsh or the Board, many eyes were slowly starting to open. But for me it was another battle lost and, seemingly, the club with it. As in July, the resistance had been almost non-existent. Only one person had taken up my fight from the floor of the AGM – a young lad called Jordan Blackburn with whom I was barely even acquainted. Where was the outrage when Walsh was propagating his lies? Why did no one have the balls to challenge him? I was fuming when I heard what had gone on. I'd been promised support and yet again it hadn't materialised. At that point I'd had enough of FC United, and everyone to do with it. But I quickly decided that if this was how Walsh wanted to play things, then fine, I was game. If I wasn't going to be allowed to be part of the club I'd created, then neither was he. I was going to force him out, however long it took.

From the very start of the drawn-out dispute, I had been faced with whispers and accusations by people loyal to Walsh. One of them, Peter Shaw, had written: 'I assume that the previous constraints preventing you from seeking election to the Board have disappeared with the passage of time, hence your re-emergence to discredit the majority of the current staff and Board members.' As the club rules bar anyone standing for election who has a criminal conviction for an indictable offence, it was obvious what he was falsely insinuating. Okay, it's possible that he might have been suggesting I was barred due to some other factor such as a mental disorder – and he might have had a point! – but I don't think so. It was an easy accusation to throw about and, wedded to the constant claims of 'threats' and 'abuse' that were circulating, it would gain a lot of unwarranted credibility. After all, it helped to explain everything to those who knew only that the 'nice' Andy Walsh was coming under scrutiny if they could think: 'Now we've got a ground, some thug is trying to force him out and take over the club.'

Another Walsh ally, Anthony Holland, similarly attested on the club's forum: 'In the past he has threatened members of the club. Allegedly he cannot run for the Board as he has form. His agenda is to destroy the management of the club and run it his way.' All this was nonsense, but nothing was done to dispel it – it seemed just the opposite. Following the Board's statement about me, and the implications which had been made, Mike Sherrard was asked online, 'Have threats been reported to the police?' Sherrard confirmed in reply: 'Threats to staff have varied and have been reported to the police when appropriate.'

I consulted a friendly solicitor and was pledged *pro bono* assistance to challenge the club. The following week, letters were sent out informing the Board of possible defamation proceedings in respect of Sherrard's post, and to Richard Searle, in respect of his comments at the AGM. Sherrard was forced to issue a humiliating clarification:

'It has been brought to the Board's attention that my post on the thread "Board Statement on JP O'Neill" may have been misinterpreted. I

would like to take this opportunity to clarify that the incidents involving physical threats to staff and any reporting or otherwise to the police are entirely separate to the status of JP O'Neill's membership.'

The reaction from duped members spoke for itself: Martin Bain decried the Board's 'utterly shameful behaviour'; Jason Smith wondered how much the association of my name with 'threats' had affected the voting, 'but maybe this was always the intention'; Stuart Rogers blasted the Board's 'total lack of transparency and honesty. I am more and more believing that, from the very top downwards, this club is being run by an elite for an elite. Jobs for mates. Banning of memberships for dissenters. This club is not what we imagined ten years ago.' Chris Porter referred to the 'underhand and dishonest attempt to discredit critics'; Mike Eden asked why the membership application *had* been blocked: 'The only obvious answer to me is that they didn't want him to speak at the AGM. [If so] the whole "democratic" process within the club is flawed.'

Whether it was by accident or design, I viewed the Board's move as yet another calamitous error. Far more than anything else that happened in 2015, this incident was what really woke supporters up to how FC was now being run. After all, if I could be banned without making any threats, why weren't those people banned who did make threats? The Board refused to say.

I had no intention of letting the matter lie. On the back of the general wave of disgust at Walsh and the Board's conduct, I was pledged financial backing by other members to pursue an apology from the club via legal means. I instructed a barrister to review the matter and, while the libel threshold of 'serious harm' had not been crossed by the club's false claims, I realised that by maintaining a pretence of libel action, it would be possible to force the Board to fully retract what had been alleged. FC's recently released financial update revealed the scale of the problems the club faced, and I wagered that the Board couldn't risk becoming involved in an expensive legal to-and-fro. I asked the barrister to draft a letter making it clear I was prepared to sue, and requested he continue ramping up the threat until the Board apologised. Who would blink first?

I also tried to expose the Board through the media. The likes of Andy Walsh and Adam Brown had long preached the virtues of democratic fan ownership, with *The Guardian*'s David Conn having always been a big advocate, covering FC's story from the very start. Surely *he* would be interested in the news that the club's democracy barely extended beyond the first sign of dissent, and that the founder of FC had been barred? No such luck. Conn told me:

> '*I do understand that you are raising some issues at the club at the moment, which I hope you resolve amicably; overall my view is that the story of national and international interest remains the landmark achievements of all the supporters who formed their own club and have made so much progress since, to the point of building the superb new stadium at Broadhurst Park.*'

I was unimpressed. 'You're a cheerleader, not a journalist,' I replied, and, believing Conn was allowing his friendship with Walsh and Brown to impinge on his professional integrity, suggested, 'Perhaps you should change your name by deed poll: David "The Big" Conn would be rather apt I feel.'

The *Manchester Evening News* was similarly uninterested. In his book, *Not For Sale*, Walsh had complained about the paper doing nothing to help United fans' protest against Sky's proposed takeover. Seventeen years later it was Walsh benefiting from their lack of action. With no mainstream outlet to do the job, I wrote a lengthy article published on *Red Issue*'s twitter handle. Detailing the strife that had gripped the club since May, 'FC United: A Fairy Story', borrowed its sub-heading from George Orwell's classic book. 'It certainly appears to have all gone a bit *Animal Farm*,' it read. 'Given the banning of agitators and a move towards Show Trials to approve membership applications, it's hard not to think even Sepp Blatter might view it all as a touch undemocratic.' In time, this course of action by Walsh and the Board would help ensure that the internecine battle became of much wider interest.

The results of the elections were released on 1 December and came as a big blow to those hoping for reform. Kate Ramsey scraped back in by just three votes, with Rob Blow being elected by two votes.

Intriguingly for some members, 2 per cent of the ballots were deemed 'spoilt' – enough to have had a material impact on the outcome. It was a measure of the lack of trust the Board now commanded that this immediately aroused suspicion, not least because on the night Ramsey had involved herself in collecting voting papers from the membership. It didn't help that the independent scrutineer, David Bulcock of Rochdale Hornets, appeared to be pally on Twitter with Andy Walker, even if nothing untoward was ever alleged. Though many members despaired at Ramsey being spared, some were more positive. One FC fan pointed out, 'Rather than fume about the narrowness of the defeat, I would suggest that the lesson here – with reference to the pathetic 10% turn-out in particular – is how slim a thread the whole régime is hanging by.' That thread would soon be a few strands thinner.

Seeking to justify their banning of me, the previous Board had sought legal advice. The club's solicitors told them that it may be possible to cite my lengthy '*J'Accuse*' forum posting about Andy Walsh as evidence of 'bullying', even though they warned, 'he will doubtless say it represents fair comment and is factually accurate'. Shortly after the new Board was elected, the whole '*J'Accuse*' thread disappeared, after having been online for over five months. I was told that this followed a recent complaint by Walsh, who'd apparently requested the Board produce a plan to combat 'bullying' on the forum, and had even issued a deadline by which they should comply. I relished the opportunity to let members know efforts to silence my legitimate criticisms were being extended, which prompted questions to the Board as to why the thread had been removed.

Neil Boothman, now a Board member, confirmed the '*J'Accuse*' thread had been deleted, citing the Board's duty of care to 'protect staff from bullying or harassment'. When asked whether Walsh had ordered this, Boothman replied, 'The Board has not been instructed to do anything by any of FC's employees.' One member suspected a bit of semantic acrobatics: 'But has the Board been asked to do anything?' Boothman conceded they had, insisting, 'I answered the question as asked.' This seemingly deliberate attempt at obfuscation further eroded trust, and suggested more evidence of an institutionalised lack of transparency within the club. When members subsequently went to check what Boothman and others had answered in the pre-AGM online Q&A regarding their commitment to openness and accountability, they found that all the posts had been removed.

If that was a bad start for the new Board, matters didn't improve. The club's website posted a news story under the heading: 'Treasury urged to give tax breaks to community-owned sports clubs.' It highlighted a report that had been commissioned by Supporters Direct that found: 'democratically-owned sports clubs could bring a big net benefit to society if they were given tax breaks.' Recommendations included: 'creating a new tax status for democratically-owned clubs [who] would benefit from Gift Aid on donations, receive 80% rate relief and have exemption from Corporation Tax' and quoted: 'Adam Brown from Substance, an architect of the proposal and the research behind it'. It suddenly seemed as though the Damian Hinds meeting back in October, for which Brown had overturned his own rules on not allowing Broadhurst Park to be used politically, might have been as much for the benefit of the research being undertaken by his private venture Substance, as anything to do with FC. I jumped on this, and dumped the info before the membership, letting them join up any dots: 'Brown's company had been commissioned by Supporters Direct, an organisation onto whose board Andy Walker was elected following lobbying by FC United, after inveigling himself in the club due to his friendship with Andy Walsh.' While there was no suggestion of any actual wrong-doing, it didn't look good. Brown only exacerbated matters by contacting the moderators of TSIO, threatening to sue. Nothing ever came of it.

A number of FC fans quietly tried to make the club see sense on my membership status. Some emailed the new Board ahead of its first meeting on 21 December, pointing out the damage the lingering dispute was doing, and pledging to resign their own memberships and withdraw financial support if it was not resolved. Although these messages were directed to the Board, strangely, it was Andy Walsh who responded. He wrote to one, 'Please can you give me a call when free. JP is using your name to lend credence to his slurs against me and I would like to talk with you about it.' Walsh also rang round former *Red Issue* stalwarts, including Tony Jordan and Dave Taylor, in an attempt to persuade them of his side of the story. He failed to win any converts: Taylor had already resigned his membership in the wake of the AGM, while Jordan insisted, 'I've got no intention of attending again, until something sensible comes back on this [membership issue]. The whole thing is a fucking joke.' Worse for Walsh, his own power base was not only crumbling, but switching sides. Peter Thwaites, a retired HR professional, had volunteered his services to the club over the years, and had previously been highly critical of my supposed muckraking, but was now convinced of the case – even to the extent of contributing to my legal fund.

While I had little confidence in the new Board, Sam Mullock was playing a blinder behind the scenes. He'd pledged to ensure that the membership issue would be reviewed, and responded to a suggestion by Walsh that it wouldn't with an uncharacteristically steely response – 'It is up to the Board what is discussed' – insisting that Walsh would not be party to the discussions, due to his flagrant conflict of interest.

Mullock was as good as his word. For what must have been the first time, Walsh was asked to step out of a meeting while the matter was aired. It was a small, symbolic moment; even with just two or three of the 11 Board members being truly committed to reform, Walsh was suddenly not getting it all his own way.

New Board member Tim Worrall was deputed to contact me and relay the Board's decision:

> *'The Board met and discussed how your dispute with the Club can be resolved. The Board are acutely aware of your vital role in the Club's history. The Board have also listened to the members who have raised concerns about the consequences of the current dispute. For the benefit of all parties, we hope that we can find a way forward.*
>
> *'We are proposing that your dispute with the Club is submitted to an arbitrator. Significantly and as an act of goodwill the Club is prepared to:*
>
> *- waive the £500 deposit, and*
> *- meet all the costs of the arbitrator.*
>
> *'The arbitrator is decided by mutual agreement. Our proposal is Kris Stewart, founding chairman of AFC Wimbledon. Alternatively, we would be happy to hear other suggestions. You may also request that an arbitrator is appointed by the Chief Executive of Supporters Direct should you so wish.'*

As with the original Board suggestion of a meeting to discuss my membership, this was another seemingly reasonable offer that I could not be seen to reject, however much I resented the idea of submitting to it. The suggestion of Kris Stewart was an interesting one. I'd nothing against the guy but there was no way I was going to allow myself to be 'vetted' by someone to whom Walsh and Brown had a direct line of contact. He was pretty much a mate of theirs, whereas I'd only seen him once since 2005. If it was going to go ahead then it would have to be completely independent. Over the next few months, that would prove a very perceptive objection.

Throughout January and February the disillusionment of many longer-standing supporters grew. Walker's perpetual drive to increase membership numbers was widely believed to be a cynical way of impressing grant-funding bodies, rather than providing any tangible benefit. The methods used to achieve it included emails beseeching people to buy a membership for those 'friends and family' for whom 'you can't decide what to buy' at Christmas. 'Whilst a dog's for life, owning part of FC United was now to be touted around as a last-minute stocking filler,' I grumbled. 'Is this really what we set the club up for? How long until they are giving away membership with boxes of Rice Krispies?'

This dilution of the club's hardcore was evident when someone called Lee Collett gave his opinion on my membership battle on the club's forum in January 2016. 'Tell him to pick up his dummy and be on his way the clown. Then we can spend the club money on something worthwhile,' he opined. A quick Google search turned up pictures of Collett beaming at Manchester City's Eastlands stadium resplendent in their blue kit, while it appeared he'd also had a spell as an Oldham Athletic fan. On the forums a barrowload of abuse was quickly dumped on his virtual head by outraged Reds.

Des Gallagher, an FC supporter who had invested a sizeable figure in community shares, was alarmed by the club's growing financial problems. While he'd contributed to my legal fund out of principle, he was well aware that it might mean the Board using his and other fans' money to fight it. He requested briefings from me to enable him to ask questions of the Board, to try to ensure members were kept fully updated as to what the farce was costing them, and use the exposure to help force them to back down. Gallagher requested clarification as to what legal costs had been incurred in the dispute to date and it was confirmed that the sum was already £1,996.77. With the £3000 community shares repayment and proposed £500 arbitration fee on top, the 50p programme price rise was looking increasingly costly.

On an FC United Facebook group, Andy Walker tried to drum up sponsorship by promoting the club as a 'community enterprise'. While some people were happy just to see him attempting any sort of fundraising, however unimaginatively, others resented such a reference to their football club, in much the same way many had always hated the likes of Peter Kenyon talking about MUFC as a 'business'. Another online spat followed, with Adam Brown stepping in to defend Walker: 'We are a Community Benefit Society [CBS]. That is our legal form as defined under the Coops Act 2013.' Although true, this came as news to many fans, even some of those most switched-on to the club's internal wranglings, given that the club had been founded as an industrial and provident society (IPS) in 2005.

The most alarming part for many came with the realisation that, according to FCA rules, a CBS 'must be run primarily for the benefit of people who are *not* members of the society,' as opposed to being run for the benefit *of* its members. Brown insisted that this status had not changed since from the club's legal incorporation as an IPS, but it wasn't what many remembered or – perhaps just as importantly – *thought* they remembered. (It seemed reminiscent of the passage in *Animal Farm* relating to the alteration of the Sixth Commandment on the farmyard wall, when 'No animal shall kill any other animal' became 'No animal shall kill any other animal WITHOUT CAUSE' to justify the way things were now being run.) 'We have never set out to be just a football club,' Brown argued, even though many, including me and most other members of the Steering Committee, always insisted that's exactly what FC was set out to be: a football club, albeit one with a social conscience.

This argument encapsulated what was fast becoming an ideological battle over the direction of the club. Brown pointed out that FC United was tied into delivering on its CBS commitments, as agreed with the outside funding bodies who had helped pay for Broadhurst Park. It meant these bodies had a say that was equal to, or even more important than, that of the membership. The realisation dawned that the independence of the club had slowly been eroded: the club's shirt might not bear a sponsor's name but what was the difference between being beholden to faceless advertisers, and being beholden to faceless 'third sector' backers?

This compromise of the club's democratic principles had seemed to have been predicted by Brown in a paper he'd written in 2008 entitled ' "Our club, our rules": fan communities at FC United of Manchester':

> '*It is the overt aim of club, members and fans to use the formation of the club for a political purpose within football, that not only binds the many disparate views and approaches within the fan base, but also gives life to its multiplicity. The fascinating question going forward will be whether these binding political principles, which have underpinned the creation of FC United and the character of its fan communities, can be maintained as the club progresses and meets greater commercial, and footballing, pressures?*'

On the club's forum, Chris Porter expressed what many were now feeling:

> '*What we've seen are subtle changes in language and rhetoric, as well as expectations being reined in – away from the revolutionary fan politics that brought many of us to FC United, and towards a more reformist, relatively nonthreatening brand of political lobbying that makes us unwilling to be too critical or radical, because we've made choices to become so reliant on various sources of funding and support from relatively well intentioned networks, that some would say channel social causes towards the kind of safe ground that the rich and powerful can live with.*'

Brown rejected this suggestion, and ludicrously insisted that FC's formation as a CBS was:

> '*Probably the most radical thing we have done and can do. It goes WAY beyond the frankly limited confines of football politics and actually challenges the very basis of Western society. Demonstrating that that can work, encouraging other organisations in and out of sport to follow that*

lead and surviving in the hostile environment of late capitalist, post-2008 political economy is far, far more revolutionary than any fan protest, fanzine article or symbolic language.'

To many fans, the claim appeared ludicrous, and emphasised both how muddled the thinking behind the club had become, and the direction on which certain people had it set. Porter also suggested the club's principles were being compromised by chasing grants 'because we want to operate at a level that is beyond the financial reach of a football club reliant on just the money provided by a few thousand fans.' Brown was baffled:

'If that's why you have supported our aim of benefiting others, in the form of a CBS – for such limited, pragmatic and unambitious aims of raising money – fine. If you don't actually want us to be of benefit to people other than our members – and be a "selfish cooperative organisation" as many sports clubs are, then you should propose that; and accept the financial consequences.'

In mid-February 2016, members could see the extent to which Brown's 'revolution' was underway. At the same time, facilities at Broadhurst Park were being massively under-utilised, with revenues well down against budget, Andy Walker began pushing a Crowdfunder campaign, begging for donations to 'kit out the cabin'. Only a matter of months after the club had taken delivery of the ground from the builders, Andy Walsh had realised they hadn't factored in any space to house the students from the Academy, hence the procurement of a 'cabin' to do the job. Former Board member Phil Sheeran had sourced a huge (and free) old portakabin, but it would cost over £15,000 to have it installed and adapted for its intended purpose, hence the new campaign.

Peter Thwaites was one member who was increasingly sceptical of the way the club was headed. Andy Walker had produced a report for the December Board meeting of how his fundraising efforts were progressing, and this was released to the members in early February. Thwaites homed in on it:

'The targeted income for the year is £251,000, to date we have raised £59.5K? Allowing for the fact that we also need to cover the cost of the Fundraising Officer's salary, by my reckoning that means we need to raise in excess of £200K during the remaining months of the current financial year. Is this achievable?'

Thwaites also requested an update on the progress of the members' votes that were passed in November, calling for specific action by the club in relation to Walker's roles.

'If I was going to be cynical I would say we take a lot of pride in being a democratic organisation but then things that we agree, through the democratic process, appear to get knocked into the long grass, drift on for months on end until everyone forgets that we agreed them in the first place.'

Mike Sherrard attempted to reassure him that the democratic wishes of the members were not being ignored, they had just been set aside 'due to the amount of time taken on other matters'.

While Thwaites spent the next six weeks continually and unsuccessfully requesting updates on the implementation of the vote on Walker, Board member Rob Blow proudly brandished a draft code of conduct – clearly the 'other matters' to which Sherrard had been referring. It was to apply to all adult club members who, as a condition of club membership, would implicitly agree to it. Its scope included – but wasn't limited to – 'conduct at matches, general meetings, branch meetings, other club events, social media and in any situation where the member could be seen as representative of the Club.' Amongst many others, its stipulations held that members would always:

'conduct themselves in a manner of mutual respect and understanding to all other members of the Club;

while on Club property, consume alcoholic beverages in a responsible manner;

during matches not ... cause distress to any other supporter or official;

be respectful when communicating on internet forums and social media and avoid posting anything that could be construed as offensive or disrespectful to fellow members or could bring the Club into disrepute;

have respect for other individuals, even when disagreeing with each other's opinions.'

The Board requested feedback. There was no shortage. The membership ridiculed it, ripping it to shreds. It was derided as the Board's attempt to 'police the internet'. Mike Adams blasted it as a 'woolly, nanny, patronising and unenforceable abomination.' Mike Lowe was aghast: 'Parts of this are nothing more than a Charter for Censorship. I'm genuinely gobsmacked.' George Baker called it 'authoritarian nonsense'. Gary Dyer wrote, 'If in 2005 [MUFC] sent out those conditions we'd have laughed, moaned, pointed out how pointless they were and wondered what had happened to football.' More to the point, what had happened to 'Punk Football'? As Paul Cullen pointed out, 'Surely half the membership would have been banned in the first few seasons if this had been in place then.'

Mike Sherrard attempted a defence of the Board, suggesting it was actually the membership to blame for the code of conduct. Citing the vote in favour of its introduction at the AGM, he pointed out it 'was voted in by a large majority', and claimed, 'If the Board were to pick and choose which Members Votes it acted upon we would all rightly expect that to be condemned.' His argument didn't stand up to scrutiny: a resolution binds the Board to act, whereas a members' vote only gives 'guidance'. Despite this, the Board had prioritised their

Code over eight resolutions passed at the same AGM. On the forum members wondered why this was. John Manning wrote:

> *'Re-reading the proposed code I wonder if it was originally drafted during all the trouble over JP's membership and is designed to shore up the personal decisions taken at the time to refuse his membership.'*

Throughout that January and February it seemed like almost every week – sometimes almost every day! – the club was beset by a new source of self-inflicted embarrassment. 'Who has scored more own goals for FCUM?' asked Chris Leighton. 'The lads on the pitch or the Board members off it?' FC United was becoming a laughing stock, but the joke was on the members. As February turned into March, the storm engulfing the Board showed no signs of abating. Those who backed the code of conduct were being widely ridiculed as 'COCs' online, and the Board conceded a complete rethink was necessary. Unfortunately, their next self-inflicted calamity was already fast approaching.

An email pinged into my inbox. It was an update from a regular mole: 'There was a vote at the last Board meeting on another censorship issue. When the membership find out, it will make the code of conduct seem like a storm in a tea cup.'

12

RISE LIKE LIONS AFTER SLUMBER

By early March, the membership was finally waking up to the scale of the financial calamity the club was facing, which had been compounded by the cascade of recent revelations – a growing number of supporters were furious at what they saw as the betrayal of the club's principles and many withdrew monetary support as a result. One of these was Stuart Cawthray. He'd barely missed any FC United game, or previously any MUFC game, since 1988, but had not attended a single match since a furious row with Andy Walsh at a game in January. He sent a heartfelt message to both Walsh and the Board, explaining in great detail what he felt had gone wrong: 'FC United of Manchester has moved so far away from what we set up this club to be,' he wrote, calling it a place 'where racism, homophobia, bullying, and bigoted views are now tolerated,' but 'dissenting voices are hounded out, just for speaking up.' He accused the club of not caring for the support beyond the money it provided, and listed the annual donations – a total of £2,682 – that his family contributed, that had now ceased. Cawthray also had £15,000 invested in the club's community share scheme.

Others were equally disgusted. Nick Hollowell wrote:

'*[Due to] the bollocks surrounding the club at the moment, I simply can't be arsed making the trip to the game today. This club could have been everything. Instead it's being ripped apart by individuals and blinded by fuckwitted codes of conduct, think tanks, Board away days, jobs for the boys and all hosts of other bullshit. I just want to go the match, have a pint, and know that my money is being used in the right way.*'

The official attendances at games remained impressive, but only masked the reality. Figures revealed the actual crowds were – in some cases – as much as 1,300 lower than declared, after deducting absent season ticket holders. Fans' interest was waning along with their goodwill. The new Crowdfunder campaign highlighted this: two years earlier, a similar appeal lasting two months raised over £51,000; the new one, lasting four weeks, had managed less than £4,000, and was extended by another month in the hope of reaching its target. A young fan called Adam Carpenter launched a blistering attack on 'Lord Walsh' and the 'paid Prince Walker'. Carpenter was 'struggling to comprehend why the begging bowl is out yet again,' and asked why the club was not yet self-sustaining, as promised. 'We were told the idea of a function room was a great place to generate business, stand on our own two feet, yet we're still doing what we were doing when we were at Bury.' He wanted to know why the club was begging for funds in a season it had earned well over £100,000 of unbudgeted FA Cup income, and made clear he would be joining the boycotters: 'I can't and won't put another penny into it until Walsh, Walker, and some of the Neanderthals on the Board are out the door.'

By early March, my legal action against the club was approaching the conclusion I sought. My barrister informed the club that I would accept a full public apology for the comments about me, in exchange for an agreement to drop any legal action. The club's solicitors requested the wording of the apology. Just as I had gambled, the club couldn't risk an expensive legal fight. As soon became clear, they were already financially committed to a separate expensive attempt to dredge up justification for my membership ban.

The tip I had received about a new 'censorship issue' had caused much speculation, yet the Board refused to disclose what had been discussed so the details were still unknown. As the intrigue grew, I learned that the club intended to spend almost £1,000 hiring an investigator to trawl online for evidence of 'abuse'. Sam Mullock broke ranks with the rest of the Board and confirmed it was true:

> '*The Club has paid an "investigator" £900 to review forum postings on The Soul Is One and the members' forum. The "investigator" is looking to identify posts which might be abusive, bullying or defamatory.*
>
> '*This action was approved at the Board meeting on 22 February. I argued strongly against this investigation at the meeting. I subsequently asked Board members to reconsider via email the following week. In the end the vote was 7–4 in favour and the investigation has commenced.*'

Mullock also announced that the Board had spent another £600 on legal advice as to whether the club was liable for postings made on TSIO forum. As one wit commented, that was something 'anyone who isn't a certifiable cretin could have told them for nowt.' TSIO thereafter changed its masthead from 'The Soul Is One' to 'The Soul Is Gone' – with its obvious implication as to the state of the club. One supporter, Martin Bain, set these new revelations alongside the ongoing Crowdfunder to highlight just how farcical the situation was: 'The FC Board are using co-owners' cash to investigate co-owners, while begging co-owners for more cash.' The membership was aghast. And the scandal had barely even started to unravel.

Supporters demanded to know who was being paid to investigate them, and Mullock confirmed it was Dave Boyle of the Community Shares Company. Within minutes, people had discovered that he'd previously been employed as Chief Executive of Supporters Direct, from where he'd had to resign after making 'crude and offensive' posts on Twitter. Such a track record hardly qualified him as a beacon of rectitude to sit in judgment on FC's support, not least as, the previous November, he'd also tweeted during FC's FA Cup game against Chesterfield: 'A rousing chorus of "f*ck the FA" at Broadhurst Park. Warms the cockles of my heart.' Furthermore, in December he'd made abusive posts during an internet discussion about the acrimonious situation at FC, writing of one of the Board's critics:

'Quite easily the most malodorous cunt I've ever had the misfortune to read the shit-awful witterings of, on an online forum. He's a deeply unpleasant turd, prone to issuing threats of violence ... The trouble is, they're a persistent cunt, able to keep dripping poison ... having looked at all the criticisms, I've concluded that it's a fucking witch-hunt ... some of the people on the end of the criticism are firm friends of mine.'

It wasn't difficult for people to work out who those friends were. His reference to allegations against the Board being a 'grand conspiracy' was the exact term Adam Brown had previously used. If that was circumstantial, an internet blog by the journalist Andy Mitten referred to a trip to Barcelona that Boyle had made with Andy Walsh in September 2009. Boyle was a long way from being impartial.

FC fans began questioning him directly on Twitter, and Boyle suddenly claimed to have had a threat made against him: 'I'm no longer prepared to do this role, having been threatened over the phone earlier today.' He gave no indication when 'earlier today' might have been, and the timeline didn't seem to leave much opportunity: Mullock linked him to the proposed investigation at 2:42 p.m.; Boyle's tweet appeared at 4:48 p.m. He was asked on Twitter, 'Presumably you've reported them [threats] to the relevant authorities, or are you just reading from the usual Walsh script?' Boyle insisted he had informed the police 'earlier today'.

Mullock's colleagues on the Board largely kept themselves out of the firing line. Many who voted for the investigation were outraged by his 'treachery' in disclosing it. The following day, Adam Brown briefly appeared on the club's forum. With no admission of his personal links to Boyle, Brown declared him to be 'very well respected in the supporter ownership movement' and, in light of the allegation of Boyle having been threatened, blasted FC fans: 'Whether you agree with the Board decision to commission this work or not, the fact that he has had to withdraw in these circumstances is, in my personal view, shameful.' He didn't hang around to be questioned, and quickly signed off saying, 'I'm offline now.' Stuart Rogers replied anyway: 'The only shameful thing here is members of the Board and paid employees hiring their mates as spies and "fundraisers" and the rest of the cowards on the Board not only letting them but hiding away while doing it.' Thomas Turton's verdict was more succinct: 'Shameful arrogance'.

The rest of the Board kept quiet for almost a week, before eventually emailing a statement to the whole membership, lambasting the 'bullying and harassment' of staff and volunteers. In respect of 'abusive postings' online, they claimed there had been a legal necessity 'to take advice on duty of care issues that the club should consider both as an employer and also on behalf of volunteers and all members.' In case their implicit association of it all with me had not been made, they added, 'All this was in the knowledge that forum-related legal actions had already been threatened against the Club and individual members.'

The statement also attacked Mullock, effectively branding him a liar, before reiterating Boyle's claims of being targeted:

'*It is unfortunate that last weekend an incomplete version of events was made available on the co-owners' forum. This story has then become further misrepresented as some kind of plot to spy on members. Nothing could be further from truth.*

'*Furthermore, it is also an absolute disgrace that the person the Board sought to act as a reviewer, was forced to decline the offer, even before they were engaged, due to threats they received. One was serious enough to warrant informing the police.*'

The statement was signed 'The FC United Board'. Mullock had been denied the chance of any input, and three other Board members had actually voted against it being issued. In response Mullock insisted 'The statement deliberately misrepresents the legal position, and tries to imply the investigation was a legal necessity . . . the legal advice did not recommend any investigation.'

Following Dave Boyle's latest claim, I set about corroborating my belief that the talk of 'threats' was all a complete fabrication. I emailed Greater Manchester Police's press office to try and verify Mike Sherrard's claim that threats to FC staff had 'been reported to the police when appropriate'. I requested details of any complaints or reports by anyone connected with FC United to the extent that: 'any person(s) were spoken to, interviewed, or arrested by GMP, in connection with any complaints made by FC United of Manchester officials at any time in 2015.' The press office replied that GMP had nothing on record:

> *'I have spoken with the FC United police liaison officer and he said that he is not aware of any complaint of this nature based on the details you have given. I discussed this with him and had a complaint such as this been made to GMP then he would have dealt with it or at least been informed.'*

I then sent a similar request to Sussex police for information on Dave Boyle's complaint for which Boyle claimed to have been issued with a crime reference number. The response was much the same: 'I'm unable to find any reference to the alleged report with the information provided.'

At November's AGM one of my failed resolutions had called for a thorough review of the ground build. It was intended to address how, and why, it had run so far over budget and behind schedule, and ensure any mistakes could be identified and avoided in future. A commonly aired justification for not wasting time on digging up the past like this was, as Broadhurst Park was now operational, the club wouldn't be embarking on any similar projects any time soon. The reality was somewhat different: cost-cutting measures had meant the development of certain parts of the ground had been scaled back, while others had been postponed. Broadhurst Park was really only half completed.

Adam Brown had previously detailed the club's commitments to bring the ground up to planning specifications. These included:

- Developing under the St Mary's Road End: £300,000–350,000
- Installing proper terracing at the away end plus toilets: £135,000
- Completing each end of the Main Stand: £120,000
- Disabled provision: £45,000
- Terracing the stand opposite the Main Stand: £100,000

These costs alone were £750,000. Brown admitted, 'Before any of that, we still have a target in excess of £200k to raise to meet our bill for the stadium build to date.' The club was also racking up as much as £30,000 per annum in interest on the £500,000 loan from Manchester City Council, with capital repayments due from 2017. The £200,000 loan stock would have to start being reimbursed from 2018. The latest finance figures showed the club to be in dire straits. Although attendances were well above projections, almost every other aspect of the club was underperforming against the budget; the deficit for the year on function room income alone was £173,000. The simple maths meant that, even if the function room had been booked out every single day, it still would've been unlikely the Board's target could have been reached.

Despite this – or maybe because of it – the Board was ploughing on with plans to develop the concourse under Broadhurst Park's St Mary's Road End as a 'Third Sector Hub'. The idea was to fund it through a £250,000 grant from an organisation called Power To

Change (PTC) and provide 'hot desks' for people within the 'third sector' to hire. The Board calculated this would generate income of over £160,000, though quite *who* in and around Moston would be paying to use it wasn't clear – frustratingly the club was already failing to market a function room located just across the road from one of the biggest cemeteries in Manchester. Adam Brown told members that, without any development, the entire stand would not be licensed for 2016/17: 'The FA and SAG [Safety Advisory Group from the council] have said we cannot use it in its current state next season. If we don't get this funding we will need to address that asap.' Quite how they'd do so was never made clear.

Although the application to PTC had been months in the planning, there had been no consultation with the membership – it seemed that the grant and 'Third Sector Hub' plan would be presented as the only option. With the prospect of half the ground being closed down, only a year after the club moved in, it was obvious that the membership would wave it through on the Board's say-so. Yet some fans were horrified at the thought of the current 'Punk Football' bar being renovated into a sanitised, plastic, Wi-Fi-loaded 'multi-functional space'. Others had even more terrible thoughts, fearing Andy Walker might be retained as the Hub's manager! A campaign got under way, with a number of fans writing to PTC to highlight the chaos gripping the club, urging them to hold off from awarding any grant until such a time as order was restored under a new Board. Their thinking was that it was better to save the club and risk losing one stand, than allow the likes of Brown and Walker any chance to solidify their positions by sealing the funding.

Andy Walsh would have been well aware of the state of the club's finances, and also that a critical mass of the membership was turning against him. The general meeting scheduled for 24 April promised to be a very different affair to November's AGM. Since then, concerned supporters had formed a 'governance group' with the aim of providing scrutiny of the club's constitution, and bringing its rules up to date.

Coming from a 'non-partisan' cross-section of the membership, the group intended to submit a range of motions for the GM by the 20 March deadline. I left reform of the club to them, and instead concentrated on submitting votes that would further undermine Walsh's support base. I also worked to ensure people backing the votes would be in attendance on the day, and willing to speak in favour of them.

Through others who were members of the club, I submitted the following motions:

> *'The membership has no confidence in the execution of the club's democratic processes.'*
>
> *'The membership has no confidence in the transparency of the club Board or executive.'*
>
> *'The membership has no confidence in Adam Brown as a representative of the Club'*
>
> *'The membership has no confidence in Andy Walker as the Club's fundraiser.'*

Resolutions were also submitted demanding that the Board abandon any plans for implementing a code of conduct, and do the same with any plans for investigating the forums, while another again called for a review of the Broadhurst Park build project. The Board meeting to discuss the general meeting was held on Monday 21 March. The following evening, the club made a stunning announcement:

> *'Andy Walsh, general manager of supporter-owned football club FC United of Manchester, has announced that he is to step down from his role at the end of June 2016, after what will be 11 years at the helm. Walsh has been general manager since the club was formed in 2005 by Manchester United supporters after the Glazer family's take-over of their club.'*

13

MASQUE OF ANARCHY

Despite resigning, it seemed that Walsh wasn't inclined to relinquish control of the club. He was due to serve a fairly lengthy notice period, and his leaving statement made clear he was already positioning himself for the future: 'I remain fully committed to the club and will continue to be actively involved. Over the past ten years I have been closely involved in building the club, its structures and influence and I very much want to continue that in a different capacity.' The 'Walshocracy' (as Walsh's circle came to be called) was eager to give the impression that their king wasn't dead. The feeling amongst some of the membership was that Walsh had quit to save Andy Walker, and his commitment to doing so was soon made evident.

At November's AGM, members' vote 11 had called on the Board to 'explain to members what criteria they applied to the creation of a paid fundraising post and the subsequent employment of the successful applicant,' including any cost-benefit analysis undertaken. Two days after Walsh's resignation, the Board finally acquiesced to the continual requests for this information. The four-page report had been compiled by Walsh, and listed the costs involved in building the ground, and how these had been met. In many cases this was through fundraising that predated Walker's appointment. Commentary had been added that cast Walker in the best possible light.

Supporters were bemused. Jason Smith posted on the club's forum: 'Andy Walker commenced employment with the club as fundraiser on 15 December 2014. How then can he be responsible for the Buy a Brick campaign which launched in November 2014?' Even included were initiatives such as the Crowdfunder – although Walker contributed to its promotion, putting posts on Twitter encouraging donations, it was entirely managed and undertaken by Andy Whiting, a volunteer. Jonathan Grinham gave his verdict: 'Alistair Campbell would be proud of that. What a farce.' Patrick Stenson called it 'an utter disgrace'. Walsh's credibility was being shredded. Even Jonathan Kendal, heretofore regarded as one of his key allies (Kendal was chair of the club's Finance Committee until late 2015), joined in. The one fundraising effort that Walker was wholly responsible for, and which, on paper, could be viewed a success, was the 50p added to the Benfica programme price. The report failed to mention it.

One helpful thing Walsh's report did was provide a proper timeline of Walker's involvement in the club, which allowed cross referencing to old Board meeting minutes. The position of fundraiser was given the go ahead on 27 October 2014, after Walsh requested an urgent appointment be made 'to get us over the line' in terms of funding for Broadhurst Park. However, the position was not actually advertised until 27 November, and only on the club's website. Walker's LinkedIn profile revealed he was then employed as Campaigns and Communications Director for Keep Britain Tidy, whose website showed he resigned on 5 December – before the closing deadline for applications for the FC role! The same day, Walker had posted on Twitter: 'My last day at @KeepBritainTidy today. Looking forward to a busy future of 3rd sector comms, fundraising and supporter engagement projects.' When later challenged on the matter, Andy Walker rejected accusations of an old pals' stitch-up: 'I did not resign my previous role days before the FC interview. I worked three months' notice and left to go freelance.' The timings just seemed too convenient for many, especially once it emerged that Walsh and Walker's association had begun when both were 'Full-Timers' together in the secretive Trotskyite sect, Militant, whose aim had been the overthrow of democratic institutions via violent revolution.

After almost a year of infighting, speculation, accusations and retribution, the piecing together of this information contributed to a definite sense that everything was coming to a head. Walsh's scalp would always have been the most difficult one to claim, but with him now out of the way, the likes of Walker and Ramsey were especially vulnerable. 'Revolution is impossible until it becomes inevitable,' as Trotsky might have mused . . .

Peter Thwaites landed a savage blow on the club's forum by leaking an old email from Walker. Thwaites had often helped the club with assorted employment issues, and Walker had contacted him requesting advice on the new programme editor's contract. Following the kerfuffle with Tony Howard the previous summer, Walsh wanted to insert a gagging clause. Walker petitioned Thwaites:

> *'Specifically, we need a steer on Clause 8: – The Service Provider will not divulge to third parties matters confidential to either FC United Ltd or connected parties (whether or not covered by this agreement) without explicit permission from General Manager.*
>
> *'Given the issues that arose with the previous contractor sharing information on the members forum and claiming that this was not a breach of contract given his co-ownership status, we wanted to protect ourselves from something similar happening again.'*

Thwaites was baffled, telling members:

> *'By way of background, this was a completely unsolicited e-mail from Andy Walker, who I had never met, spoken to, or corresponded with previously. In the past, I have drawn up dozens of contracts for Club employees. Not one of these included a confidentiality or 'gagging' clause, nor was it ever suggested that such a restriction was necessary. So*

why is there suddenly considered a need to invoke one for the person who is replacing Tony Howard as the programme editor? What state secrets are they ever going to be party to? Margy's team selections?

'*Well the answer is in Andy Walker's own words: "Something similar" presumably being the likes of Tony Howard having the cheek to stand up and defend himself, contradicting Andy Walsh's and Andy Walker's interpretation of events.*

'*Let's not kid ourselves here: this is nothing to do with confidentiality. This is the development of a systemic culture of secrecy, evasion and misrepresentation. Information is withheld, questions are not answered, restrictive codes of conduct are drawn up, and attempts are made to stifle or silence criticism on the forums. Anyone who voices criticism of the way things are run is apparently viewed as an enemy of the club.*

'*You might think that the Board would be interested in this information? Well, since it was shared with them over two weeks ago, only two of them (Sam [Mullock] and Tim [Worrall]) have bothered to respond with concern. Either some Board members are completely missing the point or else they actually believe this is the way our football club should be operating.*'

It wasn't just the FC United Board which appeared indifferent to Walsh and Walker's authoritarianism. The board of Supporters Direct, to which FC United had quietly nominated Andy Walker the previous summer, was similarly untroubled. The organisation's *raison d'etre* is to facilitate democratic supporter engagement, and it is provided with grants and public money to help achieve that. Despite this, Walker had ignored the democratic wishes of FC's membership, as passed at the AGM, calling for him to be removed as the club's communications officer. Thus, a SD Board member was demanding democracy of others while setting it aside when it impacted upon him. I raised the matter with Brian Burgess, chair of the organisation, and member of the FA's 'Compliance Monitoring Group'. Burgess replied, saying, 'it is not appropriate' for Supporters Direct to comment. Walker hit out on Facebook: 'The thugs and haters will never win. They will be exposed for what they are.' Yet the only people being exposed were the beneficiaries of the Walshocracy's excess – through past Board reports I pieced together those on whom finance and favouritism had been lavished.

The previous December, Andy Walsh had asked for £3,000 for 'a staff training programme' which the Board approved without any objection. The training was to be carried out by Richard Gilling, a person who Walsh said was 'well known' to him 'for a number of years'. Gilling's LinkedIn profile revealed him to be the owner of 'The Golf School' in Altrincham, while his qualifications appeared to have been attained at 'The Washington School of Clinical Hypnotherapy'. There was no indication that the contract was put out to tender, which was in breach of official club policy.

Phil Frampton was another friend of Walsh, and another former Militant 'Full-Timer'. Many members believed him to be a volunteer, but his own website boasted: 'For the last 5 years I have acted as a PR consultant for FC United, building up the clubs' fundraising activities, sponsorship and co-operative profile.' These were the very same areas supposedly covered by Andy Walker's brief. His website revealed at least one of his consultancy 'workshops' had incorporated a 'study tour of FC United's new stadium led by Andy Walsh'. Questions from members as to how much Phil Frampton was paid for his involvement in the Minithon – an annual grassroots-led, sponsored fun run to raise money for both FC and local charities – were batted away by the Board:

> '*Phil Frampton is a paid contractor of the club. He is responsible for a range of activities one of which is the arrangement of the Minithon. Other paid staff are also involved in arrangements for the Minithon alongside club volunteers. Payments to staff, contractors and volunteers are confidential.*'

Another paid member of staff was Robin Pye, who worked for FC from 2008 until 2015, when he was ordained. He had no history of being a football fan, was also a former Militant figure, and had long been a friend of Walsh. The curate's new role spreading God's word didn't preclude his ongoing loyalty to the word of Walsh, and as a result, Pye didn't receive many blessings on the club's forum. There, Paul Shay launched an eviscerating attack on him on the forum:

'*You probably don't remember me but I remember you very well. You personally pretty much ended my proud and deep involvement with FC in one rude and arrogant swoop.*

'*Try and remember Youth United Day [YUD] when it added a raucous few thousand to the gate each year. This was not an accident. Vinny, Gally, Lucy, Maureen, myself and others worked deep into the night after work to make it happen. We created the artwork, leaflets and emails. We approached everyone we could think of and organised the whole shebang ourselves with the good natured help of each and every other member we roped in.*

'*If you poke around the photo archives you'll see pictures of grinning young kids from Old Trafford mosques with self-made red, white and black banners, you'll see kids from housing estate youth clubs that no other organisation would touch with a bargepole due to their well-founded reputations for lawlessness. We had mini-vans from schools across the city turning up. If it was young, Mancunian and unloved, we signed them up. They came in droves and left with smiles on their faces.*

'*How were we able to drag all this to Bury, and ignite young people's imaginations? We were different. We were not the same old axis of charities, local government employees and the church. We were outside all that. We were them, and they were us. They knew that instinctively. That made our task easy as we were knocking at an open door. It was glorious, new, revolutionary, and worked. You'd call it "social cohesion". We'd call it a giant fuck off to an uncaring world.*

'*Jump forward a couple of years, and we hear that there's a new guy in charge of FC's community efforts. Who the fuck was Robin Pye? No idea, but he's an old mate of Andy's so he must be alright.*

215

'*YUD comes around and overtures are made. I was asked by Robin for a list of contacts from previous years. Now, this list had been built up by myself. I'd spent hours collating names and contact details of church groups, synagogues, junior football clubs, school heads, college heads, athletic clubs. This was not just a list, most of them had replied and we were forming relationships with them. I sent them over to you Robin.*

'*Robin, you sent me a curt email asking if they could be re-ordered in Excel format and re-submitted to you otherwise they'd be useless. I never heard from you again. Not one fucking word. Like I could afford MS Office at the time anyway. And what were we left with? A few middle class kids who were unfortunate enough to be dragged along by Robin's god bothering mates, marching round our ground with a rainbow flag.*

'*It was a laughable disaster. However, from the point of view of the new professional community team it was a rip-roaring success. Why? Money. Robin is a grant magnet. He knows the old charity/local government/church junta inside out. In a blink, we had become everything we were meant to be against. Old, money-grubbing, self-satisfied and sanctimonious hypocrites. We'd lost it. We were no longer of the people but rather just another arm of charity. Parachuting into communities to patronise and "improve" them in our image.*

'*Just another of Andy's Old Mates who nobody asked for. Another of Andy's Old Mates who takes the applause and then sends in his invoice. Just another of Andy's Old pay-cheque-taking Mates like Walker, Frampton et al who never understood who we are. We are not here to suck on the tits of charity. That's your addiction.*

'*Go now. Leave us to try and be what we wanted to be. Proud, defiant Mancunians who want to build something counter to what you lot are. Not a pale imitation of the Premiership's "foundations" but a new way of bonding our community together.*'

Pye's response was patronising and hilarious in equal measure:

'I hope the opportunity you have taken to shower a load of abuse on my head has gone some way to make you feel better. Some of the things you have said in your post are, in my opinion, just plain wrong. However, there are also some fundamental truths in what you are saying.

'When Paul says I took over Youth United Day and turned it into a middle class Christian event, he is talking bollocks. It is astonishing bollocks because it is contradicted by what is going on in front of the very eyes of anybody paying attention at to what is going on at our club.'

To emphasise his 'bollocks' point, Pye took some of the replies Shay's post had received, and addressed each in turn:

John Simpson wrote: "Thanks for posting that Paul. What a bloody sad story." Yes, Paul. Thank you for making John feel sad by posting bollocks.

'Daniel Schofield wrote: "He's done you there, Pye." No he hasn't Daniel, because what he has posted is clearly bollocks.

'Peter Munday wrote: "Well done Paul." Because this is the kind of bollocks that Peter likes to read on the forum.

'Frank Brady wrote: "Can't be summed up better than that." Frank, this is bollocks. There is your summary.

'Matthew Charnock wrote: "I give credit to Paul for saying how it is." Yes, well done, Paul for writing such bollocks on the forum.

'Mark Lawton wrote: "We need more people who think for themselves." But surely we don't need people who think up bollocks for themselves and confuse people like you Mark?

'And Malcolm Pelham wrote: "If you ran for the Board you'd get my vote all day long." I think the consensus is that we want less bollocks being talked at Board meetings, not more. So, if Paul does stand, don't vote for him.'

Despite Pye's vehement denials, many believed Shay's points rang true, and saw it as uncanny how three former Militant friends of Walsh all just happened to be the best candidates for well-paid positions within the club.

As all this information seeped out, people began to view Andy Walsh's oversight of FC United through the new perspective of his old Militant links. On the club's forum, Gareth Veck attempted to enlighten people how it worked:

'*Former Militant members may have ditched their politics but their methods and tactics remain the same:*

'*Secrecy – they wish very little of what they actually do will be held up to scrutiny.*

'*Subterfuge – what the wider public is told is rarely what is happening in reality.*

'*Conspiracies – critics are characterised as "bullies" i.e. an unspecified "other" is seeking to overthrow the democratic principles of the party we've just infiltrated.*

'*Intimidation – fear of the unspecified other is then used to increase authoritarianism.*

'*Protectionism – placing their own people in jobs in order to shore-up their position.*

'*A former member describes them in the following manner: "not trying to convince people by rational debate, but by clichés more than anything else." *'

As if to demonstrate that final point, two days after Walsh's resignation the club's Trafford branch issued a statement decrying 'the bullying and harassment on the forum'. By a unanimous 19–0 margin, they offered 'full support for the Board in tackling this issue'. Apparently, the TSIO forum 'has become a "no go" area for the majority of our membership. We as a branch believe this aggression and bullying is having the effect of destroying the democratic values that this club was founded on.' Their meetings were held at St Ann's social club in Stretford, virtually at the end of the road where Andy Walsh lived. A joke quickly went round: 'The 19 consisted of Grandad Walsh, Grandma Walsh, Mr Walsh, Mrs Walsh . . .' and so on. Yet the Swiss Family Walsh being behind the statement wasn't very far from the truth: despite him not having been in work following his resignation announcement, Andy Walsh had surprisingly been present at the meeting.

At the end of March a big exposé of the club's problems appeared in *The Guardian* under the heading 'FC United of Manchester: how the togetherness turned into disharmony'. Much to the Walshocracy's consternation, Danny Taylor, recently named football journalist of the year, was persuaded to look into the story. He'd initially viewed it as not a big enough draw to get past his editor, but given the volume of issues coming out of the club – especially since Walsh's resignation – that had changed. The myriad strands of the story would have overwhelmed many hacks, and Taylor's initial verdict was: 'This actually needs an hour-long Panorama on it!'

With so much to cram in, Taylor's article ran to treble the intended length. Andy Walker was reportedly in a desperate flap trying to get the piece spiked, with petitions made to Taylor's *Guardian* colleague David Conn – a friend of both Walsh and Adam Brown – to try and bear influence. Post-publication, Walker got in contact with Taylor, insisting his facts were wrong and even demanding to know the name of his editor. Taylor was unfazed: 'I told him I'm used to dealing with professional PRs, not his kind of timewasting – a strange mix of evasion and stupidity.' On Twitter, Taylor had been dreading the reaction, fearing he'd be drawn into vicious crossfire between the warring sides, yet he received only a single message of complaint against 'several hundred' in favour. That evening, he tweeted, 'Thanks for all feedback on FCUM. Sheer volume of tweets shows me how much dissatisfaction there is. Even more than I realised, to be honest.' Despite fears the story would be too niche, it zoomed into *The Guardian*'s Top 10 most-read list, ahead of reports of Donald Trump's latest antics. Taylor earned a 'herogram' from his sports editor for his efforts.

Of all the points *The Guardian* article made, Walsh's backers appeared most upset by a reference to me as 'the man credited with setting up the club in 2005'. Pete Crowther moaned on TSIO: 'O'Neill did not "found" the club. That's an absurd notion.' So absurd was it that, within the week, the Board said as much on the club's website:

> '*Around the time of November's AGM, personnel connected to the Board and staff of FC United of Manchester, inadvertently and without intent, caused the mistaken impression to be circulated amongst club members that the matter of FC United's founder John-Paul O'Neill being denied renewal of his membership of the club was in some way connected to a wholly separate incident of threats being made to club staff.*
>
> '*It should be made clear that the matter of these threats was nothing to do with John-Paul O'Neill. We would like to take this opportunity to apologise to Mr O'Neill, and to put the record straight for anyone still under the mistaken impression about previous misguided rumours regarding his culpability in this regard.*'

The retraction was seen as total humiliation for the Board and for Walsh. Andy Walker did his best to bury the apology, following it with 11 other news stories within 24 hours, ensuring it quickly vanished from the website's front page. Walker also deleted the statement from the club's Twitter account, after a volunteer had linked to it without his say-so.

Even in the wake of *The Guardian* piece, the *Manchester Evening News* were still not spurred into covering the club's crisis. Andy Walsh's resignation *had* been reported, but only to the extent of the paper regurgitating the club's rose-tinted press release. Instead, battle was waged on the letters page. In mid-April, Walsh wrote a letter to the *Evening News* in reply to one which had been critical of FC. He accused its author of 'unsubstantiated claims and outright falsehoods', claiming 'the club is going from strength to strength . . . As for your (unnamed) correspondent's claims of "money problems" at the club, nothing could be further from the truth. Transparency and openness, delivering real community value. That's supporter ownership – and it works.'

The fallout from *The Guardian* article helped pile further pressure on the Board ahead of the general meeting. Power To Change confirmed that they would have to reassess the grant award to the club 'in light of the information that has come forward since our original decision'. This was a demoralising blow to Adam Brown, who'd done so much work on the application for the funding. Meanwhile, the arbitration process into my membership application was also causing the Board hassle. After I rejected Kris Stewart as arbitrator, the Board asked Supporters Direct to find someone suitable, but it was mid-March by the time a solicitor called Nicholas Eyre was appointed. The drawn out timescale suited me as it meant the process would still be hanging over proceedings by the time a new raft of motions were voted on at the general meeting, for which a bumper turnout was expected.

In a stunning development, just six days before that meeting, Adam Brown quit the Board, thereby avoiding having to face my vote of confidence. Rather than announce his resignation on the website, Brown requested an email be sent to the membership. In it he moaned, 'it is no longer possible for me to remain on the Board', citing 'an orchestrated campaign against the Board, the staff, the club collectively . . . debate has increasingly been conducted in a fashion that is not acceptable.' Brown also alleged 'personal attacks and a hate campaign with the spreading of libellous, baseless and inaccurate information' had taken place.

Brown insisted, 'The Board's work is being hampered by the multitude of resolutions/votes [which] is harming the good governance of the club'. To the incredulity of many members, the great advocate of supporter ownership was moaning that the Board was being undermined by the club's democratic set-up! He went on, 'Arthur Hopcraft wrote in *The Football Man* in 1968 that football reflects the kind of society we are. It's up to all of you to decide which one FC United will be.'

Around the same time, a press release appeared on the website of Supporters Direct, announcing the launch of a project funded by the European Community: 'Clubs and Supporters for better Governance in Football' ran the headline, 'kicking off two years of exchange, collaboration and cooperation across seven EU member states.' Its aim was to address 'three core topics: good governance, financial sustainability, and member/volunteer engagement and democratic participation. Substance [Adam Brown's company], a research organisation based in Manchester, will examine the priorities and interests for each partner and finalise the agenda for the next two years.'

If it wasn't yet another cosy carriage on the Walshocracy gravy train, then people could be forgiven for thinking it looked like one.

14

YE ARE MANY, THEY ARE FEW

Sunday 24 April brought forth the general meeting. It was yet another tumultuous day, though plenty had also been happening in the build-up. After Adam Brown quit, it was spotted in filings at Companies House that Alison Watt had resigned on the same day. In the absence of any official announcement, *The Guardian*'s Danny Taylor broke the news online, 24 hours before FC officially confirmed it.

A series of questions about the running of the club were published by *Red Issue* on Twitter, many of which had gone unanswered, despite being asked of the Board on the forum over previous months. Titled '101 Damnations', it echoed Coolmore's '99 Questions' to MUFC's plc Board in 2004, and 'aimed at getting to the heart of the corruption, nepotism, and cronyism that is threatening to destroy the club.' FC's fanzines *Under The Boardwalk* and *A Fine Lung* also came together to highlight the club's problems, producing *The Pamphlet* (so-called in a nod to the Levellers during the English Civil War, who articulated abuses of state power and calls for political freedom). Under the headline 'Co-owners need to reclaim and restore our football club', it urged fans to get involved in the club's democratic process at the general meeting, and explained the issues behind the troubles, with recommendations of how members should vote.

These factors helped ensure an unprecedented turnout for the general meeting. The Broadhurst Park function room was packed, dangerously so in some people's view. As the anticipation built, discrepancies with postal votes were spotted by a member and led to the meeting being abandoned almost immediately. A Board statement released later that afternoon read:

> 'Concerns were raised regarding the receipt of votes cast prior to the meeting. As this issue could not be resolved to the satisfaction of members, it was agreed that this matter would need to be investigated further.
>
> 'As this situation has no precedent, the Board are now looking into the next steps required in accordance with club rules. Independent advice will be taken on this matter and shared with members in due course.'

Some postal ballots had not been accounted for, a fact brought to light when a number of members were allocated another voting form upon signing in at the registration desk. This meant that some forms had gone missing and/or some people had the opportunity to vote twice. The farce only reinforced the case of those calling for change. Peter Thwaites was in attendance:

> 'The question was raised as to whether we should just discuss the resolutions today and vote at a later date, but the room was seriously overcrowded and the layout not conducive for a proper debate. I was stood behind the top table and they were completely at a loss in the face of a seriously pissed off room full of people. It was a complete shambles. If FC was a school, we'd be in special measures now.'

With no independent scrutineer in attendance in the event the votes had gone ahead, one wag mused, 'It made elections in African dictatorships look slick and legit.' Fans who'd given up their Sunday to attend noted the lack of an apology from the Board for wasting everyone's time – it was a PR disaster.

John England, a retired teacher who acted as the club's match-day secretary, was put in charge of investigating what had gone wrong. He discovered duplicate voting forms had been issued after 14 ballot papers sent in by post had been placed in a drawer by the club secretary, Lindsey Howard, who'd since unexpectedly been off work. The forms were forgotten about, and hence unaccounted for. Rumour had it that Howard's absence from work came in the wake of Andy Walker bawling at her in the office and, though it was never announced to the membership, she made official complaints against Walsh, Walker and another staff member, Christine Cottrell, alleging bullying by them. An investigation was carried out by Rob Blow but found 'no evidence' to support the claims. Howard then resigned, becoming yet another founder member ostracised after falling foul of Walsh.

The final game of the season approached the weekend after the abandoned meeting and, though fans could be forgiven for hardly noticing, given all the upheaval off the pitch, it had been an awful season. The FA Cup exit to Chesterfield had come in the middle of a record run of eight consecutive league defeats. The team rallied when it was least expected, away to high-flying Nuneaton, where they conceded an injury time equaliser to draw 2–2. A victory away to local rivals Stockport followed, before a thrilling 3–2 win at home in the return game against Nuneaton in December. It looked like the players had finally adjusted to the higher division but, by February, despite an incredible comeback from 3–0 down to beat Harrogate Town 4–3 at Broadhurst Park, FC were facing a desperate battle against relegation.

A series of thumpings followed, including a record 5–0 defeat away at Harrogate, and the gloom around the club deepened. There appeared little hope of any respite from a trip to championship-chasing Solihull but, just as they'd done at Nuneaton earlier in the season, the players came good and FC won 2–1. Four more wins from the following seven games meant FC United had eased to mid-table safety by the time Solihull turned up at Broadhurst for the last match of the season to celebrate winning the title. The match marked Andy Walsh's last in charge as chief executive and I was determined that it would only be the visiting team who should take the crowd's acclaim. The evening of the aborted general meeting, I rallied troops on *Red Issue*'s forum, calling on them to mobilise that coming Saturday. I joked, 'I'm coming out of exile and there's only room for one Napoleon in this *Animal Farm* story. Whose Waterloo it will be is yet to be written.'

By the following afternoon, the surrender had already begun. Walker was first to give up, after clinging on like a dingleberry for so long. A statement announced he would relinquish his role as 'fundraiser' at the end of April (although there was no mention of his position as communications chief also being abdicated). By the Thursday, with grassroots calls for an EGM growing, the rest of the Board announced it would also quit:

> *'It is in the best interests of the club to call an Extraordinary General Meeting as soon as is possible. All remaining Board members will either stand down permanently or stand down and seek re-election. This will provide members with the opportunity to vote for a newly formed Board with a fresh mandate to represent the club's best interests and best serve the club going forward.*
>
> *'In the meantime, the current Board members will stay in their roles to help with the running of the club until the EGM. Details of the date, time and location of this meeting will be communicated as soon as possible.'*

The club's plight was increasingly desperate. The latest financial figures had just been released and, despite the season's FA Cup and TV windfall of over £120,000, the club's surplus to the end of March was only £30,485 – over £23,000 down on budget, with the full year forecast projected to end up £82,909 below. Board member Tim Worrall even admitted the club had resorted to an overdraft to help tide over the finances. The abandonment of the general meeting meant members hadn't approved ticket prices for the following season which, in turn, led the Board to claim they couldn't let people renew season tickets until it was resolved. This froze a crucial revenue stream, with the knock-on effect that Karl Marginson's staff were quietly complaining they'd not had a playing budget approved for 2016/17, leaving the team in a state of uncertainty.

In the midst of all the chaos, the Board having called an EGM meant that, by the time the season's final game against champions Solihull came round, the perception amongst fans was that matters had temporarily been resolved, and that everything could be sorted out via the ballot box in due course. But I was in no mood to let up, arguing that unless Board members like Ramsey, Sherrard and Lynch were forced out once and for all, they'd inevitably stand again and little progress would be made. When the day came round, the rabble I'd roused headed into the ground to symbolically 'retake' the club bar from the Walshocracy and its supporters.

There, it struck me what we were up against. The clientele seemed so far removed from the proponents of the 'Punk Football' ethos which had carried FC since 2005. It was all so sanitised and I barely recognised anyone. That said, it worked both ways – I was stood by the bar when a bloke came up to the lad I was with. 'I've heard that fucking JP's here today,' he growled, thinking he was talking to a confidant. 'Yes I am, mate. What's it to you?' I interjected, leaving him spluttering for words and looking like he'd seen a ghost.

The main thing that had got to me over the course of the season was the complete absence of any protest at games. I was determined that was going to change. I'd been quietly rallying many of the old guard, especially Rob Brady's bunch, urging them to turn out. Some of the younger lads had been encouraged to make banners targeting the Board, and calling for transparency. Organisation was key. On the terraces people assembled together and, lubricated by a couple of pints beforehand, it was suddenly easy to get things happening.

Boosted by the belief that they were part of something bigger, dissenters felt more emboldened. During the game, chants calling for Andy Walker's head finally got a proper airing. Despite this, there were still no delusions that the protestors were in the majority in the stadium. At half-time I was confronted by one pro-Walsh supporter, drunkenly demanding I talk through the issues. Her idea of 'talking' quickly morphed into her screaming over and over 'JP's a cunt! JP's a cunt!' in my face. It was a point I was happy to concede. Quite what Walsh himself would have made about such blatant 'bullying and abuse' was anyone's guess. Walsh was nowhere to be seen, however, his absence ensuring there was no proper focal point for any protests. The day was in danger of petering out.

Late in the second half, in an echo of the anti-Glazer protest at Altrincham in 2004, a dozen protestors invaded the pitch to interrupt the game, drawing abuse from parts of the 3,914 crowd. One of the FC players, Harry Winter, even went to rip their banners which demanded the Board quit. Two pro-Walsh fans also ran on the pitch to try to physically confront them. After a couple of minutes, and with their point made, the protestors headed off down the players' tunnel and out of the ground. A statement was released on their behalf justifying their actions:

> *'The club preaches democracy but the FC Board refuses to enact democratic decisions passed by the membership, especially in relation to communications officer Andy Walker. When democracy is undermined in such a way, the only answer left is direct action.*
>
> *'This Board has overseen a financial catastrophe, and the people who will have to pay for it are ordinary members, who risk losing their investments. The time to act is now, otherwise the club will struggle to survive the summer.'*

FC United had been 2–0 down before the game was interrupted. In the few minutes remaining after the restart, the players rallied to make it 2–2. At the final whistle hundreds of fans of both teams invaded the pitch.

In the bar after the game, Brian Slater, the club's head of security, approached me and asked me to leave, by instruction of the Board. I told him if the Board wanted me out they'd either have to do it themselves or get the police to do so. Slater returned with three police officers. In fairness to him, he said I could finish my drink. The police weren't so patient, and ordered me out of the bar immediately. I knew full well how the situation would play out but, regardless, I told them I'd go when Slater said so and that they should butt out. That was the cue they wanted . . .

The police hauled me out the door and down the stairs, informing me that I was under arrest to prevent a breach of the peace. By the main entrance, a number of fans objected to the officers' heavy-handed treatment. Surprisingly, this included John Bentley, a long-term club volunteer and friend of Walsh. Rather than throw me in the van, the police decided to take me back inside the ground into a room off the main atrium. As the outraged onlookers were bundled away, Bentley was allowed to stay and he provided the bit of calm that defused the situation. The police suddenly seemed open to reason, and explained that a complaint of assault had been made by a Board member. I suggested that if there had been any such incident then CCTV would corroborate it, and an officer was despatched to check. On his return, the officer in charge informed me that I was to be 'de-arrested' on condition I immediately left the vicinity of the ground. The deal was agreed without much need for negotiation.

The day hadn't exactly gone to plan, and the reception the protestors had received left me wondering if there was any point to trying to save the club. At Altrincham in 2004, United fans invaded the pitch at a reserve game to protest against the Glazers' possible takeover. A crowd consisting mainly of families and kids largely applauded. Against Solihull, fans invaded the pitch to protest against the FC Board's lack of democracy, and the crowd largely booed them and chanted, 'Wankers! Wankers!' How could it have come to this, for a club that was built on protest and rebellion? Online, the verdict from one onlooker was similar: 'They've basically gone from blindingly support-ing one status quo at OT, to another one at Broadhurst Park.'

Less than a week after the pitch protests, those of us pushing for change had our wish. The club announced:

'With effect from 5pm on Friday 6 May 2016, Board members Mike Sherrard, Kate Ramsey and Des Lynch will resign from the Board of FC United of Manchester.'

An email to members stated:

'It is with great regret that we have come to this decision. At the April Board meeting, we all agreed to continue in post until an extraordinary general meeting could be held.

'Since that meeting, however, we have witnessed a continuation and indeed escalation of the ongoing campaign to remove individual Board members. The actions of some members, and non-members, fly in the face of the democratic principles our club is founded on and have no place in civilised society. We deplore the use of physical and cyber intimidation and have done our best to withstand it for many months, but enough is enough.

'The fact that staff members and volunteers alike have at various times come to fear for their own safety, and for the safety of their fami-lies, is appalling.

'In addition, the repeated leaking of confidential Board discussions to those who are waging a campaign of hatred means that it has become impossible for the current Board to operate in any meaningful way.

'We sincerely hope that the co-owners of this wonderful club find a way to overcome the challenges it faces, and that FC United continues to gain experience and so grow the movement of supporter ownership we all believe in.'

Another statement was released only minutes later:

'The club has been informed by Andy Walker that he is no longer in a position, due to pressure of work, to continue his volunteer role as Press and Communications Officer for FC United and has therefore stepped down from the role with immediate effect.'

The rout of the Walshocracy was complete. When banning me the previous November, the Board probably thought they'd headed the protests off. Five months later, my own victory over them could barely have been any more comprehensive – only vindication in the arbitration process remained. Ramsey and co. had quit only after ensuring they'd lodged the Board's case against me. In line with the agreed process, the arbitrator forwarded their accusations to me to allow me a chance to respond. Their list of claims to justify the banning decision included:

'Two examples of name calling of a club employee as Factual Andy on the Club's official forum.'

'Posting on the Club's official forum a resignation letter sent from a former Club Secretary who left the club in 2006.'

'Text of request for members of the Club to support John-Paul O'Neill's resolutions for the November AGM, shows they were not given the opportunity to see the resolutions and were not required to actually agree with the content.'

'Reference to two Board members as Tweedledum and Tweedledee.'

'Second reference to two Board members as Tweedledum and Tweedledee.'

'Calling an employee [Andy Walsh] a liar.'

The overwhelming majority of the Board's 'evidence' to support their case postdated the imposition of the membership ban. The justification stated in the minutes of the October 2015 Board meeting had been: 'There were concerns over the content [of] postings made on the forum.' Any other evidence was therefore surely irrelevant. Sam Mullock independently wrote to the arbitrator, highlighting a number of issues he had with the Board's submission, not least their having overridden the legal advice they received. This had stated the Board's options were: 're-admit [JP] or investigate his conduct by putting allegations to him and hearing his response.' Neither happened.

By this time, many members were confused why the four Board members remaining in place until the EGM didn't simply overturn the banning, and allow the club to move on – after all, not a single one of those who had actually made the decision were still in post. Mullock stuck to the line that it was 'in the club's interests' to see the process through, even at the risk of more unnecessary expense. I viewed this approach as more to do with him not wanting to have to make any controversial decision himself, hoping that the arbitration process could render all things to all men. This was demonstrated by Mullock's request that the process's findings: i) accept my membership application; ii) accept the Board's right to ban me; iii) issue me with a warning; and, iv) call on me to apologise to Walsh for my '*J'Accuse*' post! Mullock didn't appear to understand the process – while points i and ii were contradictory, points iii and iv were outside the arbitrator's remit.

The abandoned general meeting was rearranged for Sunday 15 May. Two days beforehand, Andy Walsh appeared on BBC Radio Manchester to discuss recent events at the club. He was still absent from work but, despite having refused to answer any questions from the membership, Walsh was happy to put his case in the media. The presenter introduced him as appearing solely 'in a personal capacity'. I had learnt about the programme a couple of hours beforehand and requested to also be invited on, to be given the chance to put the counterargument. Walsh refused to appear if that happened, so the presenter offered a compromise: I could do a prerecorded interview to be interspersed with Walsh's live comments.

On air, Walsh once again came out with his all-too-familiar claims of 'abuse', repeating claims for which the club had already been forced to apologise. At one point, the presenter had to cut him off mid-flow, following numerous warnings not to personalise matters. On the club's forum, members interpreted Walsh's action as just another egregious attempt to influence votes ahead of the general meeting. Angela Kholy said, 'This is most concerning. The audience that should be addressed first and foremost is our membership.' Peter Slack posted, 'What respect and sympathy I had for him has just disappeared. The Board should be pulling him up on this.'

There was little chance of that. Rather than any hint of Walsh being hauled into line, Rob Blow targeted an unlikely scapegoat: 'I would say the BBC have behaved disgracefully, though it's not something that surprises me that much.' Two days later, Walsh failed to show at the general meeting, helping it pass off a lot more calmly than might have been anticipated. The volume of resolutions and votes saw it drag on for hours, but much of the debate was just for show. Following all the resignations, the Board elections in June were what would truly decide the club's future.

The night after the GM, matters took a darker turn. The 'board' username on the club's forum, previously used by the likes of Kate Ramsey to post club communications, made a number of posts about one of the backers of my resolutions, linking to an old newspaper report detailing a conviction this member had received. The posts were swiftly deleted by another Board member and, within minutes, Kate Ramsey appeared, posting in her own name: 'Interesting. A post about criminal activities by a member who spoke at the GM briefly appears then disappears. Who is censoring this forum?' This was her first post since November's AGM, and Ramsey was so animated by the matter she went on a relative spree. When she was accused of having made the posts under the 'board' log-in, Ramsey tried to deflect responsibility saying, 'several people had the "board" details.' She then reposted the deleted link, adding, 'Integrity is everything when you stand up and say how our club should be run.'

Coincidentally, around the same time Ramsey was exposing this FC fan's past, he and his wife were receiving racially abusive, anonymous text messages. saying: 'Pakis not welcome', 'JP's Paki cock sucker', and another threatening his wife that her husband 'better not show his face at FC again'. Ramsey vehemently denied any responsibility. The next morning, Sam Mullock confirmed Ramsey had admitted to making the posts as 'board', claiming, 'She was automatically logged in and posted under that name by mistake. She then reposted as herself.' Two days later Rob Blow made an announcement on Ramsey's behalf: 'Further to my recent resignation from the Board of FC United of Manchester, I would like members to know that I have now ceased all volunteering activities at the club and will not be renewing my membership.' It was never uncovered who was behind the racist text messages.

Another whose association with FC had concluded was Walsh's ex-Militant mate, Phil Frampton. Lesley Peake, a member who had helped raise hundreds of pounds for the 2015 Minithon event, spent two months enquiring how much the club raised from it after she discovered that Frampton was remunerated for his role overseeing it. Board member Tim Worrall eventually tracked down the figures, and it turned out Frampton had received 40 per cent of the amount raised for the club. This led Worrall to ask Frampton what, exactly, his role was, with their exchange subsequently being recounted on TSIO forum:

> *Worrall: 'What are you working on at the moment, Phil?'*
>
> *Frampton: 'Oh, I can't tell you. There's too much to go into.'*
>
> *Worrall: 'What do you mean? What work are you currently doing for the club?'*
>
> *Frampton: 'No, no, I can't go into it all now. There's just too much detail.'*
>
> *Worrall: 'OK, give me one detail. What work are you doing this month?'*

Frampton: 'Sorry, I just don't have time to go into it all right now.'
Worrall: 'OK Phil, name one thing you are currently involved in.'
Frampton: 'No, there's too much. I don't like how this conversation's
  going, I'm being bullied.'
Worrall: 'I don't like how this conversation's going either. I tell you
  what, you've got three days to gather the info together and we'll
  speak again on Friday at 10 a.m.'

Friday arrived: half an hour before they were due to speak, Frampton resigned his post.

Joining him out the door was business development manager, Amanda Tudor. She'd been appointed to her £30,000 per annum post in March 2014, but there was little evidence of any aspect of the club's business having been developed since. Almost no new revenue had been generated. There was not even a database of contacts to show for approximately £69,000 of members' money that had been spent on her position.

The extent of the shambles the Walshocracy had bequeathed was only just starting to be uncovered. The Board contacted Walsh to ascertain whether the club's main sponsor was on board for the 2016/17 season. It turned out that the club didn't actually *have* a main sponsor, despite income from them having been accounted in the 2015/16 budget. Walsh had been responsible for the club's relationship with the company in question, and had seemingly just assumed they would carry on their agreement from 2014/15. A few months earlier, the club's finance committee flagged up their account as still unpaid and it emerged that the club didn't have an agreement with them – no contract, nothing. A hefty five figure sponsorship sum was instantly written off, and this in a season offering exposure through the new ground, huge crowds and a televised FA Cup run. Not only was the revenue lost for 2015/16, the club was now desperately trying to fill the void for 2016/17. Ultimately, it would cost two years' worth of revenue.

What's more, the calamity appeared to have been hushed up. There was no mention of it in the minutes of any Board meeting, nor was it flagged up in the financial report issued to members after the mistake was realised. At the time this had been slowly unravelling, Walsh had recommended Christine Cottrell, the club's finance manager, be awarded a two-tier pay rise. The proposal was unanimously accepted by the Board.

Eleven days after the general meeting, the results of the votes were announced. They were a strangely mixed bag, though notably, votes of no confidence in the Board's transparency and democracy were passed. Had an EGM not already been called, one would have surely been forced. Nineteen people now put themselves forward for the eleven Board roles, far more than had stood for election at any point since July 2005. Only two of these were sitting Board members – Tim Worrall and Sam Mullock – while Alison Watt and Tom Stott had previously been on the Board and were re-standing. Watt submitted her candidacy less than a month after feeling compelled to quit, and despite insisting 'very little seems to have changed' since 'attacks' had rendered Board roles 'impossible to fulfil'.

On 15 June, just ten days before the EGM, my membership arbitration process finally concluded. Nicholas Eyre delivered his report and his concluding verdict was unequivocal:

'[JP]'s previous rejection should not stand; he was let down by the process and I believe the Board should be open about this and issue an apology. On the assumption that [JP] still wishes to be a member he should be invited to re-apply.'

The damning judgments stacked up: 'The process around the governance of the Board investigation was flawed'; 'I do not think it appropriate to treat him differently'; 'If the general manager was party to any decision to exclude [JP] I would regard this as highly inappropriate'; 'It is difficult to escape an appearance of bias'; '[JP] sought details of the allegations against him ... no satisfactory explanation was forthcoming'; 'The stark contradiction between the minutes of 23rd November and the Secretary's letter of 26th November is wholly unexplained'; and 'There is some suggestion that [JP] was behind inappropriate postings but these suspicions were not put to him nor are they fully substantiated in any evidence I have seen.'

The EGM passed with minimal fuss. Neither Stott nor Watt were re-elected. The results were regarded as a resounding victory by those seeking change, in favour of a new leadership that would instil confidence and competence. Walsh's notice period had been served, and his acolytes were no longer in control. But anyone who thought the club could finally move on were very much mistaken; the Walshocracy and their legacy would continue to undermine the club for a long time to come.

15

BY WISDOM AND EFFORT

Alison Watt's candidate statement putting her case for re-election had provided the membership with an insight into the problems the club now faced. 'An entirely new Board and a loss of many staff may suit the purposes of some,' she wrote, 'but instability is likely to cause far more problems than it solves . . . particularly as a major problem in the club is reliance on memory, not written procedures.' Her reference to a lack of paperwork underpinning the club would prove something of an understatement. The club had no proper legacy or handover documentation in place, meaning the new Board was essentially starting from scratch.

Fans were alarmed that Watt had been part of a Board that oversaw a £6 million development run solely on 'memory'. There were no reference manuals for a crisis or emergency, nor even mere staff absences, yet Watt considered this a campaign pitch. Walsh's infamous 'winging it' philosophy seemed to run through every aspect of the club's operations. The new Board – consisting of George Baker, Jim Brunt, Paul Butcher, Peter Cranmer, Nathan Ellis-Scott, Lawrence Gill, Sam Mullock, Michelle Noonan, Adrian Seddon, Peter Thwaites and Tim Worrall – could barely have imagined the scale of the task they were taking on.

The immediate problem they faced was bringing in much needed revenue. Both season tickets and sponsorship were crucial in that regard, and the club's marketing in both areas was already at least two months behind schedule. Amanda Tudor's time at the club had largely passed under the radar, and she'd departed as much a stranger as she arrived, but her name was suddenly emblematic of the Walshocracy's reign. As well as facing difficulties accessing her club laptop, Adrian Seddon informed members of other problems the new Board had inherited:

> *'Over 50% of the advertising banners around the ground last season were for services given during the build. Very few were sold. Very few match packages were sold, and almost all to supporters, forums, branches. We do not have a sponsorship database as such, just some details of companies, often just the company name with no proper contact details.*
>
> *'We had to arrange for the ground staff to go around the ground noting down the companies who had banners, so I can add those not on our database. I have made getting a proper database a priority.*
>
> *'There is currently no one properly selling advertising for us. I am contacting all last season's sponsors, and David French is contacting all the 127 business club [a group of various FC United sponsors]. David, Sam and I are contacting a few new clients in our spare time when our full time work obligations allow.'*

In Tudor's two years at the club, she had failed to produce any sort of promotional brochure to help entice prospective sponsors. The new Board commissioned two volunteers to come up with one and they cobbled something together within a week. The new regime discovered the entire set-up to be a shambles: companies had been issued three season-long adverts when they wanted one for three seasons; other companies' adverts were in place even though the proposed partnerships hadn't developed.

A review of the club's staffing structure was undertaken by Peter

Thwaites. His report to the Board was scathing: 'It would be difficult to imagine a more challenging starting position. I believe many organisations would simply have folded in similar circumstances.' Despite all the employees the club had, no caretaker position had been established: 'It's almost inconceivable that, 13 months on following the opening of Broadhurst Park, such a fundamental gap had been left unaddressed, particularly in light of the problems it was clearly creating for other staff.' The business development manager role was deemed 'neither properly designed, nor fit for purpose.'

Thwaites reported: 'proper Apprenticeship Agreements had not been drawn up,' while there were no contracts in place with any of the club's match-day employees, including stewards and bar staff. None had undergone pre-employment background checks. Thwaites continued: 'I spoke to Andy Walsh around 12 months ago to discuss the type of contract that might be put in place for temporary workers. The failure to follow this matter through is inexplicable and represents a serious shortfall and risk to the club.' Before leaving, Walsh had whacked in a hefty claim for expenses but, as Thwaites discovered, 'There is no actual expenses policy outlining, for example, levels of authorisation, standards of verification, timescales within which claims must be submitted etc.' This absence of proper systems and processes was evident throughout the club.

Thwaites' HR background provided critical expertise, but it still took until the end of July before the club was in a position to advertise for a new CEO. Manchester City Council, increasingly concerned by the upheaval at the club and what it meant for the prospects of their loan repayments, requested a place on the interview panel. The new role merged the previous positions filled by Walsh and Tudor; the pitch to potential candidates was unequivocal: 'Make no mistake, this is a significant challenge.' In early September, Damian Chadwick, the venue controller at Bolton Wanderers FC, was announced as the successful applicant. Thwaites told the membership, 'He exactly fits the profile of the type of person that the Board were looking for.'

Chadwick was an FC founder member, and under no illusions as to the scale of the job facing him. He acknowledged that it would likely take until the end of the 2017/18 season to fully turn things around, and was clear about what was expected: 'Everyone needs to be sure of their role but the buck has to stop with the CEO. I'm accountable to the Board, the Board are accountable to the members.' In a clear dig at his predecessor he added, 'I'm not going to be trying to cultivate a media image, I'm here to get on with the job of running a football club.' Unfortunately for FC's immediate prospects, Chadwick first had to work two months' notice at Bolton. The club limped along in the meantime, hoping things held together.

A few months earlier Chadwick had offered his thoughts in a discussion on TSIO regarding Walsh's resignation, saying how he'd offered advice and assistance during the development of Broadhurst Park:

> '*I wrote to A[ndy] W[alsh] during the planning and build, offering my expertise on running large venues. My email was ignored so I phoned the office and left my details. No one ever had the courtesy to even say "thanks but no thanks" so I left it at that.*
>
> '*I know the football circuit very well and have to go on seminars, and you'd be surprised how many times AW popped up as guest speaker. A very old football chairman spoke to me once when we chatted about addressing large crowds, and he said: "some people get addicted to it and they're the fuckers you should avoid."*
>
> '*I thought of that conversation at a football do at Lancashire County Cricket Club last summer when AW popped up to roll out the same old mantra. Nine months later and he's gone after presiding over debacles like this, can't say I'm surprised.*'

Tales of Walsh having spurned expert help from within the membership continually cropped up. To many it now seemed that either he thought he knew best, or was just a control freak. Over the coming months multiple incidences emerged, while the new regime seemed to be spending more time combatting problems they'd inherited than building for the future.

Once the new season got underway Walsh still attended games, much to my amazement. He was absolutely shameless, swanning around and accepting the messianic acclaim his dwindling band of devotees still showered upon him. Many of the club's staff were known to be extremely hostile to the new Board, some even having convinced themselves I'd vetted the new CEO's arrival. Walsh continued to haunt the corridors like some latter-day Lady Macbeth, his corrosive influence affecting staff morale.

Before the match against Stockport County in August 2016, Tim Worrall requested a meeting with him: the Board could not locate the club's security contract anywhere in the office files. Walsh also still had some keys that were club property, while other documentation that should have been handed over upon expiration of his notice period had not been returned, two months on. Despite this, the club had already paid up his historic expenses claims, as well as another £5,000 settlement that he'd been provisionally awarded back in December 2013 as a 'bonus' for delivery of the finished Broadhurst Park.

In early October, one senior club official turned up at Broadhurst Park and was stunned to find Walsh in the office, holding court with his former charges. When asked to explain what he was doing, one observer said he mumbled incoherently and scuttled off.

It seemed that moves were being attempted in certain quarters to target those who'd helped overthrow the Walshocracy. TSIO forum mysteriously went offline for a couple of days and, on its return, the site admin reported:

'*I've just had a conversation with a nice man from Nominet, who tells me he was contacted last year by "FC United of Manchester", who said they had the legal ownership of thesoulisone.co.uk domain. This "FC United of Manchester" asked for the domain to be cancelled, and it did*

indeed expire two days ago, rather than being auto renewed as per nor-
mal. I have explained the situation, and the domain is being
re-instated.'

On the basis of an 'anonymous complaint', FC's GMP liaison officer –
whose previous points of contact at the club had been Andy Walsh
and John England – got in touch with the Board to demand all those
who had invaded the pitch at the Solihull game in April be barred
from the club. No evidence was offered in support of any particular
person, yet he specifically requested that I be one of those banned.
The Board regarded this as completely unenforceable – hundreds of
people had invaded the pitch at some point or another that day. The
process of identifying them would have been virtually impossible at
the time, let alone months after the event.

Encouraged by the new Board to increase dialogue with supporters,
Karl Marginson agreed to conduct a Q&A session in early September,
one evening after training. During all the off-pitch turmoil Marginson
had attempted to stay neutral, but many had no doubts where his
loyalties lay. He'd described the previous season's protests as 'distaste-
ful' in an interview on local TV, outraging members who'd been part
of the fight to save the club. Marginson was very much Walsh's man,
as Stephen Bennett, one of the FC Radio volunteers, explained:

> *'Walsh used to have people listen and report back what I had said; he*
> *would confront me if he thought I wasn't being pro-Karl enough. Once,*
> *Karl was made to confront me by Walsh regarding my comments on*
> *Dave Carnell's debut away at Ilkeston. I said he was bobbins basically.*
> *Karl said that Carnell was gutted by my comments and I had a duty to*
> *be positive about the team. We were all in it together, and I didn't help*
> *by slagging players off.*
>
> *'I later went up to Carnell and told him I was sorry if I had offended*
> *or upset him. He asked me why, and I said: "my comments on your per-*
> *formance against Ilkeston". He said: "I was shit and cost us two goals so*

you were right." He then told me he never listened to the radio and didn't know what I was talking about. It was just another way Walsh was trying to control everyone!'

I attended the Q&A session and, with a few exceptions, the audience was largely what you might expect of a Walshocracy convention. They were intent only on offering oleaginous, platitudinous nonsense to the manager, rather than any serious probing of the club's long-term coaching aims. Walsh himself was in attendance. FC had finished the previous season in the club's highest ever position – 13 in the National League North – but many supporters were concerned about the team's dire and seemingly directionless style of play. There was also a belief that Marginson was averse to bringing through graduates from the youth team, preferring to pad out his squad with experienced trundlers cast off by other clubs.

One youngster on FC's books who had never been given a chance in the first team was Justin Johnson, snapped up by Dundee United on a professional contract. Despite him arguably being the most notable 'graduate' from FC's youth ranks, his move to Scotland never got a single mention on the club's website. This fact was put to Marginson, resulting in him giving a drawn-out response abdicating responsibility and making a number of allegations about the role of his former assistant Chuks Akuneto in Johnson's move. Watching on, I immediately rang Chuks to ask for a response. As he was in the Moston area, Chuks said he'd come down and confront Marginson on the matter himself. The ensuing set-to was definitely not what Marginson had bargained for, as Chuks furiously contested the claims and accused him of lying.

Marginson was reeling. Prompted by a player's info, I asked about his coaching methods, and how often he practises set-piece drills, such as corners or free kicks. Marginson was forced to admit that he *never* practises them, claiming it is 'too laborious' and 'players don't want to work all day and then stand around doing drills in training.' In fact, that was *exactly* what the players wanted: a couple of weeks after the Q&A they took it upon themselves to start conducting drills in their own time after sessions ended.

Further questions left Marginson increasingly exposed. Walsh, sitting nearby, tried to shout me down and his acolytes willingly joined in. One demanded, 'Go and watch another team if you hate this one so much.' Someone else stepped up to slam my ingratitude and suggest no one had the right to question Marginson, apparently failing to grasp the concept of a 'Q&A' event.

At the end of the evening, Walsh made a beeline for me. After berating me, suddenly he was all nice and suggested that we ought to meet to talk over 'our issues', claiming that we both want what's best for the club. I told him my 'issues' were him handing out £30,000 willy nilly to his mates, and that I had nothing to discuss with him. I said, 'You're yesterday's man, a complete irrelevance. I'll do any talking to the new CEO.'

I was convinced this was all part of Walsh embarking on a campaign for election to the Board, an intention he'd indicated in his resignation statement in March. The following morning James Quinn, the actor and FC Radio commentator who'd compered the Q&A, texted me: 'Andy says he spoke to you and is ready to meet. Am happy to sit in and mediate, clarify some of the lessons and sort out a way forward for the club.' I realised that if I refused to agree to a meeting Walsh would spin it as 'JP has no interest in working things out', so I offered to meet any time during the following week. Over the next few days Quinn left messages with Walsh but heard nothing back. Instead I went through John Bentley (the club volunteer who'd intervened when I was arrested following the final game of the season), and a 'sit-down' with Bentley mediating was arranged for the café at Manchester Art Gallery.

A fucking mediator, deary me! I turned up and Walsh proposed that he record the meeting: 'Just so there's no dispute about what is said.' I immediately thought, 'He's hoping to try and trap me here.'

Why else would he want a record of it? It's not like a transcript had to be submitted to Hansard! Walsh requested: 'a cessation of the hostilities so we can actually talk about the contribution both of us can make to this club because I believe you can make a positive contribution'. His words were dripping with condescension. I asked him if he wanted to run for the Board. He replied, 'I probably will, yeah.' I asked what he envisaged contributing and he claimed – seriously! – 'strengthening the democracy of the club'. Obviously I found this hilarious. He wasn't happy: 'What's funny about that? Why's it amusing?'

Walsh went on, laying out his 'vision' for the club, patronisingly adding:

AW: 'You're an intelligent bloke, I think you've got a lot to offer. I'd like to talk to you and talk through the issues.'

JP: 'I don't see any issues, I see the club moving on. I see you, yesterday's man, clearly trying to cling on. You've had 11 years to do all this.'

AW: 'I don't think I've done too badly over 11 years.'

JP: 'Apart from bringing the club to the brink of bankruptcy, when it should have been at its strongest?'

AW: 'That's the accusation? That I've brought the club to the brink of bankruptcy?'

JP: 'That's not my accusation, it's what the figures say in black and white.'

AW: 'I've not heard that from anyone else.'

JP: 'You don't hang around with people who challenge you very often.'

AW: 'Well maybe people should challenge me. I don't mind being challenged. What I don't approve of is people being abusive.'

JP: 'I don't, and that's why I started having a go at you – because of how you treated Tony Howard.'

AW: 'This is all down to my treatment of Tony Howard?'

JP: 'No, but you're a hypocrite.'

AW: 'How am I a hypocrite?'

JP: 'By your treatment of Tony Howard, and then you wail when you get the slightest bit back.'
AW: 'What did I say or do to Tony Howard?'

The conversation was going nowhere, but I had what I wanted: Walsh's admission that he intended to stand for the Board. The fact that Walsh had requested a ceasefire suggested he didn't have the stomach for any election fight. When news of Walsh's intentions spread, even friends of his quietly advised against it. Him standing for the Board would do further damage to the club, ensuring that the issues of the previous 18 months were all dragged up and relived. Many people were relieved when the October deadline for candidates passed and his name was not on the list.

Walsh had already taken a job with an IT company in Manchester, and the week after his meeting with me, the Football Supporters Federation (FSF) appointed him as their new national game development officer. The FSF describes itself as 'the democratic organisation representing the rights of fans and arguing the views of football supporters in England and Wales' and Walsh's brief was to 'lead activity, develop campaign work and build membership.' The FSF's chief executive was Kevin Miles, a long-term friend of Walsh's who had also been a 'Full-Timer' in Militant.

While Walsh moved on, FC's Board continued to wade through the issues he'd left behind. The club was continually hit with unexpected liabilities that further undermined its finances. The council sent in an invoice demanding £17,000 for works undertaken on access roads to the stadium – FC had apparently committed to paying the sum when Walsh was in charge. Another agreement the club had been bound to was in respect of a 'capital allowances calculation' – an accounting procedure which allowed the club to offset future tax payments against expenditure on the ground. In an astonishing deal struck by Walsh, the club's auditors had been guaranteed £62,000, with a £25,000 fee up front. The deal was never run past the club's finance committee, even though its remit was specifically to provide specialist advice on just this sort of arrangement.

Walsh's signature was not on any of the capital allowance calculation documentation, and that fitted a general theme. Despite his influence and control throughout the club during 11 years in charge, the new Board struggled to locate any paperwork or agreement bearing Walsh's name. Even the contract with the club's new academy partner didn't bear his signature, although he was still CEO at the time it was formalised. Instead, on Walsh's request, Tom Conroy had signed it, only two weeks into his role as the club's football development manager. If that was surprising, the news that Walsh's club laptop had been completely wiped of all records, information and emails before being returned, was doubly so – not least because none of it had been backed up on the club's IT system. It seemed inconceivable that the wiping of the laptop could have happened accidentally. After all, Walsh had since taken up a job with an IT company, and was clearly experienced in the industry – the acknowledgments of his 1999 book *Not For Sale* referred to him being employed in IT then, too.

As Damian Chadwick set about trying to put the club back on track, he struggled to conceal his incredulity at what he'd inherited. Only a year after the club had taken ownership of the ground, his view was that if he had £7 million to spend it would be better to 'knock the place down and start again.' His initial report to the Board referred to 'ongoing emergency maintenance' being necessary in a number of areas, while he carried on 'chipping away at the mountain of operational processes and procedures currently not in place or not documented'. Operating manuals for alarms, CCTV and lighting were either nowhere to be found or still in the sealed packets in which they arrived. Chadwick highlighted one absurdity:

> '*We have now discovered, after I suggested we looked, that the 3G [pitch's] floodlights have a timer system so we can remove the need for the*

*caretaker and office staff being pulled away turning these on and off.
Yet again there is no OM [operating manual] so it's back to Google to
help with our paperwork.'*

At the end of November, the Board tried to convey to members the
severity of the difficulties the club faced:

*'Further to disappointing financial results for the first quarter and a
review of the club's cash position, the Board need to alert supporters to
the possibility that the club will need to apply for an overdraft around
December 2016. We're now halfway through the second quarter and our
finances are still behind where we expected in a number of areas, which
will put further pressure on our cash flow.*

'We are in a worrying financial position.'

The Board warned that the club expected to record a loss in the current financial year; that it would be unable to finance planning
stipulations to develop under the St Mary's Road End and complete
the main stand; and that, if the situation failed to improve in the new
year, the club would not have the cash to meet its obligations to
lenders. The reasons for all this were: the escalation and deferment of
costs on the building of Broadhurst Park; the underperformance of
the club's commercial revenue expectations since June 2015; the club's
staffing structure being 'neither fit for purpose nor performed in line
with the club's business plan', which was deemed 'unrealistic'; and a
failure by the previous regime to put in place 'adequate financial control systems, HR processes and delegated contract sign off'. The Board
called on supporters to rally together and help turn things around:
'So many of us have given up much, so to consider anything other
than that is not an option.' A big crowd was expected for the following day's FA Trophy game against Nuneaton, only for an overnight
dip in temperatures to leave the pitch frozen. The game was called
off, costing the club thousands.

At the following week's AGM, Andy Walsh made an appearance, rehashing his long-debunked claims, and ludicrously singling out Board member George Baker – possibly the most mild-mannered man in the room – as being one of those guilty of the 'abuse' to which he referred. Given Walsh's habit of running away when he knew questions would be asked of him, it was little surprise that he was nowhere to be seen after the voting procedures had been conducted, when the Board began a detailed presentation of the club's financial plight. For many of those present it was sad to see what Walsh had now become. A friend of his later spoke of Walsh having become 'extremely bitter' over the previous couple of months, as the Board had gradually made clear to the membership the extent of his calamitous regime. (Walsh's solipsism subsequently reached its peak when he reacted to some FC fans' banner at a game in honour of their friend's tragic death – 'RIP Adam, mate' – by texting a Board member to ask if such a thing was acceptable, seemingly believing it could only have been referring to Adam Brown.)

While Walsh appeared to be stuck in 2015, still squealing about 'abuse', most FC-ers were doing what they could to help the club progress. Sam Mullock had been instrumental in helping 'Course You Can Malcolm' to return and, during the season, the group put on a number of events, raising thousands of pounds for the club and helping to revive the match-day 'feel good factor'. Volunteers were rallying round to help the new Board, with fans like Paul Haworth, Helen Goldsmith and Jonathan Allsopp bringing a level of professionalism to the club's communications that was unthinkable under Walker's stewardship. Meanwhile, I offered assistance to Peter Shaw, a volunteer who oversaw much of the building, maintenance and repairs required at Broadhurst Park, helping out with some labouring jobs, and perhaps managing to dispel some of the Walshocracy's lingering suspicions about both me and my motives.

In February, the Board took a gamble on filling a free weekend by organising a fundraising friendly game against SV Austria Salzburg, along with a beer festival. With the wintry weather holding off, both were a great success. The increasingly good vibrations had already left the Walshocracy ever more resentful. The previous week, former Board members Adam Brown, Des Lynch, John Nicholson, Phil Sheeran, Mike Sherrard, Tom Stott, and Alison Watt looked 'to clarify a number of matters' by issuing a lengthy, rambling statement. It amounted to little more than self-pitying self-justification that bore little resemblance to reality:

> '*Despite the current Board's claim to the contrary, the financial plan for Broadhurst Park was robust and extremely well researched . . . A solution to the current problems at FC United cannot happen without a recognition by the current Board of the destructive campaign waged, leading to the loss of years' of experience at Board level, and apologies to those whose reputations have been unjustifiably traduced.*'

Many members reasonably wondered: 'What reputations?' On the club's forum the statement was derided. 'Utterly ludicrous', 'despicable' and 'shameless and deluded' were just some of the kinder reactions. Their intervention could scarcely have undermined them any more than if I had orchestrated it for them. The day after their statement had referred to unspecified numbers 'who have left in disgust due to the viciousness and rancour of the last 18 months,' the club recorded its highest home league crowd since the club's inaugural season, as 4,158 attended a game against Salford City. If the Walshocracy's credibility hadn't been completely shot to pieces beforehand, it was now. But, once again, the statement showed that they weren't going away.

Further evidence of this came in the form of a new internet forum, the intention of which was declared by its anonymous administrator: 'Pack in the snide comments to and about people who've already been bullied out of their positions. Current regime is fair game.' They were after revenge, pure and simple. It was relatively easy for seasoned Walshocracy watchers to decipher who the people behind the anonymous usernames were, given their deployment of regular catchphrases, and oft-aired, wrong-headed arguments. Some were even adopting multiple usernames in order to converse with themselves, and to make the backing for their counter-revolution seem greater than it really was. Anyone who bothered to try to challenge their one-eyed, illogical arguments was swiftly banned.

Chadwick, the new CEO, undertook his own review of the club's staffing structure to see what improvements could be made. His eventual report was highly confidential: it contained staff appraisals, recommendations for new roles, and details of employees who should be placed at risk of redundancy. The document was circulated solely to the 11 Board members, but within days it appeared in its entirety on the new Walshocracy forum, posted by one of Walsh's cheerleaders, even though placing this information on the internet could only damage the future career prospects of those it mentioned, i.e. some of Walsh's former staff and allies.

While it had been suspected for a while, the incident seemed to prove that the Board had a leak which urgently needed plugging. Every Board member denied responsibility, including the newly elected John Davies, a friend of Christine Cottrell, one of those in line for redundancy. After local media outlets started sniffing around the report, a journalist informed Tim Worrall that he had been sent it by Andy Walker who, coincidentally, had urged the same journo to write up a story about the club's financial problems following the Board's statement about the situation that was made to members in November 2016. 'I get the feeling he does not like Andy Walker one bit,' Worrall told his colleagues. It wasn't clear where Walker had sourced the report. Certainly, there was no evidence that he was responsible for the leak – he could easily have come across it on the forum. The Board resolved to take the matter up with Supporters Direct on the basis that it was inexcusable for one of their committee to undermine the running of a member club in this way. Walker resigned his position with the organisation on 24 February.

The mole hunt led the Board to suspect that the club's IT system may have been hacked, and a thorough review was conducted. This confirmed that the club had an alarming vulnerability: Board members' email passwords were not encrypted, meaning everyone with access to the system could see what anyone's password was. Theoretically, they could then use the passwords to remotely access club email accounts. Other than the contractor who ran the system, only two other people had recently had such access: the club's office manager and, before he quit, Andy Walsh. There was no proof, nor even any suggestion, that either of them had engaged in this activity, but the mere fact that it was possible meant the security of the system was compromised. It was added to the long list of items that needed addressing. In the meantime the Board called in the police and passed over to them the investigation of how the structural review ended up being disseminated.

The club was becoming well acquainted with various members of GMP. FC United's club liaison officer had not given up on his mission to have me banned, blaming me for the pitch invasion the previous April. He put another request to the Board, demanding that the club act, this time specifying a ban of at least six games. Any failure to do so came with a threat to report the club to the council's Safety Advisory Group, the body responsible for licensing the ground. The police officer further claimed that I had admitted two criminal offences during the time I'd been under arrest. It wasn't clear what these supposed offences were and, if true, only added to the mystery of why the officer had decided to 'de-arrest' me at the time. When a Board member asked me about the claim, I replied it was complete nonsense. John Bentley corroborated this. It turned out that the police officer pursuing the matter was due to be transferred from his role covering FC, and his replacement, who had already been appointed, had no knowledge of it. In the absence of any evidence, the Board refused to comply with the demand, and it was the last they heard of it.

The Board was still desperately trying to get a proper grip on the club's financial situation. In attempting this, they were reliant on the club's finance manager, Christine Cottrell, who had worked alongside Andy Walsh from her appointment in 2012 until his departure. Towards the end of January 2017, Adrian Seddon reported to the membership that the Board had discovered that Cottrell had made an interest-free, unsecured loan of £15,000 to the club in December 2014 which was due to be repaid within 30 days of her handing over the money. It was a *highly* unusual arrangement, no details of which had previously been shared with the membership. The club eventually repaid Cottrell £5,000 in January 2016 – the same month Walsh recommended her for a two-tier pay rise – with Walsh arranging the repayment of the remaining £10,000 before he left the club in June 2016. Most alarming about this was the fact that the liability was never highlighted to investors in FC's community shares or loan stock.

Following the structural review, Cottrell's role was placed at risk of redundancy, with the club seeking a more qualified, more experienced person to oversee its finances. Cottrell's only prior financial experience appeared to be as a bookkeeper for a launderette she used to be involved with, yet, following her Walsh-backed promotions, she was now effectively fulfilling the role of finance director. Cottrell didn't take news of the review well and was never seen at Broadhurst Park again. She subsequently claimed for unfair dismissal against the club, before accepting a redundancy settlement.

In late-February, the Board published details of the lease for Broadhurst Park that the club had signed with Manchester City Council. This followed a meeting between Damian Chadwick, Dave Payne, FC's project manager, and council officials at which the council made clear its dissatisfaction over numerous breaches of the lease that had occurred since the ground was signed over in June 2015. These included: a failure to obtain the landlord's permission for alterations and additions to the stadium and its surrounding areas; the installation of an advert on the site without authorisation; applications for various planning permissions that were obtained without the separate landlord's permission required; the installation of fully grown trees on the site without permission; and the ongoing failure to adhere to deadlines for the completion of building works that were a condition of the original planning application.

All this came as a demoralising shock to Chadwick and the Board. The required building work included the installation of another seating and terracing block at either end of the main stand which had been part of the ground's original plans, but had been altered by someone on the project team that Andy Walsh oversaw in order to 'save' the club £70,000 on construction costs. In May 2015, when the council discovered what had happened, they allowed a temporary extension for compliance with the planning application but, due to complicating factors involved in undertaking the work post-construction, the cost to put it right had risen to £170,000 – the supposed £70,000 'saving' would actually cost the club an extra £100,000.

In their January statement, the former regime had claimed of their proposed St Mary's Road End development: 'The Power to Change bid was fully costed with a business plan showing increased income of £160,910 for [this] year, which is revenue lost to the club.' The reality was that they hadn't applied for landlord's permission for the development – presumably not even realising it was required – and, without it, any planning permission was completely worthless. As a result, there was no revenue 'lost to the club': the scuppering of the Power To Change bid had actually proved to be a huge blessing.

Other clauses in the lease left members baffled. One of the benefits of Moston that Walsh and Brown had continually trumpeted over Ten Acres Lane was Broadhurst Park's scope for development. The capacity of any stadium in Newton Heath was restricted by the lack of space, they said, which wasn't a problem at Moston. However, the Broadhurst Park lease clearly stated that stadium capacity was capped at 5,000. Most worrying was the apparent veto that the council had been handed over aspects of the club's budget and business plan which, *prima facie*, undermined the club's founding principle of one man, one vote. In May 2016, the membership had voted: 'the Annual Business Plan should be approved by members.' Following the lease's publication this appeared to be effectively meaningless, given that the council could reject what the members approved. It was inconceivable – surely Walsh and Brown hadn't really signed this away? But then the implication of these budget clauses had never been shared with the membership, let alone explained . . .

In hindsight, it was all there in the minutes of contemporaneous Board meetings. In January 2012: 'there are some very restrictive conditions [which were] critical in the future development of the club.' The Board was seeking: 'some reassurance that 10 years down the line these issues will be dealt with amicably because MCC representatives will have changed.' Even after the loss of the Newton Heath site, it seemed those running the club could be sweet-talked and persuaded to overlook legally binding 'restrictive conditions'. These minutes inspired less confidence as they went on. 'MCC policy will probably be the same,' the Board guessed. 'The relationship between MCC and FC United at the moment is more important than winning a line in the lease.' In March 2012, Howard Bernstein from the council addressed the Board and the minutes reported: 'All areas of concern were explored and reassurances given in many instances.'

Council 'assurances' over Ten Acres Lane had cost the club hundreds of thousands of pounds yet, just a matter of months after that had fallen through, the Board was brandishing 'reassurances' as though they were written on tablets of stone. Less than two years into occupancy of the ground and what were they worth? The council officials overseeing the matter could point to the lease and say, 'Well, this is what you agreed.' Two of Chadwick's main ideas for some quick revenue generation to help keep the club afloat had been subcontracting the car parks to a car-boot sale company and long-term sponsorship of the individual stands. Deals had been lined up, until the details of the lease came to light. The council advised the FC delegation to go away and consult legal advice ahead of a further meeting in March. They also warned that any breaches of the lease should be rectified as a matter of urgency.

When Chadwick reported back, a number of Board members were left despondent. A couple of months earlier one had commented that, given the scale of the problems the club faced, it was only the prospect of good people losing their investments that was keeping him involved. Following these new revelations, and all the effort that had been expended, it wasn't clear where the club would – or could – possibly go now.

On the pitch, it had been another largely uninspiring season in which the team again looked set to become embroiled in a relegation battle before pulling clear to safety in the closing weeks of the season. There were early exits in both the FA Cup and FA Trophy but despite the overall gloom, there were still some bright spots: a home win against Stockport County, home and away victories over the league's runners-up Kidderminster, and a 3–2 win at Gloucester from a 2–0 half-time deficit. There was even a cup win to celebrate – the Manchester Premier Cup (for non-league teams affiliated to the Manchester FA) was won with victory over Stalybridge, but there was no disguising the overall disappointment, even if 13th position and 54 points represented a very slight improvement on the previous year.

Regular poor performances were unlikely to aid the club's most immediate need: generating cash to pay back the bank overdraft and attempt to get the club back on an even keel. Power To Change were still willing to issue a £300,000 grant to help meet the cost of renovation of the St Mary's Road End concourse, although it was now predicated on the club putting up £100,000 of its own money. This was money the club didn't have. Most frustrating about this was – as revealed at one Board meeting – that the club had 'historical debtors of around £30k dating back as far as 2013'. Members were informed: 'Ideally we should make every effort to chase up all of this debt [but] in reality, given the period of time elapsed and in some cases the lack of paperwork, we will be forced to write some of it off.' In July, with the deadline for accepting the grant fast approaching, seven members stepped in to provide short-term loans to the club, meaning the grant could be released. The development that the Power To Change money is funding is scheduled to begin in November 2017.

I was among a number of volunteers who helped organise a fund-raising gala dinner, alongside former Steering Committee colleagues Luc Zentar and Martin Morris. This was held in mid-May at the Midland Hotel in Manchester, with former MUFC manager Tommy Docherty the main speaker, and the evening raised over £20,000. It was a welcome injection but just a small portion of what was required, especially given the ongoing overdraft. A three-year season-ticket ini-tiative was launched, with the club asking its wealthier members for £1000 backing to help it stabilise. The number of these was to be capped so the club wouldn't be cannibalising too much of its future income; as of early July it had raised over £60,000.

A meeting of the club's members voted to approve the Board's business plan for 2017/18 which, following the restructure and other cost-saving measures implemented by the new CEO, suggests the club will turn an operating profit of over £180,000 in the year to June 2018. After all the upheaval, there's a belief that the underlying business is now on the right track, but there are still big challenges to overcome: August brought with it a deadline for the club to find £80,000 for an interest payment to Manchester Council. And, to think it was as a protest against the crippling interest bills the Glazers sad-dled on Manchester United that FCUM was set up in the first place . . .

EPILOGUE

My Sunday league football team's last game of the 2016/17 season took place at Ten Acres Lane in Newton Heath. I was aware the venue had undergone extensive refurbishment, but to actually see it was quite enlightening. As well as having a brand new football pitch, the complex is now also the home of the British Taekwondo team and could scarcely be better resourced. Certainly, there was little evidence that any corners had been cut in providing the state-of-the-art facilities, despite Manchester City Council's claim in 2011 that FC United would have to abandon its own proposed development of the site due to central government funding cuts. (The council still owns the site through its 'Eastlands Trust' – Eastlands being the original name for the site of Manchester City's Etihad Stadium). Six years on from the fateful decision, it all represents a big contrast to Broadhurst Park.

Just over a year after walking away from running FC United, Andy Walsh has his new job as national game development officer at the Football Supporters Federation. (One example of his role there saw him attend a 'Clubs In Crisis' presentation in Blackpool which largely focused on the local club's travails, with Walsh interjecting at the end to offer his advice and expertise – a somewhat equivocal privilege for those in attendance.) In April 2017 it was announced that Walsh had also joined something called Telcom as a Director and board member: 'to support our journey towards redefining the connectivity standard for the property sector, and setting a new level of ambition for the country's internet speed.'

The company's press release further stated: 'We want the UK's internet infrastructure to enable and speed up future innovation, rather than constrain it,' whatever that means. The buzzword bullshit bingo continued as they told the world: 'Born disruptor, Andy Walsh is the former General Manager of supporter-owned football club FC United.' A similar puff piece in the *Manchester Evening News* informed readers: 'Having helped to redefine how football clubs are run, Walsh hopes to support Telcom's mission to disrupt and redefine the future of internet connectivity in Manchester and the UK at large.' Strangely, there was no mention of the 'disruption' FC United underwent in the wake of Walsh handing back his club laptop wiped of all records and information.

In August 2017 it was announced Walsh had joined the board of the Manchester league club, Wythenshawe Amateurs, who are aiming to move up to the North West Counties League. (This was viewed as ironic by those FC fans who remembered him reassuring members after Ten Acres Lane fell through, "Don't worry, we won't be going to Wythenshawe." All in all, Walsh appears to be doing quite well for himself. Another of whom that can be said is Howard Bernstein, chief executive of Manchester City Council at the time the offer of Ten Acres Lane was withdrawn, and an honorary president of Manchester City FC. He retired from the council in March 2017, having set up a company, The Office Of Sir Howard Bernstein Limited, the previous month. He and his wife are its two directors. Bernstein immediately became a 'strategic adviser' to Deloitte, the accountants who also operate as planning consultants, and the website www.placenorthwest.co.uk revealed that 'the company was listed as advising on 80% of large-scale planning applications and development frameworks in the city centre.' This included projects by Manchester Life Development Company, a partnership between the council and Abu Dhabi United Group – the owners of Manchester City FC.

The council's willingness to do business with Abu Dhabi would appear to be a betrayal of the city's heritage. Adorning the pedestal of a statue of Abraham Lincoln in the city's Lincoln Square is an extract of a letter the US president wrote to the people of Manchester in 1863 during the US Civil War, following cotton workers' vote to continue their support for Lincoln's naval blockade of the Confederate states' slave-picked cotton – the vast majority of which had previously headed to Lancashire's mill towns. With the resulting economic depression the blockade caused, there were said to be more confederate flags flying in Liverpool than Virginia, yet in Manchester the vote amongst workers at the city's Free Trade Hall was for solidarity, even at the ongoing cost of personal hardship. Lincoln praised the 'instance of sublime Christian heroism which has not been surpassed in any age or in any country.' He acknowledged 'the sufferings which the working people of Manchester and in all Europe are called to endure in this crisis,' and touched on 'the attempt to overthrow this Government which was built on the foundation of human rights, and to substitute for it one which should rest exclusively on the basis of slavery.'

Yet from 2008 onwards, the likes of Howard Bernstein had no qualms about signing up Manchester to grubby financial deals with Abu Dhabi's rulers, despite the United Arab Emirates' record on slavery, sexual equality, and religious and sexual freedoms being in complete contrast to those espoused by the city's supposedly liberal council. In hindsight, it's no wonder that a small democratic club founded on principles and out of opposition to the pursuit of mammon should have been unable to put down roots too close to the autocratic Emiratis' colony in East Manchester.

In 2017, set against some of the other Premier League club owners, the Glazers admittedly don't appear all that bad. After all, their only 'crime' is to be voracious capitalists eager to milk Manchester United for all they can. At the last count, they'd squeezed out well over £1 billion – not at all bad going over the 12 years since the takeover. The debt remains over £400m. The Manchester United Supporters Trust has seemingly come to accept the Glazers cannot be beaten economically and have opted for cooperation. A statement by the group in March 2017 said:

'The past is the past. We believe the focus must be on maintaining the present level of investment in the playing side and expanding the stadium so that Manchester United remains one of the biggest clubs in world football. Our priority and purpose has always been to fight for, and protect the club in the best interests of the fans, and the execution of that strategy has seen a shift from early day protests to a robust but co-operative relationship.

'Ultimately, we remain of the view that a significant proportion of a football club's shares should sit in supporters' hands. Football clubs are social and community institutions as much as they are private ones, and a significant proportion of supporter ownership ensures their interests are taken properly into account, and the club as a whole takes a sufficiently long-term view over decision-making. We believe that this represents the best ownership model for Manchester United and football clubs the length and breadth of the country.'

The continuing increase in the value of Premier League and Champions League television rights has inflated Manchester United's value far beyond the £780m it was in 2005, meaning that the type of supporter ownership MUST covet is more out of reach than ever. With the big clubs' incessant craving for ever greater financial returns, it seems inevitable that improvements in mobile technology will provide the means for clubs like United to sell their games direct to viewers rather than relying on collective, league-wide deals through platforms like Sky or BT Sport. One view of the future has the top clubs actually owned by companies like Amazon, Apple and Sony so they can cash in on the expected bonanza.

Another, far less widespread view has the former Manchester United player Gary Neville one day looking to front a consortium to buy out the Glazers. Already well aware of the potential for United's individual

TV rights, Neville could currently be said to be serving his 'apprenticeship' through his involvement in Salford City – a club currently in the Conference North alongside FC United. He and his 'Class of 92' Manchester United colleagues have set Salford an ambitious target of promotion to the Football League. Following one of its many tip-offs, and despite vehement denials at the time from Neville, *Red Issue* revealed in early 2014 that the money behind their Salford takeover was provided by the Singaporean billionaire, Peter Lim. This was confirmed months later when it was announced that he had bought a 50 per cent stake. Lim had previously held the franchise for a number of Manchester United-themed cafés in the Far East, while in 2010 he had bid to buy Liverpool FC after the Americans Tom Hicks and George Gillett were forced to sell the club.

In October 2014, Lim bought the Spanish club Valencia and the following year appointed Gary Neville as manager, though the latter's tenure lasted only four months. Intriguingly, only a month into the role, Neville gave an interview in which he indicated his future ambitions lay beyond just running a team: 'I'm not going to say where I want to end up, and it isn't in management or head coaching, so I want to be clear about that. That's not my ultimate goal of where I want to be.' Neville's current main business interests are in property, with some huge developments planned in Manchester, while the 'Class of 92' group and Peter Lim also own Hotel Football across the road from Manchester United's Old Trafford stadium. In February 2017, Howard Bernstein described Neville as 'a man of total integrity', adding, 'I hope he will continue to play a very strong role in Manchester's strategic direction for the next couple of decades.' Three months later, the pair were both guest speakers at a charity fundraiser staged by Manchester Maccabi Sports Club – Bernstein's position as patron of the organisation suggesting that the city's Jewish community have chosen to overlook his dalliances with the bigots of the UAE, a country which refuses to admit Israeli citizens.

In early 2015, almost a year after Neville had taken over Salford

City, I arranged for him to visit Andy Walsh whilst Broadhurst Park was still under construction, so he could see how FC United were doing things. Neville later said to me that he'd seen big warning signs about how the club was being run and, perhaps only half-jokingly, suggested that I was to blame for things going wrong. His argument was that the level of debt with which the club was now saddled could have been prevented by inserting a clause to prevent it into the constitution right at the start. Perhaps it's a valid point, but it's certainly not one that I, nor any other member of the Steering Committee, ever considered being necessary. The thought never crossed anyone's mind. What's more, the nature of the club meant that it would go where the members took it, even if that eventually meant they (democratically) went against all the principles on which it had been founded. One of the reasons I stepped back and didn't stand for the Board in 2005 was that the club had to develop its own identity. Up to that point it had largely been delivered in line with my blueprint and my input – no one became part of the Steering Committee without my say-so. Once it was set up, it seemed only right it should stand or fall by itself.

In the spring of 2016, in the wake of Andy Walsh's resignation, a link to the phenomenon known as 'Founder's Syndrome' was posted on the various forums. The relevant Wikipedia entry describes this as 'an organisation where one or more founders maintain disproportionate power and influence following the effective initial establishment of the project, leading to a wide range of problems for both the organization and those involved in it.' Some of the symptoms are listed as follows:

> '*The organization is strongly identified with the person or personality of the founder.*
>
> *The founder makes all decisions, big and small, without a formal process or input from others . . . little forward planning . . . There is little meaningful strategic development, or shared executive agreement*

on objectives with limited or a complete lack of professional development. Typically, there is little organizational infrastructure in place . . . There is no succession plan.'

'Key staff and Board members are typically selected by the founder and are often friends and colleagues of the founder. Their role is to support the founder, rather than to lead the mission. Staff may be chosen due to their personal loyalty to the founder rather than skills, organizational fit, or experience. Board members may be under-qualified, under-informed or intimidated and will typically be unable to answer basic questions without checking first.

'The founder responds to increasingly challenging issues by accentuating the above, leading to further difficulties. Anyone who challenges this cycle will be treated as a disruptive influence and will be ignored, ridiculed or removed. The working environment will be increasingly difficult with decreasing public trust.'

Of *Animal Farm*, George Orwell once wrote: 'I meant the moral to be that revolutions only effect a radical improvement when the masses are alert and know how to chuck out their leaders as soon as the latter have done their job.' One hesitates to suggest Orwell was preaching a version of 'permanent revolution' but it's a moral that will hopefully be heeded in future. There's little doubt that FC United's members have been anything but alert to the direction the club began to take, and it represents a collective failure that might appear to some observers as having undermined the achievements of 2005. But there's a good case for taking an opposite viewpoint. The failures came from an abandonment of the club's founding principles and, whereas in *Animal Farm* the animals are doomed to servitude once more, in contrast FC United was able to undergo a second revolution by re-embracing the spirit on which the club had been created. The Walshocracy won't see it that way, of course, but the very fact that change was eventually achieved is testament to how fan-ownership can operate: even if in this instance the process wasn't strictly along typical democratic lines – with Board members quitting rather than being voted out – it was still an outcry about the absence of proper transparency that members were due that provoked much of the original outrage. And from there, the popular tide turned against the Walshocracy largely thanks to information that was gleaned from internal reports members could only rightfully access on account of them being owners of the club.

There are countless examples of football clubs having been run into the ground over recent years but, to take just one famous case, if Leeds United had been owned by its supporters then perhaps them having access to details of its internal workings, and the fortune being frittered on goldfish, might have helped avoid the extent of the financial meltdown that followed. Equally, it might not have done, but it's interesting that it takes just one crisis or power struggle to beset a supporter-owned club before critics line up to declare 'Told you so! It'll never work – too like *Animal Farm*!' while no end of Leeds or Blackpools or Blackburn Rovers would ever convince those same sages that private ownership structures might not be in clubs' best interests. Such is life.

Walsh has moved on, the council's loans are well secured. The people with most to lose from FC United's current predicaments are the ordinary fans who believed in the club and ploughed their money into Community Shares to build Broadhurst Park. (Draw your own parallels with the Glazers' plans for fans to pay for their leveraged takeover of Manchester United back in 2005.) So here we are embarking on the 2017/18 season and, a month in, early results suggest it will be a long slog: FC United still has a long way to go to properly turn things around but, after all the turmoil, the club at least has a chance of one day seeing its own *golden future time*. Which is all it really had back in the summer of 2005.

League Structure

Premier League
Championship
League One
League Two
Conference National
Conference North (2015/16 – present)
Northern Premier League Premier Division (2008/09 – 2014/15)
Northern Premier League First Division (2007/08)
North West Counties Division One (2006/07)
North West Counties Division Two (2005/06)

National Cup Competitions

FA Cup – participants include all teams from the Premier League down to 'Division 10' (NWCFL Division 2, and any other equivalent division in the different regions).

FA Trophy – participating teams are from the Conference National down to 'Division 8' (Northern Premier League Division One, and any other equivalent division in the different regions).

FA Vase – participating teams are from the various regional leagues at 'Division 9' and 'Division 10' of the pyramid (for FC United this meant NWCFL Divisions 1 & 2).

FC UNITED STEERING COMMITTEE

Mike Adams
Phil Bedford
Rob Brady
Adam Brown
Russell Delaney
Andrew Howse
Tony Jordan
Martin Morris
Peter Munday
John-Paul O'Neill
Tony Pritchard
Phil Sheeran
Julian Spencer
Vasco Wackrill
Andy Walsh
Luc Zentar

EVOLUTION OF THE FC UNITED BOARD

2005 EGM	2006 AGM	2007 AGM
Adam Brown	Adam Brown	Adam Brown
Russell Delaney	Scott Fletcher	Scott Fletcher
Scott Fletcher	Alan Hargrave	Alan Hargrave
Martin Morris	Martin Morris	John Manning
Peter Munday	Peter Munday	Martin Morris
Tony Pritchard	Tony Pritchard	Ian Robertson
Phil Sheeran	Phil Sheeran	Phil Sheeran
Julian Spencer	Julian Spencer	Julian Spencer
Joe Tully	Mike Turton	Mike Turton
Vasco Wackrill	Vasco Wackrill	Vasco Wackrill
Andy Walsh	Alison Watt	Alison Watt

RED REBELS

2008 AGM
Adam Brown
Scott Fletcher
Alan Hargrave
John Manning
Martin Morris
Ian Robertson
Phil Sheeran
Mike Sherrard
Julian Spencer
Vasco Wackrill
Alison Watt

2009 AGM
Adam Brown
Scott Fletcher
Alan Hargrave
Helen Lambert
John Manning
Martin Morris
Steve Pagnam
Phil Sheeran
Mike Sherrard
Julian Spencer
Alison Watt

2010 AGM
Adam Brown
Scott Fletcher
Alan Hargrave
Helen Lambert
Martin Morris
Rob Nugent
Steve Pagnam
Phil Sheeran
Mike Sherrard
Julian Spencer
Alison Watt

2011 AGM
Adam Brown
Chris Hammond
Alan Hargrave
Martin Morris
Rob Nugent
Steve Pagnam
Phil Sheeran
Mike Sherrard
Julian Spencer
Alison Watt

2012 AGM
Adam Brown
Pete Burke
Paul Farrell
Paul Farrell (resigned
the day after)
Chris Hammond
Alan Hargrave
(resigned the day after)
Des Lynch
Steve Pagnam
Phil Sheeran
Mike Sherrard
Julian Spencer
(resigned the day after)
Alison Watt

2013 GM
Adam Brown
Pete Burke
Chris Hammond
Des Lynch
John Nicholson
Steve Pagnam
Kate Ramsey
Phil Sheeran
Mike Sherrard
Tom Stott
Alison Watt

2013 AGM
Adam Brown
Pete Burke
Alan Hargrave
Des Lynch
John Nicholson
Steve Pagnam
Kate Ramsey
Phil Sheeran
Mike Sherrard
Tom Stott
Alison Watt

2014 AGM
Adam Brown
Andy Davies
Alan Hargrave
Des Lynch
John Nicholson
Steve Pagnam
Kate Ramsey
Phil Sheeran
Mike Sherrard
Tom Stott
Alison Watt

2015 AGM
Rob Blow
Neil Boothman
Adam Brown
Blaine Emmett
Des Lynch
Sam Mullock
Kate Ramsey
Richard Searle
Mike Sherrard
Alison Watt
Tim Worrall

2016 EGM
George Baker
Jim Brunt
Paul Butcher
Peter Cranmer
Nathan Ellis-Scott
Lawrence Gill
Sam Mullock
Michelle Noonan
Adrian Seddon
Peter Thwaites
Tim Worrall

2016 AGM
George Baker
Jim Brunt
Peter Cranmer
John Davies
Nathan Ellis-Scott
Lawrence Gill
Sam Mullock
Adrian Seddon
Peter Thwaites
Adam Wood
Tim Worrall